Teacher Careers

Issues in Education and Training Series

Editors: Stephen J. Ball and Ivor F. Goodson
University of Sussex

Issues in Education and Training Series: 5

Teacher Careers
Crises and Continuities

Patricia J. Sikes / 2 / 35527
Lynda Measor
Peter Woods

 The Falmer Press

(A member of the Taylor & Francis Group)
London and Philadelphia

UK   The Falmer Press, Falmer House, Barcombe, Lewes, East Sussex, BN8 5DL

USA   The Falmer Press, Taylor & Francis Inc., 242 Cherry Street, Philadelphia, PA 19106-1906

Copyright © P. J. Sikes, L. Measor and P. Woods 1985

First published in 1985

Library of Congress Cataloging in Publication Data

Sikes, Patricia J.
  Teacher careers

  (Issues in education and training; 5)
  Bibliography: p.
  Includes index.
  1. Teachers—Vocational guidance—Great Britain.
2. Teachers—Great Britain—Psychology. I. Measor,
Lynda. II. Woods, Peter. III. Title. IV. Series.
LB1775.S54 1985 371.1′0023′41 85-10364
ISBN 1-85000-066-2
ISBN 1-85000-067-0 (pbk.)

Jacket design by Leonard Williams

Typeset in 10/12 Bembo by
Imago Publishing Ltd, Thame, Oxon

Printed in Great Britain by Taylor & Francis (Printers) Ltd, Basingstoke

Contents

Acknowledgements

We are grateful to the Economic and Social Research Council for financial support in the later stages of the research on which this book is based. Our thanks, once more, to Mrs Meryl Baker for expert secretarial assistance, and to the Open University for administrative support. Above all, we are indebted to the teachers who took part in this study, and who gave so generously of their time and knowledge. This book is dedicated to them.

Introduction: Teachers Careers in Context

Careers

A career is sometimes seen as 'a succession of related jobs, arranged in a hierarchy of prestige, through which persons move in an ordered, predictable sequence' (Wilensky, 1960, p. 127). Such a view locates careers within the framework of bureaucratic organizations. In this book, we look at careers from individuals' points of view, which see them 'as the moving perspective' in which people see their lives 'as a whole' and interpret the meaning of their various attributes, actions and the things which happen to them' (Hughes, 1937, p. 409). Some teachers no doubt do see their careers in terms of a structured sequence of posts. But, equally, many do not. Some may have such a strong vocational commitment that they see their job and their futures purely in terms of the educational effects they have on children — their careers are their pupils' careers. Some, more instrumentally, may see it as a useful job from the point of view of pay, holidays and conditions of work, settling for a reasonable non-progressive position, with, perhaps, a major commitment in some other area of life — perhaps the family. In between is a whole range of adaptations.

Such a perspective on careers has the following major characteristics:

1 It is subjective. The structure and content of a career depends on how the person concerned sees it. This in turn involves considerations of a person's interests. All teachers have careers, and there are many different kinds of them, as many, in fact, as there are teachers, if we get down to the finest detail. Inevitably, however, many interests are shared among groups of teachers.

2 It takes a whole life view. Careers are seen within the entire longitudinal perspective of a life. Interests that an individual holds, certain aspects of the self that formulate those interests, the way in which one attributes meanings to events — such matters are developed over time. One needs to see sections of a career properly located within the dimension of a life-span.

3 Similarly, it takes a whole personal world view. That is to say it considers all of a person's interests and activities, in, for example, job, family, hobby, or alternative job. This is the latitudinal dimension. Segments of a career need to be located within the whole, if their nature and relative importance within a person's life are to be properly understood.

4 It is concerned with on-going development. There may be immediate, short- and long-term perspectives on this. They may be clearly or hazily perceived. Development may be multi-faceted, with differential progress along different routes, and differential realization of interests.

5 It is concerned with a person's identity. As Becker and Strauss (1956, pp. 262–3) argue

> A frame of reference for studying careers is, at the same time, a frame for studying personal identities ... central to any account of adult identity is the relation of change in identity to change in social position; for it is characteristic of adult life to afford and force frequent and momentous passage from status to status. Hence members of structures that change, riders on escalators that carry them up, along, and down, to unexpected places and to novel experiences even when in some sense foreseen, must gain, maintain, and regain a sense of personal identity.

From this viewpoint, personal change is not necessarily a smooth, unilinear development. Nor is it one that sees either personal will or external constraints as solely determining. Rather, the adult career is usually the product of a dialectical relationship between self and circumstances. As the result of meeting new circumstances, certain interests may be re-formulated, certain aspects of the self changed, or crystallized, and, in consequence, new directions envisaged.

This general model underpins the research reported in this book.

Teacher Careers in Crisis

A study of teacher careers might appear timely for two main reasons. One is that there are few such studies, especially along the lines indicated above. Work reported tends to be sectional, with particular interest in the early years of initiation into teaching (for example, Hannam *et al*, 1971; Hanson and Herrington, 1976; Lacey, 1977); or in the impact of certain events or policies, like secondary school reorganization (Riseborough, 1981). Or they are concerned with teachers as a body, or as groups (for example, Purvis, 1973; Ginsburg *et al*, 1980; Lawn and Ozga, 1981). There is a notable American work (Lortie, 1975), and one British study (Lyons, 1981) with a similar approach to ours, but there are important differences between American and British teachers and the latter has a restricted methodology (single interviews), and consequently a rather thin data base.

The other reason is that teacher careers (like almost everything else in education) are currently held to be in crisis. The term indicates a disjuncture of one sort or another, for example between past and present career perceptions large enough to render the future problematic, to disturb teachers' sense of well-being and to threaten their teaching efficiency.

In a sense, however, there have been problems of different kinds in teacher careers for some time (Grace, 1972). For many, the initial trauma of socialization into the role is the biggest crisis in their lives (Taylor and Dale, 1971; Hanson and Herrington, 1976). There are disjunctures at this stage between ideals an practice, expectations and actuality, requirements of the role and personal predilections, capacity (of knowledge, skills and work load) and demands. Most teachers overcome this hurdle, but for many stress continues to be a prominent feature of their everyday work. Hargreaves (1978) talks of the 'debilitating occupational disease' of teaching. Kyriacou and Sutcliffe (1979, p. 89) found a third of their respondents (130 comprehensive school teachers) rating being a teacher as either very or extremely stressful, and two of the likely sources appeared to be 'poor career structure' and 'inadequate pay' (see also Dunham, 1977). And the International Labour Organization (1981) reported stress, low morale, and insecurity for teachers throughout the world, but especially in Western countries.

Teaching has been represented by some as having very little career structure, in the objective sense. Purvis (1973) for example, argues that most are faced by 'flat, dead-end opportunities', and Lortie (1975) described teaching in the USA as 'career-less' compared with most other kinds of middle-class work, and thus ideal for those women whose prime commitment was to the family, and for whom teaching offered the appropriate kind of unstructured 'in-and-out' kind of engagement (see also Krause, 1971). Blanche Greer (1971, p. 231) would agree, pointing out that, 'the number of positions available in a given school, as in any organization with a two- or three-step hierarchy and relatively undifferentiated work, is small in relation to the number of people ... on the bottom rung of the ladder. In this respect, teaching is a dead-end job without the traditionally compelling valuable — promotion. Consequently, according to Dreeben (1970, p. 172), 'The occupational irony of teaching is that teachers must renounce their occupation in order to advance'.

It is doubtful, however, whether the position is quite so stark in Britain, and certainly the greater majority of our sample, both men and women, as we shall see, expected some kind of promotion. For the most part, this would be within the framework of the Burnham scales. These have gradually taken over from a comparatively egalitarian position that had held since the war, marked by an emphasis on basic pay. In April 1982, 31.5 per cent of all school teachers were on scale 1, 21.3 per cent on scale 2, 14.9 per cent on scale 3, 6.3 per cent on scale 4, 1.4 per cent were senior teachers, and 13.6 per cent deputy heads or heads. Thus, nearly two-thirds of all teachers were on either scale 1 or 2, though it is a considerably lower proportion for secondary school teachers (especially male), with which this study is concerned. Despite this flattened pyramid, it is a hierarchical structure that was justified at the time it was introduced as offering opportunities and advancing professionalism. As Roy (1983, pp. 78–9) notes:

> ... the advocates of the basic scale faded away, to be replaced by new leaders wanting a fair deal for every teacher, linking promotion to different salary scales and thus enabling every teacher to see clearly the existence of a promotion ladder; you start at scale 1, move to scales 2 and 3, and if you are lucky, with good qualifications and happen to teach in a secondary school (and, he might have added, if you are male) to scale 4.

However, Lacey (1983) has suggested there is a basic contradiction here. He argues that this hierarchical structure represented an advance in bureaucratization, which in some important respects is at odds with professionalization, especially in the area of relationships. Lacey draws attention to a distinction between organic and mechanistic styles of management (Burns, 1966). 'Mechanistic' could be applied to the current structure of teacher careers, in that it involves specialisms, hierarchies, rules. The organic style by contrast is characterized mainly by 'lateral consultation rather than vertical command', and posts are defined in terms of tasks facing the organization as a whole, rather than duties and powers, and is, claim its advocates, more adapted to change. Burns relates the organic style to professionalization, and sees the mechanistic style as alien to it. Lacey concludes, therefore, that the development of a hierarchical career structure and claims for greater recognition as a profession are basically contradictory, and work against each other (see also Dreeben, 1970). Add to this a number of other factors that traditionally impede teachers' claim to professionalism — a poor public image, reluctant, coerced clientele, depressed pay scales, the nature of their work — adults in a children's world (Waller, 1932) — the absence of a general teachers' council, the intangibility of the product which make them 'particularly vulnerable to the self-doubt and status panic that characterize many white-collar workers' (Webb, 1983; Lewis, 1979) — and teachers can be said to have regressed in recent years in their aspirations for professional recognition. Further, Lawn and Ozga (1981) argue that teachers in general are now more workers than professionals, a change reflected in the increased emphasis on trade unionism as opposed to professionalism (Ginsburg *et al*, 1980). Lawn and Ozga claim that teachers have become increasingly proletarianized, arguing that they have lost many of their former benefits which traditionally distinguished them from other workers; have become more vulnerable to extreme pressures; and are losing control of the work process.

Herein lies another disjuncture, for, some argue, the trend towards greater centralization and growing demands for accountability are basically contradictory (though see Sockett, 1983). The moves towards a centralized curriculum, new forms of assessment, particularly those under the aegis of the Assessment of Performance Unit, the demise of the Schools Council with its teacher majority, and its replacement by Curriculum and Examination bodies answerable to the Secretary of State, the newly-proposed General Certificate of Secondary Education (with its nationally agreed criteria formulated by the examination body) — all are symptomatic of the centralization which will displace the kind of localized teacher knowledge and expertise which goes into, for example, the construction of and preparation for CSE Mode 3.

Teacher power is being challenged in other ways. The 1980 and 1981 Education Acts increased the statutory rights of parents and governors. The education of the older adolescent, particularly the non-academic pupils, is increasingly being channelled away from schools. Teachers have been made more accountable to further and higher education, and to the world of work. Their teaching is becoming increasingly open to inspection and assessment. But, Roy (1983) has argued, 'if you have direct control, you cannot have accountability, for accountability implies the exercise of judgment and discretion, control simply means that you do what you are told. Thus control of the educational process, and the accountability of teachers to the various interest groups, are incompatible' (p. 97).

However, the disjuncture that probably runs deepest at the moment is that arising from the economic crisis, falling rolls and government policy which have promoted cuts in educational resources and blockages (and in some cases stoppages) and re-routings in teacher careers which contrast greatly with the comparative days of plenty in the 1960s. The scale of this change can be judged by the figures. In 1983, 6350 opted for premature retirement or accepted redundancy, making a total of about 30,000 since 1977, at an average age of 56.8. Government estimates suggest that 65,000 will have retired before the official age by 1989 (DES statistics). For those who are left, there is almost a moratorium in some areas on teachers' chances of promotion. And many are having to bend their talents in hitherto unsuspected directions, for example in multi-subject teaching (Briault and Smith, 1980).

Contrast this with the halcyon 1960s. In 1948, there were 198,234 teachers; in 1972, 395,219. This reflected the rise in pupil numbers from 5.4 million to 8.5 million. Educational expenditure rose from £200 million in 1948 to £2,000 million in 1972, from 2.8 per cent of the gross national product to 6.6 per cent (see Dennison, 1981). Promotions were comparatively plentiful, over half of those in the late 1960s and early 1970s resulting from the creation of new posts. During this whole growth period, some teachers just walked into jobs:

> *R:* So after you left art college, you got the job in South Wales?
> *Mrs Castle:* It was a mixed grammar school, small grammar school, it was advertised, and I applied, they were very short of art teachers,

and it was offered to me through the post, it was I who insisted on an interview.

R: It's inconceivable these days isn't it.

Mrs Castle: Yes indeed it is! (64, retired, art)

Thus, teachers beginning their careers during that period geared their future expectations to a growing area of high priority. For many, those expectations have now been dashed. For middle-aged teachers — those who began teaching in the 1960s and early 1970s — the crisis is particularly acute. Previous career 'timetables' (Roth, 1971), whereby a teacher might expect normally to be on a certain scale or in a certain post by a certain age are no longer appropriate. These teachers suffer from the general implication in bureaucratic careers that

> there was something 'wrong' with the person who was in the career phase usually characteristic of people at a different life-cycle stage from him, at any rate characteristic of those younger than him. It is socially acceptable, so to speak, to beat one's age-graded career status by being young for the phase or status, but not the other way round (Sofer, 1970, p. 55).

However, Corrie's (1981) teachers did feel that one could advance too fast as well as too slow. He concluded (p. 22) that 'there is a reasonable and just rate of movement within teaching'. Unreasonable movement, especially delay, could bring on an identity crisis. As Strauss (1959) notes: 'An essential part of this critical experience is that a man's naming of himself is disoriented. He is not what he thought he was. This is a classificatory disorientation'.

This has brought on what Cole (1984) has termed a 'motivation crisis'. This is further aggravated by increasing dissatisfaction about pay. Teachers are currently (1984) claiming that their earnings have dropped in comparison with other non-manual groups from 137 per cent of the average in 1974 (the year of the Houghton Report) to 110 per cent in 1983. They further claim that the average professional salary has increased by 270 per cent compared with the teachers' increase of only 198 per cent, reflecting the 'marked deterioration in the financial and hence social standing of teachers in society' (*Times Educational Supplement*, 17 August 1984, pp. 10–11). Some of our sample felt these changes keenly. All of them felt that teachers' status had declined.

> Declined, I'm absolutely certain of that. I think society generally is down on and against authority, and I think teachers come in to that category. (Mr King, 63, retired, science)

> It has declined, very badly. When I began teaching, people thought quite highly of it as a career. When I retired, I began to think it was going downhill. (Miss Nott, 67, retired, art)

Teachers who had grown up in rural areas felt this particularly strongly.

Well being brought up in a village, you had the local factory owner, and the clergy and the teachers. They were the sort of upper class. (Mr Shaw, 45, scale 3, Head of Department, rural science)

For teachers who had spent their childhood in the country, getting themselves into the teaching profession had seemed an enormous achievement.

Mr Shoe: We lived in a rather feudal system. I remember the rector at the time. He was more or less the lord of the manor. When my mother put myself and an elder brother through college, he said 'Isn't she not rising a bit out of her station?' 'How dare my mother put her sons through college!' Mother felt that she'd like better for us, than what she'd had.

R: And being a teacher was that?

Mr Shoe: Oh yes, and better than what the rest of the family had. In those days a school master was someone you stood to attention — almost — he had the respect you see, and he was a figure in the community. People who had gone to university and come out with a degree were gods in those days. It wasn't for me, much as I'd have liked to have done it. I think it is sad to think that the respect that kiddies had for the image of a teacher is going. I am sad to see it. (63, retired, science)

What is interesting, is that teachers perceived the status of their job as declining at precisely the same time that their salaries began going up. However, many teachers complained bitterly about the salary levels when they had first begun teaching.

At first, well I had to go out and do things. I wasn't beyond digging ditches and cutting corn, I helped out on the farms. (Mr Shoe, 63, retired, science)

I remember the first salary I had, having tried to pay everything that one had to, left me with about a pound to keep a family on. (Mr Quilley, 67, retired, art)

The pay was so bad, that I used to pick tomatoes, drive lorries, anything. (Mr King, 65, retired, science)

Teachers had felt that in their early career, the security of the job was some compensation.

I think I came from a generation where parents tended to instil in you that you wanted a secure job, and not to be too venturesome. Maybe this was a bad thing, I don't know, you didn't take risks. You said 'This is a secure job, a pensioned job, it's a job for life'. (Mr Shoe, 63, retired, science)

This, however, no longer holds. Several of our younger teachers questioned the security of their job situation in the current context and felt that their status as professionals was also in question.

> In earlier days, teachers were certainly treated with more respect locally. But now, I always remember one laddie saying to me in a pleasant sort of way 'my dad's earning thousands more than you'. He had contempt for a teacher's position. (Mr King, 65, retired, science)

One consequence is this:

> The young chap in my department, he's good. I don't want to lose him. He's been here four years and I think he ought to be on a two but I am told that he cannot be on a two, we haven't got any points to spare. So what'll happen? He's young. He wants a family — in fact his wife's just learnt she's pregnant, he needs the money so as soon as he can he'll go. It's like that all the time now. If they want good teachers they should pay for them. But do they heck as like! (Brian, 44 scale 4, Head of Art)

Teachers, therefore, experience blockages, finding not just one avenue closed in the school they are in, but also alternative ones. Those who suddenly find their promotion chances nullified no longer enjoy the option of changing schools. Many are stuck where they are, therefore, with all the escalators having broken down, facing frustration, 'staleness', lowered ambition, drive and performance (Hunter and Heighway, 1980, p. 475).

Thus, as well as a search for new career maps and timetables within teaching, we might expect a search for alternative careers elsewhere. Teaching is traditionally a kind of profit and loss engagement, where difficulties are balanced out by advantages, failures by successes. But in the current straitened circumstances, there is little to balance out the losses. Even the centrepiece of the intrinsic rewards teachers say they gain from their job — pupil response and progress — is under threat, being increasingly under the cloak of teenage unemployment and the general 16+ crisis. 'What are we teaching for?' thus becomes a question that relates not only to career, but to educational goals in general.

There may be a generational aspect which aggravates this problem for some. According to one of our informants:

> Of course teachers have changed, course the demands on teachers have changed ... In the sense that if you go back to the conditions between the two wars, by and large teachers knew what they were doing. I mean nowadays I think they're not quite sure. There's so many people with ideas about what education should be that you get teachers not really being quite sure what they're about. I think also the vast expansion of education since the war has meant that all sorts of people have got into education who not really, never ought to have

been there. They've not been really sought out as what?, no doubt some of them should never have got into, actually been let loose with children ... Those who had come through the teacher training systems that were in operation, well, 1918 sort of times ... they were, what? They were fairly sure of their own importance for one thing, they thought being a teacher was something. They thought it was a thing that was important in the community and I think that gave them a sense of being able to cope with just about everything that was put on their plate, and when you take that generation who were the people who went into the last war in the teaching profession and coped with all the exigencies that occurred during that period, I think they stood up to it enormously well ... I think they were surer, more secure of themselves than a lot of modern teachers are ... for my generation of teachers I don't think expectations of us were as well defined as they had previously been. (Jim, 65, retired, science)

For some, the motivation crisis has been aggravated, and indeed dominated, by other concerns, for example secondary school reorganization. Riseborough (1981) has shown how a particular group of secondary modern school teachers lost status and indeed all sense of previously held notions of career, when their school amalgamated with a grammar (see also Sikes, 1984b). Young, highly qualified teachers were appointed over their heads and their own general teaching skills were devalued. In fact they lost all their identity in this new organization — another case of 'classificatory disorientation' — and their main source of gratification came not from teaching but in tormenting the headmaster, thus forming a counter-culture among the staff. As one of them said, 'If you take this status away, not all the money in the world will make (a teacher) feel content with his job, and this is what teaching is all about, you've got to feel right'.

One might argue here, following Lacey (1983), that the bureaucratic structure of the school was ill-suited to handle the changes involved. Counter-functions developed, the bad feeling being projected upward to the top of the hierarchy. On the other hand, it could be argued that this was simply a case of bad management, which may have resulted from policy and/or under-resourcing. Either way, reorganization caused problems for some of this group, though it should be noted that for others, including some in our sample, it opened up new prospects, particularly on the pastoral side.

Another group who may not 'feel right' as a result of reorganization is that of some ex-grammar school teachers, who came into teaching through their interest in the academic pursuit of a subject, and who now find that not only may they be required to teach more subjects, but also to groups of mixed ability. In the comprehensive school, with a different kind of organization and ideology from the grammar school, they find themselves being asked to do basically a different kind of job from the one they joined up to do, and having to undergo some fundamental identity change if they are to manage it.

With the comprehensive intake everything changed. I didn't like the job any more. I mean I'd definitely never have chosen to go into teaching as a comprehensive school teacher. I liked the traditional academic emphasis, and ethos of the grammar school. It's not that I'm not prepared to teach people lower down the ability scale, but if they don't want to learn or can't understand then that's not something I wanted to be involved with. (Mr Count, 54, retired, science)

We reorganized from the little elementary school to the 2000 pupil comprehensive. From the sublime to the ridiculous. Two thousand on roll. The staffroom was like a station waiting room. Nobody knew anybody. I mean I'd been there thirty years and a lot of the teachers at the comprehensive were strangers to me. And I eventually moved out and went into Lincolnshire to get away from the comprehensive system which I didn't agree with and I still don't. But it caught up with me in the end and I left, I retired. (Arthur, 69, retired, art)

Teachers trained for years at university to pass on specialist information to eager pupils can no longer hope to impart what they know for more than a small percentage of their time, if at all. I know from experience that I shall never see a single 'O' level class. I may never teach another 'A' level group. Yet this school has over 1000 pupils. Instead I shall try and help a few while drowning in a mass of disruptive and hopeful leavers. I find this frustrating. It isn't at all something I would have chosen to do with my life. (Male, 47, scale 4, ex-grammar school)

I think the kind of science teaching we were taught to teach was the kind of science that one would do at a selective grammar school. Probably because the teacher trainers were ex-grammar school teachers and their expectations were based on the sort of school they'd taught in. It's very difficult, for me at any rate, and I still haven't learnt how to control a class and create a learning situation with the less able kids. I don't really quite know how to do it. (Keith, 38, scale 1, chemistry)

This, of course, is not necessarily an argument against comprehensive education, though the points made above are often used to that effect. Our argument is, rather, that it is, partly at least, a product of the impact of particular education policies on particular points of the teacher career.

Mid-career teachers are the group more likely to be adversely affected, for they have been well settled in their previous job and are required to make a profound change. Moreover, they have little alternative, for they are not qualified to do anything else, and it is too late for them to re-train (see Woods, 1981a). Older teachers, perhaps, like Arthur above, have the option of retirement, while the younger generation coming into teaching, that have been coming in over quite a period of years now, this mix of pastoral and academic is part of what they've seen around them all the time ... and I think that will improve more in time as more of the oldies go. (Kath, 59, retired, science)

So there are problems coming at teachers from all sides, and they compound one another. For example, an organic or participatory school organization might be expected to handle some of these changes, possibly in an educationally productive way. But a bureaucratic one, as Riseborough's study vividly shows, can make things very much worse. Again, teachers are required to be more accountable, to teach more subjects (including several new ones), but with fewer resources. These incompatibilities and disjunctures, therefore, combine to produce an unprecedented crisis in teacher careers.

The Research

The research was guided by interactionist principles (Woods, 1983). We were interested in how individuals adapted to, or sought to change, situations; how they managed roles and constraints; and, as we have noted, *their* perceptions of their careers (Hughes, 1937). We wondered how the 'crisis' was affecting teachers' views of their jobs, whether, for example, it had weakened their sense of commitment, or caused them to re-define the teacher role or to search for new career routes and timetables (Roth, 1963). We hoped we might be able to suggest how 'spoiled careers' (Goffman, 1961) arising from these developments might be averted, and what structural changes might be made within schools to help meet these problems.

Inevitably, as we investigated deeper and deeper into teacher careers, we journeyed beyond the present crisis, and beyond the social, political and economic factors discussed earlier. For there have been other crises and critical points in many teachers' careers, and other powerful influences. Gradually, therefore, we built up a picture of teacher careers consisting of typical ages and stages, and of critical transitional periods, in which the present crisis must be situated. In our account we have concentrated on this overview, for it is only within this general framework that current events can be understood. Indeed, the major theoretical interest in the present crisis derives from the fact that it highlights the more long-term aspects of teachers' careers. Career structures are more usually loosely and hazily held in teachers' minds (Lacey, 1977). Uncommon events or difficulties bring them to the forefront and give them shape, making them more amenable to research. Thus the crisis is a touchstone to deeper and wider investigation of teacher careers, during the present situation — and in the future.

The preliminary theoretical cast of the research emerged from recent work on teacher strategies. Most work on teacher socialization focusses on constraints, and the initial years only of teaching (Hanson and Herrington, 1976; Taylor and Dale, 1971; Hannam *et al*, 1971). Recently Lacey (1977), though also concentrating on the initiation of teachers, has elaborated a model which is designed to facilitate a more balanced study of the process, which would include the individual teacher's own impact. This proposes three major orientations

1 Strategic compliance, in which an individual complies with a senior's definition of the situation, but holds private reservations.
2 Internalized adjustment, in which the individual complies but changes one's own views to believe it is for the best.
3 Strategic redefinition, in which the individual seeks to change the situation. Further investigation of this area on a wider basis is of crucial importance in two respects.

First, educationally, intending and practising teachers have much to learn from such a study. The critical question is: what degree of freedom do teachers have to achieve their own personal aims? Lacey's broad model allows for consideration of both those who will personally adjust to any situation, and those who will seek to change radically any situation they find. However, between these two extremes, there are a variety of adaptations. There has, as yet, been *no* systematic study of these. We do not know the range of possibilities. The present evidence is that initial teacher socialization is traumatic, involving deep changes in self and perspectives. Knowledge of how others have come to terms with the system, coped with the problems and made their individual contributions might increase the prospects for personal satisfaction, and the redefinition of situations more in line with personal aspirations.

In terms of Lacey's model, our research would include an empirical test of the conceptual mode of adaptation he terms 'strategic redefinition', addressing such questions as — does it occur? If so, under what conditions? and what is its nature? The research should also afford insights into how individuals employ redefinition, compliance or personal adjustment, or any other mode, in different circumstances.

The essentially strategic cast of our teachers is illustrated in this response:

It's perhaps a survival instinct. I don't know, it is just a feeling, at times, that in order to survive and in order to protect and I am not thinking of being purely conservative, with a little c, but in order to protect perhaps what I value — but in terms of things like my subject, within a committee room, in order to protect that and let it retain some kind of status you have got to be open and you have got to lay your cards on the table but I think at times you have got to be bloody minded, you have got to dig your heels in and say 'enough is enough', or 'no' or 'yes', or whatever. You have got to be, and I think it is very closely related, if you want to use a word like I do, 'devious', you have got to be. That sounds very scheming and underhand and I don't mean it in that way. You have got to be willing to look at the problem and try and work out what the opposition is going to be. It is just like playing chess, though I can't play chess. You have got to try and work out your opponent's next move . . . because if not, some rather astute guy is suddenly going to wipe you clean off the board and you are going to think later, 'God if only I had done (so-and-so), that situation wouldn't have arisen' . . . I think this approach is something that's grown, something I've developed over the years as a response to circumstances you might say. (Brian, 44, scale 4, head of art)

Secondly, sociologically, such a study holds much promise for developing theory concerning the relationships between micro and macro processes, a matter currently of much debate within the discipline. One of the developments addressed to this problem is the construction of a model of teacher socialization arouind the concept of *coping strategy* (Hargreaves, 1977, 1978 and 1979; Pollard, 1982; Lacey, 1977; Woods, 1979). In essence, this allows us to envisage what exactly has to be coped with and its origins on the one hand, and the creative act of coping on the other. The latter aspect has been less well studied than the former. In particular, we do not have teachers' own views of coping, nor are any of the studies to date situated within the context of the entire teacher career and biography. We proposed to make these (teacher views and biographies) the central features of the research.

Method

The method deemed most suitable for this kind of research was that of the 'life history'. Denzin (1970) remarks that the 'life history may be the best method for studying adult socialization, the situational response of self to daily interactional contingencies'. Its chief feature is the 'prolonged interview', which in fact consists of a series of interviews, in which the subject and interviewer interact to probe and reflect on the subject's statements. The interview is supported where possible by documentary evidence and reports from persons other than the subject. The method, popular amongst 'the Chicago school', but largely out of fashion since, is due for a rebirth, for the promise it holds of situating ethnographic studies within a broader perspective (Goodson, 1980; Faraday and Plummer, 1979; Bertaux, 1981).

The advantages of the approach for this present research are as follows:

1 It is 'holistic', that is to say concerned with a teacher's total life and career, and not just a segment or aspect of it. For a full understanding of teacher interests and motives, we need as near complete a biographical picture as we can acquire. Three examples illustrate the importance we attach to this:
   (i) Nearly all studies of teachers consider them only in their

professional roles, and neglect informal processes. Yet the teachers we have interviewed have emphasized the overwhelming importance of the latter.

(ii) Mardle and Walker (1980) have suggested the importance of latent culture as sedimented in biography for any teacher model of strategy, but none have so far pursued this suggestion.

(iii) The HMI Report *The New Teacher in School* (HMSO, 1982) identified personality traits as no less important than academic attainments for success in teaching (and, incidentally, concluded that 25 per cent of new teachers were not satisfactory by the end of their probationary year).

Another aspect of this holism is the fact that life histories can embrace various modes of consciousness (Giddens, 1979). Cole (1984) has drawn attention to the possibility that what some studies have taken to indicate a change of attitude in teachers, may simply reflect a change in mode of consciousness which some methods are not equipped to trace. Again, this is recognizing the crucial interactionist point about the influence of situations, and the need to contextualize findings within them.

2 It is 'historical', and hence promises to add depth to our ethnographic case studies.

3 It bestrides the micro-macro interface. In studying a life-history, one is forced to consider its historical context and the dialectical relationship between self and society. As Goodson (1980, p. 74) puts it:

> Through the life history, we gain insights into individuals' coming to terms with imperatives in the social structure ... From the collection of life histories, we discern what is general within a range of individual studies; links are thereby made with macro theories but from a base that is clearly grounded within personal biography.

However, life histories do not present themselves to us as a fully-fledged method ready for use. There is, as yet, no substantial body of methodological literature to support life history studies, as there is now in ethnography. Development of the method, therefore, was also a research concern, and has been reported in detail in Measor (1984) and Woods (1985). In these papers we discuss the central life history method of conversations, the possibilities for educational theory and its grounding within the data (Glaser and Strauss, 1967), and respondent validation. We emphasize the importance of the negotiation of access in such intimate work, the building of a relationship within a fixed time constraint, and the significance of the researcher's appearance and personal style. We also thought it important to consider images that were held by the teachers of the researcher.

Interviews (or, rather 'conversations') lasted on average for one to one and a half hours, and varied in number from two to seven, with an average of four-five. This number depended either on availability or the lengths to which the teacher was prepared to go. Generally they were very cooperative. The interviewer would adopt an unstructured approach, pursuing themes jointly with the teacher. The early meetings were largely factual, composing a 'career-map'. Then, aspects of it that appeared of particular importance to the teacher were taken up. The interviewer's task here was to aid the teacher's recall, and not to lead or suggest. Thus the interviewer would seek to fill gaps, test information given in various ways, act as devil's advocate on occasions, draw on their own experience and career, and those of others, to spark off other lines of thought. The conversations were tape-recorded with the teachers' consent, and transcribed.

The Teachers

In organizing our sample, we were guided by the principle that numbers must be small, in the first instance at least, because of the intensive detail required of each individual life; but large enough eventually to yield a comparison, and to permit a measure of generalizability. The sample, therefore was organized as follows:

1   Area

Local authorities differ considerably in policy and resource input into education, and this can have a markedly different impact on teacher careers. We therefore selected two areas, one Southern and Conservative-controlled, and the other Northern and Labour-controlled.

2   Age

The three key points indicated in pilot work were

(a)   three years into teaching;
(b)   mid-career;
(c)   retirement.

Previous research has concentrated heavily on teacher training and the probationary year. We aimed to counter-balance this by including a fair proportion of older teachers selected from other critical career points.

3   Subject

We selected an equal number of art and design and science teachers. These subjects were chosen because of their contrast in methods, environment, pedagogy and thought processes, and status and social position within the school, all of which might be reasoned to have a markedly different impact on self and career. An additional reason for selecting art teachers was that there have been very few studies of them.

4 Sex

It is well known that men and women have very different kinds of teaching careers (see, for example, Lortie, 1975; Purvis, 1973).

For these comparisons to hold, all were to have taught for the most part in secondary schools, and to be in positions below deputy head teacher. The sample in each area would therefore be composed as follows:

	MEN	WOMEN
	(2 Artists,	2 scientists)
Near retirement	4	4
Mid-career	4	4
Three-year teachers	4	4

In each area, therefore, there would be a total of twenty-four teachers, making forty-eight as a whole.

Such neat symmetry is unusual in qualitative work, and it turned out to be unrealistic in ours. It was difficult to find women science teachers. Older art teachers were not all that common in the Northern area either. In fact the whole task of assembling the sample and negotiating access proved a formidable one, and we were forced to cut a few corners. The sample thus lost its quantitative neatness, but the original categories were all represented.

A second problem with the sample as it stood was that the art teachers had much more to say than the scientists. This was to be expected to some degree, since we were operating in a medium that held biasses in favour of the artist. In some areas this difference does not matter since they were of accord. Elsewhere, we have tried to counter-balance by including a higher proportion of the scientists' accounts than of the artists'.

Another feature of the sample was that where possible we chose teachers in small groups who knew each other and had either shared some previous teaching experiences or had taught at different historical periods in the same school. This constituted a form of triangulation, whereby we were able to get more than one view of a particular incident or situation.

Throughout the book, we have adopted a means of identifying teacher quotes on the lines of the four major indices by giving teachers' ages, subjects, and names. The latter are pseudonyms, but they indicate sex and area, the Northern teachers being referred to by their christian names (except for Mr Bridge and Mr Count), the Southern by surnames. This, significantly perhaps, is how they chose to be known to the two researchers.

Full details of the sample are as follows:

Southern Sample

(a)   Retired teachers

    Art   Mr King, 65, (Valley Boys)
               retired, art, degree and PGCE

               Mr Quilley, 67, (Hartford Grammar School)
               retired, art, art college and teacher training

               Mrs Castle, 64, (Valley Girls)
               retired, art, art college and teacher training

               Miss Nott, 66, (Jameson Secondary Modern)
               retired, art, art college and teacher training

    Science   Mr Ladyhill, 67, (Valley Boys)
               retired, science, degree, PGCE

               Mr Shoe, 63, (Ambrose School)
               retired, science, certificate of education, college of education

               Miss Evans, 70, (Valley Girls)
               retired, science, degree, PGCE

(b)   Mid-career teachers

    Art   Mr Shark 45, (Ambrose School)
               scale 4, Head of Department, art, degree, PGCE

               Mr Redford, 33, (Linkfield Comprehensive)
               scale 4, Head of Department, art college, teacher training, MA

               Mrs Think, 38, (Prospington School for Girls — private
               school)
               scale 4, Head of Department, art, art college, no teacher
               training, MA

               Mrs Armitage, 35, (Lands' Comprehensive School)
               scale 2, art, certificate of education, college of education

    Science   Mr Shaw, 45, (Hopton Comprehensive)
               scale 3, Head of Department, rural science, certificate of
               education, college of education, BA, MA

               Mr Ray, 38, (Cityside Comprehensive)
               scale 4, Head of Department, science, degree, PGCE, MA

               Mrs Vicar, 39, (Valley Girls School)
               scale 3, certificate of education, college of education

(c) Young teachers

Art   Mr Indus, 28, (Finwood Comprehensive)
scale 2, art college, teacher training, MA almost completed at the time of interviews

Miss Lavalle, 27, (Downland Comprehensive)
scale 2, art and technology, certificate of education, college of education, craft, design, technology diploma

Miss Judd, 25, (Jayne Comprehensive)
scale 1, art, art college and teacher training

Science   Mr Tucks, 29, (Hingleys Grammar School)
scale 2, science and maths, degree, PGCE, MA

Mr Hardy, 27, (Merton Comprehensive)
scale 2, City & Guilds qualification, work in industry, BA, PGCE

Mrs Boyd, 26, (Linkfield Comprehensive)
scale 2, science, degree, PGCE

Northern Sample

(a) Retired teachers

Art   Arthur, 69, (Roman School)
retired, art, certificate of education, college of education

Mr Bridge, 58,
retired, art, degree

Science   Jim, 65,
retired, science, certificate in education, college of education

Mr Count, 54, (Roman School)
retired, science, degree, PGCE

Kath, 59,
retired, science, degree

(b) Mid–career teachers

Art   Brian, 44, (Hedge School)
scale 4, Head of Art, certificate of education, college of education

John, 44, (Roman School)
scale 4, Head of Art, degree, PGCE

Helen, 40, (Rural School)

scale 3, Head of Art, certificate of education, college of education

Ann, 43, (Roman School)
scale 1, art, certificate of education, college of education

Sally, 44, (Roman School)
scale 3, art, Head of Year, degree

Science   Dave, 44, (Rural School)
senior teacher, Head of Science, degree, PGCE

Mike, 46, (Rural School)
scale 3, Head of Physics, degree, PGCE

Ray, 38, (Rural School)
scale 3, Head of Biology , BEd, college of education, MEd

Keith, 38, (Roman School)
scale 1, chemistry, degree, PGCE, late entrant

Margery, 45, (Roman School)
scale 3, Head of Chemistry, degree

Christine, 33, (Classic School)
scale 3, Head of Physics, degree

(c)   Younger teachers

Art   Jan, 25, (Classic School)
scale 1, art, BEd, college of education

Sarah, 25, (Waterlands High School)
scale 1, art, BEd, college of education

Chris, 28, (Hedge School)
scale 1, art, degree, PGCE

Science   Pete, 25, (Rural School)
scale 1, biology, degree, PGCE

Structure of the Book

We begin with an overview of the life-cycle of the teacher. There are, of course, many careers within teaching, but it seemed to us that there was a general framework of age-stages and tasks appropriate to them suggested by our sample. Our material had affinities with a model of adult development proposed by Levinson *et al* (1978). On the basis of empirical research, derived from a biographical interviewing technique, they argue that 'the life structure evolves through a relatively orderly sequence (of eras) during the adult years' (*ibid,* p. 49), and that each era is characterized and identified by 'its own distinctive and unifying qualities which have to do with the character of living'. We found five distinctive eras among our teachers, (a) those between 21–28 years old; (b) 28–33; (c) 30–40; (d) 40–50/55; and (e) 50–55+, and we investigate the character of each of these in Chapter 1.

This does not mean that the teacher necessarily experiences smooth career progression. Rather, a typical career is marked by critical incidents or phases (Chapter 2) which either give it a beneficial boost, deal it a savage blow, or both at the same time. One such period is that of initiation into teaching, the first two to three years in post. This is well known, and there have been several works that relate the traumas of this induction (Taylor and Dale, 1971; Hannam *et al,* 1971; Hanson and Herrington, 1976). We see it, however, within the context of the whole teacher career, and examine its implications for teacher identity and for future teacher career lines.

From our conversations with teachers, certain well-defined themes emerged. As might be expected from the cast of the study, one of these was to do with coping with the demands, pressures and constraints involved in teaching over the years (Chapter 3). The accumulation of strategical knowledge is, in fact, one kind of career. Previous work in the area of teacher strategies has not considered the career dimensions. But, one might argue that a very salient part of a teacher's (or anybody else's) career lies in strategical development. Teachers call it 'experience'. It is the ability to match means to ends in complicated equations involving abilities, resources and constraints. It is not learnt in a day, but gradually acquired over the years. How teachers develop strategies to manage constraints is discussed in Chapter 3.

One of the most important strategical requirements teachers face is meeting the expectations others are seen as having of the teacher role, when their own personal predilections may be at variance with it in some respects. In our research, we become aware of repeated references to 'becoming' or 'being a proper teacher'. We were eager to delineate the main features of such a type, as they perceived it to be, and to investigate their own accommodations to it over their careers as a whole. What does it mean to resist the role? What scope do teachers have for alternatives? What factors are associated with being, or not being, a proper teacher? What implications does this 'teacher deviance' have for education; and for teacher careers? These matters will be investigated in Chapter 4.

In the present straitened circumstances, teachers may have to develop not only new attitudes to roles, but new career routes within the organizations they are in. Since lateral and vertical avenues are blocked, these need to be of a different nature from those traditionally viewed as making up a teacher's career structure. All the more reason, therefore, why we should consider the management of schools, the power structures and the organization of relationships. Here, our sample endorsed the greater personal rewards and gratifications to be gained from an organic, participatory system, and the heightened tribulations coming from a mechanistic bureaucratic one. In a sense, the participatory model is still an unfulfilled, and somewhat deviant one (Hunter, 1981; Hunter and Heighway, 1980). In the latter respect, therefore, it matches our findings about, and analysis of the role, at an institutional level. This will be discussed in Chapter 5.

Managing the role, and status and power within the institution, are crucial elements in the composition of a teacher's identity. There were two others, we discovered, of critical importance — the subject one teaches, and the pupils. Curiously, pupils have received little attention in their impact on teachers and education, other than in a normative framework (see Riseborough, 1983). Yet for many teachers, this is what the job is all about — teaching one's subject to children (Lacey 1977; Lyons 1981). Further, while it is no doubt the case that many enter teaching with a strong positive attitude toward children, there are many unforeseen situations and interactions wherein pupils bring their influence to bear, from the trials of 'sussings-out' (Beynon, 1984; Ball, 1980) to the kind of redemptive support that gives teachers their greatest rewards (Lortie, 1975). On the other hand, they have been known to drive some teachers out of teaching altogether. In between are a multitude of accommodations.

There has been some incidental work on this. Hargreaves (1972) has referred to the well-known staffroom 'norm of cynicism'. Pupils invariably fall short of one's initial, ideal, expectations. Cynicism is one way of coping. Teachers have been heard jokingly complaining that they have 'lost their sense of mission', but the joke is a thin veil over a quite basic reorientation and change in commitment. We see teachers coping, too, with recalcitrant pupils in studies of staffroom humour (Woods, 1979) and ideology (Hammersley, 1984). Some teachers have been noted excluding pupils from their lives altogether, through absences, manipulation of the timetable, or subtle tricks of consciousness (Woods, 1979). Type of pupil may constitute the main factor in a teacher's career, rather than any structured promotion. Clearly, then, pupils are a crucial influence on teachers' careers, as was evident from the testimony of our sample, and we shall consider this in Chapter 6.

The importance of the subject to many teachers is well recognized (Ball and Lacey, 1980; Goodson, 1981). It is the acquisition of specialist knowledge and skills that stamps the teacher as a person of special worth. That relating to one's subject rides above the problems, intricacies, pitfalls, and blocked opportunities of the hierarchical structure. It is a counter-vailing force against bureaucracy, giving one a firm foothold in the semi-autonomy of the subject department, affording status within it, and bolstered by a like-minded community.

However, as with pupils, one's relationship to subject does not stand still for all time. Knowledge advances, skills can decline, priorities and commitments change. With their crowded timetables, teachers — especially those of knowledge-based subjects like the sciences — find it difficult to keep up with the latest development. So that while they may remain an expert in that area in the context of the school, their expertise within their own reference group of scholars may become increasingly jaded. Furthermore, subjects are not taught in a vacuum. They vie with other subjects for teaching time, for resources, for clientele. Some fight for survival, or at least contest unwelcome amalgamations, in a rationalized curriculum. The meaning of the subject to teachers within their careers we examine in Chapter 7.

Finally, in Chapter 8, we seek to draw out the main theoretical implications and policy recommendations emerging from the research.

Chapter 1

The Life Cycle of the Teacher

They stay young, they stay young and they stay young, and you get older and older and older, it's the same old pattern. That's what I dislike about teaching. (Emlyn, 33, scale 3, biology)*

Pupils, like policemen, continually get younger — or so many teachers say. By virtue of the nature of their job it is difficult for teachers, as it is for obstetricians and lollipop people, to avoid recognizing their own mortality. As social systems, schools are affected by the processes occurring within them. The ageing of members is one of these processes and, as a consequence of falling rolls and contraction, the teaching profession becomes, on average, older, is one which is likely to assume increasing significance for the cultures, ethos and outcomes of schools.

This chapter presents an overview, not an exhaustive description, of the ways in which secondary school teachers perceive, experience and adapt to growing old.

Age and Occupation

Ageing is both a unique and a universal experience and as such is an important source of personal and social identity. In Western culture, and particularly for men, paid work tends to take up a large proportion of the life cycle, and occupation can and often does, confer identity (see Mulford and Salisbury, 1964; Havinghurst, 1964; Super, 1981).

Ageing, occupational development and identity are inextricably linked. Sofer suggests that

the variations in meaning attached to work at different phases of the personal life cycle can be expected to be associated with variations in

* One or two quotes in this chapter are taken from teachers in a related piece of research and not in our basic sample.

what the person expects at different phases and what is expected of him. We associate particular ages with particular statuses and with each status go characteristic and legitimate hopes, expectations, rights and duties. Age–status expectations constitute an important link between the personality system of the individual and the social system in which he participates (1970, pp. 118–9).

These meanings and expectations are likely to be further differentiated when, as in teaching, there is an hierarchical career structure and 'position mobility follows patterned sequences (and) different motivations ... become appropriate and inappropriate at each stage' (Strauss, 1959).

Research (for example, Peterson, 1964; Newman, 1979; Rempel and Bentley, 1970) has variously shown that different experiences, attitudes, perceptions, expectations, satisfactions, frustrations and concerns appear to be related to different phases of the teacher's life and career cycle. This is the case for other workers (see Glaser (1968) for examples). However, teachers are in the almost unique position of working with a fixed generation, which they progressively move further and further away from.

There is no standard definition of the age span of a generation. From our standpoint, age parameters are only of relative importance because 'generation' is conceptualized as being essentially subjective and experiential. Thus, a generation shares cultures and similar experiences during a specific period of time, within the same historical context. We move out of one generation and into another when, because of various extra- and intra-personal influences it no longer feels appropriate or comfortable, physically as well as subjectively perhaps, to share and participate in particular cultural activities.

For example, reflecting on his, relatively brief, teaching career, one man said:

> It's interesting, the sort of changing relationship with children. When I first started, when one was, sort of, young, 22, 23, children treat you as an older brother, whereas now they start to look on one more as a parent, sort of thing. You know I find, particularly in this school where the parents are often not much older than meself, there's a change in the sort of relationship and I suppose that will come about more. (Arnold, 31, scale 2, drama)

At the same time, and more usual within the work situation, age relationships vis a vis younger colleagues shifts from child to parent. Cain's (1964) concept of age status asynchronization usefully describes the imbalances or discrepancies which can occur and can be a source of personal and social strain if a teacher is in a low scale, low status post that is generally regarded as being appropriate for a younger person.

A Framework for Comprehension

Teachers do not all follow the same occupational career path, nor is the progression of their life career necessarily similar in other respects — each has their own idiosyncratic biography. Yet their accounts do suggest a common developmental sequence of stages or phases each of which seems to be associated with an evaluation and perhaps a redefinition and/or re-ordering of interests, commitments and attitudes which are not necessarily consequent upon events and experiences arising directly out of the work situation.

In considering these different stages in context, that is in terms of the teacher's total life experience, it became clear that our data broadly supported Levinson *et al's* (1978) conceptualization of life development, and we therefore use their model as a structure for the coherent presentation of evidence. The Levinson model has its weaknesses. For example, it was limited to males and his sample was really too small to justify the prescriptive calendar described. Yet, because the model is predicated on the notion of the 'character of living' which encompasses all aspects of life — biological, psychological, sociological — it can accommodate differences of gender, race, occupation, culture and historical and geographical context, which can be expected to have an influence upon the individual's various life experiences.

It was this holistic approach which we found relevant to our concerns because we wished to concentrate on occupation, on the personal and shared experiences of being a teacher, without diminishing the personally perceived importance and occupational significance of being a mother, of fighting in the war, of being an artist or a physicist, of having a degree or a Certificate of Education, and so on.

The concern in this chapter is to outline what appear to be definite, identifiable phases of the teacher's career as perceived and experienced by teachers themselves. These phases have not been rigidly defined in terms of age for people's experiences inevitably differ. There are also cases when, for example, a late entrant of 40 has similar occupational experiences to a 21 year old although in other respects their experiences are totally different. Thus, what the late entrant has to say may, in some instances and in relation to their occupational development, be representative of a person in a younger age group, while on other occasions their accounts reflect the concerns of their age peers.

Our approach is rather more flexible than Levinson's and our focus, being on a particular occupational group is more specific; we have, therefore, used his model as a supporting, rather than a confining, framework.

Phase 1: 21–28

According to Levinson *et al*, the major tasks facing those in the 21–28 age group are 'a) to explore the possibilities for adult living: to keep options open, avoid strong commitments and maximize the alternatives . . . (and) b) . . . to create a stable life structure: become more responsible and "make something of my life" ' (1978, p. 58). This phase, which he calls 'Entering the Adult World', is in many respects something of a trial period, and it seems that teaching is a career which allows scope to attempt and to accomplish both of its tasks.

Hanson and Herrington (1976) note that it is difficult to determine the real degree of career commitment among student and probationary teachers and research findings vary considerably. For instance, about 50 per cent of the college of education students studied by Lomax (1970) 'drifted' into teaching, while a further 25 per cent had really hoped to go to university. Smithers and Carlisle (1970) found that over 50 per cent of their students would ideally have liked to enter another occupation. Yet Carr (1972) and Taylor and Dale (1971) reported that teaching was the first choice career for around 75 per cent of their respective samples of students and probationers. While the situation may have changed since it has become harder to get on to a teacher training course (because of higher entrance qualifications and the drastic cut-back in places available) these figures suggest that, initially at least, a considerable proportion of teachers do not see teaching as a particularly desirable job.

Even among those for whom actually becoming a teacher is the realization of a long-term ambition many young teachers do not see themselves as committed to a life-long career in teaching (see Nias, 1984; and Cole, 1984). Intention to leave and numbers actually leaving teaching is considerably higher among the under-30s than for any other age group (Kyriacou and Sutcliffe, 1979; Lortie, 1975; Dale, 1976; Lacey, 1977). School teaching is something they are trying out before going on to other things, which they may or may not have ideas about:

> I am now wanting to get, still with an element of teaching but being
> able to carry on with things, personal, individual work of my own at
> the same time. My ideal is to get a job part-time teaching in an art
> college — like it is for most other art teachers. (Chris, 28, scale 1, art)

Jan (25, scale 1, biology) was less specific:

> I don't know whether I see myself being in school in ten years time. It
> depends a lot on circumstances, personal circumstances. I just don't
> know yet. I don't plan that far ahead.

Pete (25, scale 1, biology) hoped to go into business, and Margery (45, scale 3, chemistry) had chosen teaching rather than take up an offer of a job as a research chemist because she was getting married and saw her career becoming relatively unimportant. Very few actually have any specific career plans (Dale, 1976; Lyons, 1981); this is probably because they are unaware of the possibilities, for, those who do, often have a family background of teachers — they know the culture (see Super, 1981). It is also true that at the present time when there is teacher unemployment and when many teachers can only get temporary posts, actually having a scale 1 job is something to feel fortunate about, and can seem to be sufficient career. Promotion, especially when opportunities are so limited and the future so uncertain, may appear as an extremely remote prospect.

For the majority, if not all new teachers, the immediate concern is coping, and being seen to be able to cope, with the job itself:

> It worries me, it still worries me . . . when you go into English classes or whatever, they're all sitting down, quietly working, but they don't in art, they're all over the place, and I don't like people coming in and thinking they're not working. I mean they all are. (Sarah, 25, scale 1, art)

In order to survive they have to learn the skills, the craft technology of teaching. But first, if they are to succeed they have to come to terms with the reality of the situation.

The majority of the teachers we have talked to had had grammar school or grammar school type educations. Their first contact with comprehensives or secondary moderns, and their pupils, whether it came on teaching practice, in their first job, or later on ('old' teachers can still be young in experience) came as a bit of surprise. It seems that, as Peterson found among Chicago teachers, 'there occurs in early teaching experience, a "reality shock" in coming to terms with problems of disciplining and motivating students' (1964, p. 268), and even more fundamentally, a culture shock in meeting alternate values and perspectives. For example:

> On teaching practice I went into a secondary modern school for the first time in my life and realized that I'd been living in cloud cuckoo land. All the time I'd been at school and at college I'd been fighting to keep up with people who probably had the edge on me, I'd been struggling all the time to maintain my place and so, I believe was everyone else I knew, and you get into a secondary modern school and you suddenly come across these folk who don't give a damn about anything, or so it seem to you . . . I used to come home and tell mum and dad about what had been happening and they wouldn't believe it! . . . It was a bit of a shock at the time. (John, scale 4, head of art)

> For my first five years I worked in a grammar school. It was a new experience teaching non-grammar school kids. I was aware of the difference, because my wife worked in a secondary modern but I'd never actually taught kids who were secondary modern kids and meeting these turned me upside down . . . But I survived, I learnt an awful lot. (Dave, 45, Senior Teacher, chemistry)

It was perhaps an even greater shock for Keith who went into teaching straight from industry without any training:

> I thought, I'll be a grammar school teacher. It'll be just like it was when I was a kid, and I was all sort of nostalgic, it'll be just like going back to school again ... the kids were not like I'd expected. Even though it was a grammar school it was in no way the sort of grammar school I'd been to ... I was shattered by the kind of boys that I met who couldn't care tuppence about learning, and all they seemed to want to do was mess about all the time; and by the girls who were not at all like I'd thought. They weren't at all ladylike. In fact many of them were cruder than the boys. (Keith, 38, scale 1, chemistry)

Discipline maintenance seems to be the area which causes young teachers the most anxiety. It is a curious phenomenon that particularly, although not exclusively, for women, impressions of first pupils are of how physically big and of how mature they seem:

> My first sixth-form group all seemed enormous. With regard to their maturity, I think I just got them wrong just as I think all young teachers do; they looked mature and you thought they were but they weren't any different really ... I think it was just me really, or anyone who's inexperienced. (Margery, 45, scale 3, chemistry)

Lacking the natural authority of age, keeping order is often perceived as a frightening and difficult task. In the past when more authority was, seemingly, attached to the teachers' role some were, perhaps, a little more confident:

> In the first school, the grammar school, that I was in even the sixth form, and our ages weren't all that much different, I was 23 and they were 18, 19 even then they had to be told what to do, and disciplined. And they accepted it, it was what they expected. (Dave, 45, Senior Teacher, chemistry)

But even teachers who experienced a similar situation to that Dave describes, along with those working in schools where discipline is comparatively strict, still tended to be apprehensive and usually experienced and were aware of pupils 'trying it on' and 'seeing how far they can go' with a new teacher (see Ball, 1980; Beynon, 1984).

Jan's (25, scale 1, art) experience is typical:

> I found the pupils higher up the school, my first week in this place they were all out to get me, the likes of the fourth years and the fifth years. I was new. And they do it with every new teacher I've since found out because I say to people 'well did that happen to you?' 'Oh yeh! They do it to everyone just to test you out' ... They answer back, try and put one over on you if you ... explain something they'll say 'Oh, why is that?' as if to say 'well do you really know what you're talking about?' They test you out on that ... They're just trying to see what reaction they'll get ... I did it with young teachers when I was a kid.

During their training and when they first start teaching quite a number have been advised that it is a good plan to be very strict, firm and distant at least for the first half-term in order to establish an identity as a teacher who will brook no nonsense (cf Waller, 1932). After this, it is said, it should be possible to 'let up' a little and approach and respond to pupils, who hopefully have learnt that it is not worth taking 'liberties' and 'advantages', in a more relaxed and friendly manner.

Jan followed this advice:

> Once I've got the discipline, I can relax and go round and talk to them individually. But I won't get involved with them until they are at a stage when I can go round and know if I talk to one person somebody else isn't going to start yelling ... so that's about the first half-term before I really start to get to know a class. That's what they advised me to do at college ... We have a system in this school where if they're too bad we send them to a year tutor. Well I was warned straightaway, don't do that too much because the children know, as soon as you send them out of the classroom, you've lost ... You have to deal with the situation yourself, there and then, and if you set punishments you have to follow them through. If you do that the chances are you won't have any more trouble.

There are those who try, unsuccessfully, to follow this advice, or who reject it, because it goes against their personal nature. For example:

> I'm sure I have more discipline problems than I should because I like to relax too easily, and relaxing, you can relax too much and the kids soon take advantage of it. (Pete, 25, scale 1, biology)

> I try to follow the plan of starting off strict and then soften up later ... but I'm not very good at being authoritarian so I soon soften up, 'cos I can't remember to keep doing it ... (Ann, 43, scale 1, art)

At some time during their first year, teachers often experience 'critical incidents' to do with discipline (see Chapter 2). Frequently these incidents take the form of a direct challenge to their authority, and thereby their professional identity. If teachers keep control and resolve the situation, it seems that their identity as a competent teacher is strengthened — both in the eyes of pupils with whom they are likely to have 'easier' relationships; and of other staff who begin to respect them as fellow professionals. However, this will only be the case if any anger they show is controlled. Teachers who can be easily riled are fair game for pupils who feel like a diversion and a spot of entertainment in a lesson (Beynon, 1984). Nor are they highly regarded by colleagues who are likely to see them as inept, lacking in self-control and therefore, unprofessional. In the following account Sarah (25, scale 1, art) outlines the scene she staged after pupils had misbehaved on an out-of-school visit. She suggests a potential gender difference, when she reflects that the scenario and the teacher's role in it might have been different had she been a man:

> I told them off, and I organized a sort of demonstration of disgust . . . so I just, basic acting, threw a tantrum and walked out . . . I thought I wonder what'll they do now. So I came in a few minutes later . . . and they were completely silent and so they realized by that demonstration of something that is not normal for me, that I was really annoyed . . . That was drastic action, something I've never done before . . . A man might have done something different but that's how I thought I could shock them, a shock tactic . . . The situation developed and as (it) developed this was my end plan. It worked though!

The chances of her having to use such a strategy again are probably slight. Teachers often report that following a 'critical incident' they experience fewer difficulties. This is partly because pupils respond differently learning through their grapevine that they will not necessarily 'get away' with disruptive behaviour, and partly because the teacher's confidence in their ability to cope is strengthened. Such incidents appear to be a crucial part of learning to cope with being a teacher, and it seems that those who continually 'fail' get reputations of inadequacy, and if they do not leave, are not regarded within that particular school as being competent teachers.

For the majority, on the whole, as time passes, while it continues to be an important area of concern, discipline tends to become a slightly less intimidating aspect of the job. There are various explanations for this. For instance, teachers gain experience and fairly soon establish an identity and a reputation within their school:

> After three years you'd have learnt the technique or learnt some techniques that work for you. And you begin to know the kids, which makes a difference, and they you. When you're new, you're the sort of pebble that sticks out and they react to you more. When you're sort of part of the wallpaper, you're part of the scene, part of the background, it's different . . . You're a member of the school, you've always been there. Or, at least they can't remember a time when you weren't. And it just goes on then. You've got no real, major problems. (Jim, retired, biology)

In addition, pupils are diminished in all respects, they resume normal proportions — as Dave (45, Senior Teacher, chemistry) reflects:

> I taught for five years in one school, and when I think about that the first years that I'd started teaching were then in the fifth form. But, I taught them as first years so, they grow with you and you see them growing up so they're not so much of a threat, physically in size or in personality . . . when you can remember them as tiny first years.

Furthermore, and perhaps even more reassuring, they may be surprised to learn, from a variety of sources including pupils who talk freely to them, and when they cover other people's classes, that older teachers do not necessarily have the degree of control that the young teacher had attributed to them.

In some ways coming into possession of such knowledge represents and can be regarded as a status passage (Glaser and Strauss, 1967), and an initiation into the 'teacherhood', because at least part of the mystique of the 'experienced teacher' is lifted, and they are revealed as ordinary mortals not dissimilar to oneself!

After discipline, the next major aspect of becoming a teacher would appear to be concerned with the subject (which, because of its importance we examine in detail in a separate chapter). At this stage the subject is usually personally very important. Most teachers have, to a greater or lesser degree of intensity, a special fondness for, and get a great deal of enjoyment from, their subject. It is because of the subject, in order to stay in contact with it and perhaps because of a desire to pass it on that some are motivated to become teachers (see Lyons, 1981, p. 94). The subject can provide a sense of security. It is an area the young teacher is, as Pete (25, scale 1, biology) says, comfortable with:

> I think it's very much a question of wanting to do the things that you
> feel comfortable at doing. And I think I know my subject well enough
> to be able to teach it pretty well.

With regard to the subject they are specialists, experts in the field, and it gives them an identity (cf Lacey, 1977; Bernstein, 1975). In school, however, they are inexperienced novices and one way of coping with this is to put the emphasis on the familiar. Thus the subject is likely to be perceived as the most important part of being a teacher. Teachers of all ages and lengths of experience may use the subject as a personal defence. For instance, a teacher who finds it difficult to cope with mixed ability classes may say that his subject is too difficult for the less able (see Elbaz, 1983, p. 122). It seems that those with a subject degree and a PGCE put greater emphasis on the importance of the subject than do these who trained at a college of education. A possible explanation is that the latter have made higher investments in their self as teachers, and therefore have a greater incentive, and/or find adapting to the role easier (see Grace, 1978, p. 200).

Learning how best to communicate the subject to the various groups of pupils tends to engage a large proportion of the young teachers' attention;

> It's such a struggle, especially with the older ones, to get them to sit
> down and to sweat over it, which you need to do. I haven't got the
> expertise *yet*, to get it out of them. (Sarah, 25, scale 1 art)

However, Chris' (28, scale 1, art) concern to communicate effectively is perhaps more to do with his interest in the general problem of communicating ideas and his view of the teacher's role, than with his relative lack of experience:

It is difficult to start with, a challenge if you like, but I can see things ... you know, goals, that I'd quite like to reach, being able to communicate successfully and so on ... getting across certain complicated things, you know, sort of ideas, being able to share those ideas, that are of a very complicated, sometimes, personal nature ... You just have to some way improve and cut down the time it takes you to get to some more important things that I am interested in and want to understand ... Everything's got to be so obvious and laid in front of them without any doubts about it ... well most of the time, you can't leave too much that can be interpreted wrongly ... You have to plan and go through all the possibilities before, or at least work out what could happen ... in terms of interpretation, the way they might interpret ideas that you're telling them ... how they might misinterpret or the directions they might go off in from the ideas that you give them. (Chris, 28, scale 1, art)

Usually they evolve their own pedagogy through a mixture of trial and error, from observing others (on the rare occasions when this is possible), by remembering their own teachers (who, incidentally often serve as models of bad practice), and from their own idea of what it should be like. The majority say that their professional training, apart from teaching practice, was of very limited practical value. Sometimes, in the face of cynicism from older members of staff, and an initially unpromising pupil response (often due to pupils' expectations based on experience in that particular school) they need great persistence in order to carry on with their strategies.

This was Pete's (25, scale 1, biology) experience:

It's a strategy that I've always tried to do and I've always worried about whether its working. And recently I seem to be getting evidence that it is working ... Basically its 'be positive' ... you don't slang kids, you're never sarcastic to kids, and the way to motivate people ... is to try and find occasions when they're doing something right, and tell them its right and say how pleased you are, and really encourage good things and don't gripe on about bad things. I have a conviction that it's the *right* thing to do in teaching ... And recently it really seems to be working ... I look around at other members of the staff and I see that they're doing the opposite and that makes me feel that I'm right. And they tell me that I'm stupid and that my way will never work! And I was beginning to believe them. Not now though.

Socialization into the occupational culture, learning to be a professional and a proper teacher also takes place on the job. By observation and experience the young teacher learns the appropriate codes of conduct which relate to such things as: how to address other members of staff in front of pupils; how to talk to, relate to, and associate with pupils; what constitutes acceptable dress for a teacher, and in-school expectations about marking, involvement in extra-curricular activities, and so on. If one is to have a smooth running career it is as well to fit in (see Hanson and Herrington, 1976, pp. 5–6), to internalize or at least strategically comply (see Lacey, 1977, p. 72–3) with these informal although very important rules (see Lacey, 1970). As Lacey notes, new teachers who question, reject or attempt to change what is regarded as professional behaviour, can experience 'serious problems in qualifying' (*ibid*, p. 96). However, the rules are rarely verbalized or defined, for instance:

> There are certain things, I don't think about them any more, I just, if I think it's wrong I don't do it. (Chris, 28, scale 1, art)

> I think that teachers should adopt certain standards, but what those standards are I don't know, but I must admit, when I see other teachers I think, Ugh . . . I suppose it's the middle class thing . . . just the way they conduct themselves, just that, that special thing. (Sarah, 25, scale 1, art)

This lack of definition can be problematic, and lead to miscueing, perhaps especially if, following Sarah's supposition, the teacher comes from a working class background. Once again, Keith's (35, scale 1, chemistry) experience as a late entrant provides a particularly clear example:

> When I first started teaching, I came straight from industry, my first reaction when kids messed about in class was to give them a smack round the head. And I was soon told that that was unprofessional conduct . . . but, this is it, . . . what *is* professional conduct then? . . . I don't think I've ever seen a job specification . . . But what I'm getting at is that to my recollection no one had ever said a professional teacher does this, this and this and doesn't do that, that, and that . . . What does the profession entail? What are the criteria? What are the norms of behaviour? . . . because when I was a pupil, to inflict corporal punishment was considered to be quite a professional thing to do . . . now, 25 years later it's an unprofessional thing . . . I now appreciate that it was unprofessional conduct to belt a kid . . . but until they tell me the rules of the trade as it were I don't know what's considered professional or unprofessional.

At some schools young teachers quickly learn that it is perhaps not wise to talk too much in the staffroom about problems, particularly disciplinary ones.

> In the staffroom, teachers vocalize problems that they don't really need any help for, but, just need to say it . . . They're not prepared to talk about proper problems . . . I'm not, not in the staffroom as a whole. To some people, yes, the people who I know perhaps could help me, like a head of year . . . I mean, if it is known that a member of staff is having problems then . . . the opinion goes down . . . I've seen that happen to someone. (Sarah, 25, scale 1, art)

What Sarah (and most other teachers) says, throws an interesting light on Hammersley's (1980) findings that the staffroom offers a 'ritual of self-exposure and repair and thus an expression of solidarity' (p. 48). Teachers say that the majority of staffroom conversations are at the anecdotal level and it may be that accounts of terrible classes and awful pupils are the tip of the iceberg. Telling such stories, which can often have a humorous aspect and hence entertainment value, and sharing the problem is reassuring both for the teller and the listeners who have had similar experiences. But, the real problems, the ones that cause most anxiety are kept either to oneself, or are told to the people who one trusts, and who it is felt safe to be open with. In Sarah's case, her Head of Year. However, even if only on a superficial level, it does seem that there has been a definite change in attitudes, and that it is easier for young teachers to seek help. Jim and Arthur, starting teaching just after and just before the war respectively, felt that they just had to get on with it.

> I can't ever recall sort of going to another member of staff and saying 'I just can't control this lot'. You wouldn't have dreamt of admitting your inability. (Jim, retired, biology)

> There was an unwritten law that you didn't talk shop in the staffroom. You kept your worries to yourself. (Arthur, retired, art).

Margery (45, scale 3, chemistry), who began her career in a grammar school in the late 1950s compares her experiences with the present day:

> I think actually a big difference is that . . . one hid one's incompetence, very much, from everybody I think, from oneself. I think nowadays the young teachers we have are much more happy to talk about it, and I'm not sure it's always to their advantage . . . When I started, any problems were your own affair.

Nowadays, in many schools, or within specific departments, new, inexperienced teachers are encouraged to talk about their problems and are given constructive, positive help. Yet even in such atmospheres where young teachers are told they can talk freely, it seems that there are fears (perhaps not unreasonable if there are many teachers at your school with similar views to Margery's) of appearing incapable of a reluctance to 'emphasize one's powerlessness vis a vis colleagues' (Nias, 1984), and feelings and suspicions that one's problems and difficulties are worse than anyone else's.

> You imagine it's happening, you know, everybody's in the same place but unless they actually tell you, you know you think oh, they're not having half the problems I am . . . they're actually having worse ones (laughs). (Chris, 28, scale 1, art)

These feelings are partly a consequence of the secrecy that surrounds the classroom, and they are likely to be more commonly experienced as fewer probationers are appointed during the current period of falling rolls. Both Pete and Chris had been the only probationers and the youngest members of staff at their school, and both said that for a while they had felt rather isolated and depressed because of this.

Chris (25, scale 1, art) was lucky to stay in touch with his friends from college:

> When I came here I was the only probationer . . . I had friends outside the school who were teaching, who were in their first year, and I could share a lot of the things with them . . . It's a great talking point, the first year of teaching . . . It's very reassuring that everybody faces the same problem . . .

If a group of young teachers start at a school together they may form a mutual support group, wherein they can share experiences, tips, ideas and information about pupils. This was Christine's (34, scale 3, physics) experience:

> When I came here there were three probationers in the department. We'd all started together, all got the same problems and we all used to sit after school sorting ourselves out. It was very much a self help type of group . . . We were all scientists so we very much could identify with each other's problems . . . It was quite important to me. At the end of the day we'd just collapse into a chair and thrash out the problems . . . We used to discuss lesson content, pupil ability, discipline . . . It was moral support to a great extent . . . but there was practical help as well.

They may also joke about, and criticize as 'old fashioned' more senior teachers (cf Peterson, 1964, p. 285), and this can serve a therapeutically cathartic function. As Peterson suggests, it seems that young teachers form 'generational cliques' partly in order to protect themselves from 'uncomfortable situations with mature teachers' (1964, p. 296).

Without the opportunity to belong to a generational clique young teachers may be socialized into the culture of the middle-aged, career frustrated teachers, a group which is increasing as promotion prospects are reduced because of contraction. If they are, they may come to believe and to find that teaching is not much fun or a very satisfactory career and they may bring less enthusiasm and effort to their classroom work. Also, as was previously suggested, pedagogy and curriculum development may be influenced by the cynicism of older teachers. This has implications for the quality of education generally, for eventually school atmosphere and ethos are likely to be affected and, as research (for example, Rutter *et al*, 1979; Reynolds and Sullivan, 1979) has shown, pupil outcomes may well suffer. Not surprisingly it would appear that, to some extent, the majority are sooner or later in some way affected by others' scepticism — and their perceptions of their own experiences.

Pete (25, scale 1, biology) was lucky to find a safety valve:

There's all these people in the staffroom, absolutely moaning and moaning about what they've been asked to do and what they've got to do etc ... On the last week of last term, I just had to walk out of there ... I just couldn't cope with all those people moaning and moaning about what they had to do, it just cheesed me off so much I just had to say something to someone. And it developed into ... spilling out to my Head of Department about how hard I'm having to work and how I just can't cope etc. etc and he agreed with me, said I was doing fine and is changing things so that I'm less pressurized.

Edelwich with Brodsky (1980) noted that 'attitudes like germs, spread rapidly in a stuffy atmosphere' (p. 76), and it might be that experienced teachers try to ensure that the young teacher catches their 'disease'. New, enthusiastic workers in any occupation pose a threat to the status quo. In order to avoid being shown up and made to work harder and re-examine methods, the older workers may attempt to socialize the tyros into their ways and put pressure on them to conform. This happens in schools just as it does in factories (see Woods, 1981, p. 30; and Edelwich with Brodsky, 1980) and an increasingly static teacher population may well exacerbate the situation. Even those who have universal-type ideas about education being able to have far-reaching social effects are not exempt. Indeed the idealistic face potentially greater and more painful disillusionment, especially if they lack like-minded colleagues who can help them sustain their ideals.

Within a school, teacher age distribution is not only significant in purely educational terms. Young teachers, perhaps especially if they are new to an area and if they do not have personal commitments locally, may look to the school for their social life. They may be disappointed if most of the staff are older and concerned with their homes and families. Both Chris (28, scale 1, art) and Peter (25, scale 1, biology) found this:

I'd moved to this area to get the job so I didn't know anybody in (—). I think I expected everybody to be in the same position as me, people of about my age, that they'd go to similar sorts of places and do similar things. But I found there was nobody like that ... everybody was married ... they didn't want to do the same sort of things. (Chris)

When I first came there seemed to be a big gap in age between me and everybody else ... it's a very old staffroom so there's very little social activity anyway ... it used to worry me for a time ... that there was no social life in our school. They were all talking about their mortgages and their kids and I was growing up far too fast. (Peter)

If the teacher does join a school-based social group their whole life can revolve round the school, with boy/girl-friends, husbands/wives and children being progressively incorporated.

Young teachers are of the same generation as many of their pupils. According to Levinson's model both are in the 'season of youth' which takes in ages 15–30. Being of an age, teachers and pupils are likely to have similar interests and concerns — for example, fashion and music. This 'common ground' can become the basis for cooperative, friendly, pupil teacher relationships which compensate for the lack of age and experience-based authority (cf Denscombe, 1980c).

Ann's (43, scale 1, art) point of contact, which her subject allowed her to exploit, was, and still is, clothes:

> My first job was in a girl's secondary modern . . . being young I got on well with teenage girls . . . they identified with me, and they generally like art anyway . . . Most of them didn't do 'O' level so there was no syllabus that had to be followed, no training that had to be done and so I often did things about fashion and things that they were interested in; so I managed to get them interested and then I could slip in a few things that I felt were worthwhile and they might not have seen. Plus the fact that I always made my own clothes, and they'd come and say 'I like your dress, Miss', and I'd say, 'Well, you make it like this', and they'd go home and make it; and I had a good relationship with them.

The extent to which teachers want to share their interests and identify with pupils, obviously, differs. In some schools there are few, if any, similarities between pupil and young teacher (i.e. 'educated', 'middle class') cultures (cf Peterson, 1964, p. 271). While within such schools there may well have been 'constructed an identifiable middle ground between teacher and pupil cultures upon which the official business of the school (is) conducted' (Measor and Woods, 1984b) it is likely that there is little desire on either side to associate on a social basis.

Pete's (25, scale 1, biology) feelings were that:

> We're ever so friendly but there's always that distance and I've no wish for it to be any different.

As has already been seen, during teacher training the importance of keeping 'that distance' in order to maintain discipline is often emphasized and, in any case some personally prefer to be seen primarily in the teacher role. There are exceptions. Although none of the teachers we talked to said they had ever mixed socially with pupils they said that they had heard or knew of those who did. The ones who said that they definitely would not choose to do so suggested that those who did

> were perhaps lacking something in their personal lives. (Chris, 28, scale 1, art)

Peterson found that female, American high school teachers who had started teaching in small, rural schools were more likely to report high job satisfaction from close social relationships with pupils than those who initially worked in urban areas (1964, pp. 71–2). Relative geographical isolation and community strength seem similarly to have been a factor in this country. Older teachers like Mrs Castle who taught in the Welsh valleys, and Arthur, working in a fen-land village, did not, in their early days, before the war, have easy access to transport and were, therefore, thrown back on the same social life that was available to pupils and their families. Margery (45, scale 3, chemistry) however, lived some distance from the school and she thought that this might have made a difference.

> I didn't mix socially with pupils. I didn't live in the town so I suppose that hindered ... I lived about ten, twelve miles away, so social life tended to be separate ... if I'd lived closer it might have been different.

It appears that it is part of the culture, the tradition, at some schools for pupils and teachers to meet out of school. For instance, Mr Count had worked at a relatively formal grammar school where teachers and pupils were expected to take equal turns at hosting the bridge club, and Ann's daughter went to a school where it was usual for young teachers and sixth-formers to be on christian name terms and to meet socially.

One area where there is likely to be contact and a common interest is sport, where relationships which are not pupil-teacher but fellow-team-mate may develop.

> We played basket-ball three or four lunchtimes a week and I got to know that group of lads exceptionally well, and one or two of the girl hangers-on who'd come, and score for us: I was almost on an equal footing with sixth-formers then ... Just as my wife had a netball team. She was 21 and they were 15 and they'd chat to her about their boyfriends and what have you, just as if she was one of them. (Dave, 45, Senior Teacher, chemistry)

Marriage and long-term relationships between male teachers and their pupils are not unheard of:

> Once in a blue moon some member of staff would marry a sixth-form pupil, and that happens even now. (Margery, 45, scale 3, chemistry)

But teachers have to be careful. Men are usually warned, at college, to avoid situations which could possibly be misconstrued. Dave admitted to getting quite paranoid when he was a young teacher and it seemed that he was likely to get into a situation where he was alone with girl pupils, and on more than one occasion, Arthur had felt himself to be in real danger!

> I was frightened to death once or twice. You get a 14 year old girl that is quite well developed these days and you get a girl to come to your desk for something or other or sometimes they come without being

asked and they, well you know the procedure, you know they can rub up against you in such a way that you think 'oh my god, I'm just about being seduced in front of my own class here', you know, it's a very difficult situation ... you are taken by surprise when you are younger and you can get trapped, very often they do, and you can get really in an awkward predicament ... there are such things as nymphos even in 14 year old girls, I met one or two of them, by god they are ... as I say when I first started work I used to cycle to school, seven or eight miles from home, to Squirreldray, and in the summer-time I had quite a nice run and the kids, of course they finished school before you, you always had various odds and ends to do before you leave school and I was waylaid once or twice on the way home by top class girls, you know, one of them at a time, not in groups, you know, and the next thing you know they are riding their bikes alongside you and there were various parts when you had to walk up the hills and things like that and, oh yes, the invitation was there, but by god, it would have been fatal, and you know, some of them were quite nice kids in lots of ways, others were little bitches, you had to sort them out and deal with them in the appropriate manner. (Arthur, 69, retired, art)

Sally (41, scale 3, art) who, perhaps relevantly, had no teacher training, found the role compartmentalization expected of her as a young teacher, prob-lematic:

I think the social thing at first I did find a bit difficult ... some of them (sixth-formers) wanted to come round in the evening and see me and discuss things they were doing and so on (as they had done with the previous older teacher) and an older member of staff advised me against this. Said he didn't think it was a good idea, I ought to be careful ... it was difficult to be very friendly and familiar on one side and then go back to the school teachers' role on the other side.

Young women, especially if they are attractive, may find themselves particularly popular. Not surprisingly this is especially likely to be the case when they work in boys' schools. This was Sally's experience:

When I first started, at a boys' secondary modern there was a bit of a problem with being a novelty ... with being one of two women and the other was coming up to retirement anyway, ... and when I ran a club after school about seventy people turned up for it the first session. And we got the odd graffiti and that sort of thing. But it seemed to sort itself out fairly soon ... when the novelty wore off it was better.

Mrs Castle, quoted in Chapter 2 gives a similar account. Yet the character of such incidents is not always as gentle as it was in Sally's experience and much less pleasant are sexual innuendoes which are, perhaps, particular occupational hazards for those teaching art,

> You always tend to get it a bit in art of course, with nudity being rather connected with art. (Sally, 41, scale 3, art)

and biology. Women tend to adapt by using a strategy of coolness:

> The more upset you are the more likely they are to do it. (Sally, 41, scale 3, art)

For the most part, however, young teachers just enjoy being with pupils. They tend to have fewer personal and domestic commitments which along with their 'youthful energy' enable them to spend more time with kids doing things that they both enjoy. In John's (48, scale 4, art) case, this had meant going out into the country to sketch; for Sarah (25, scale 1, art), it had been hiking trips, and in Pete's (25, scale 1, biology) own words:

> I go birdwatching anyway, I might as well go birdwatching with other people and help them to learn things and share the pleasure.

Those who do spend a lot of time taking part in and organizing extra-curricular activities might have half an eye on being seen to be committed and involved and thereby improving their chances of promotion, but this is unlikely to be their sole motivation.

Pete (25, scale 1, biology), for instance, has been able to accommodate, and hopefully further both his birdwatching and his career interests:

> From the promotion point of view it definitely helps ... when I ran the football team I thought 'Oh no, I don't fancy doing this', but on the other hand I felt quite definitely that I ought to get involved in something, and I'd been asked by the Head of PE if I'd run a football team and I'd said yes and when I went back to him I said, 'Well, look, rather than run a football team I'd rather run a birdwatching club'.

Sarah (25, scale 1, art) actually received confirmation that her involvement in extra-curricular activities was helping her career. When, on one occasion, as she frequently did, she found herself leading a walking party supposedly organized by another, more senior teacher, a Deputy Head was present:

> He said 'Well, it'll be mentioned in despatches that you did this, that and the other.' But the times you do it and there's nobody there to see you do it, you know I often wonder whether it is noted'.

Promotional ambitions are typically to become head of a subject department. Indeed this was the aim of all of the young teachers we talked with. Pastoral posts of responsibility do not initially seem to be as popular. Reasons for this include

(a)   young teachers are less aware of career possibilities within the pastoral structure;

(b)   as has already been noted, they tend to identify with their subject and are less willing to consider spending less time working with it (see Lacey, 1977, pp. 61–4); and

(c)   they are too close in age to pupils to consider taking on a parental type guidance role.

During the expansionist phase of the 1960s and early 1970s regular and frequent promotion came to be expected and it was not unusual for people of twenty-seven to be scale 3 or 4 heads of departments. While in the early 1980s they are less likely to achieve such posts, young teachers are anxious to meet socially appropriate age associated career stages, because the implications are that there is something 'wrong' with the teacher who is still on a scale 1 after six or seven years' experience (see Cain, 1964).

> It doesn't look particularly good on a record for somebody to be teaching seven years on a scale 1. It's a bit of a death knell. The natural question is 'Why has that person been on a scale 1 for seven years?' Possibly because of certain incompetencies in certain respects the interviewers might feel. (Tom, 28, scale 1, maths)

For a man, unless he is a late entrant, or there is another apparent acceptable reason, scale 1 at 28 is not regarded as really appropriate. For a woman, however, particularly if she has children, there is little social shame attached to an entire working life spent in scale 1 posts.

Phase 2: 28–33

During this phase, which Levinson *et al* (1978) call the 'age thirty transition', 'the provisional exploratory quality of the twenties is ending (and there is a) sense of greater urgency' (p. 85). For many people life becomes more serious now. Commitments and responsibilities are increasing and it becomes more important to establish a stable basis and work out and plan a life structure for the future. It can be a stressful period particularly because after the age of 30 it usually becomes increasingly difficult to start out in a new career. In various respects the years of the age 30 transition are a last chance to assess and subsequently confirm or change one's provisional life structure.

At this point gender differences can become particularly apparent. Women, who throughout their twenties had pursued an occupational career and had not had children, frequently report that they experienced their thirtieth birthday as something of a watershed. They felt that they had very little time left to decide whether to have children and, depending on such variables as personal orientation, cultural norms and economic circumstances the choice may have appeared to be an either/or one (see Sheehy, 1976, Chapter 1b).

Another very important factor to be considered is the state of the jobs market. All the mid-career women teachers we talked with who had children had been happy to interrupt their careers because they were confident that they could get a job when they wanted to start again. In the event none of them were out of teaching for more than a year at a time. Nowadays the situation is different and women are more reluctant to resign. It seems that more of those who decide to have children are taking only the statutory period of maternity leave before returning to their protected jobs.

During the age 30 transition it may be that some teachers will leave or begin to consider or explore alternatives to teaching. For others, promotion becomes a more important issue than it perhaps has previously been. By this time, teachers are likely to feel sufficiently experienced and capable of taking on greater responsibility. They no longer find their present post as satisfying or challenging as it initially was, and they begin to look for a new one. Some will already have received promotion and may, therefore, be relatively satisfied for the moment. Others may believe that they have been 'overlooked' and may feel bitter and dissatisfied when they see older people on high scales, apparently, and actually, not doing anything to earn their higher salaries. Their discontent is likely to be due partly to their increasing anxiety to achieve age appropriate positions. Teachers in this age group frequently say that they are afraid of becoming like older colleagues who 'failed' to do so, who have responded by withdrawing their effort and commitment and who are among the leading grumblers and cynics of the staffroom. For example.

> I know lots of teachers who've become rather embittered because they've served many years and rightly or wrongly feel they should have gained a promotion. Maybe they didn't deserve promotion . . . but it does tend to make people embittered I think, when they could see other people who had taught the same time as them, or even fewer years than them gaining promotion . . . I think people like them tend to do the minimum . . . they become sour, bitter and cynical, and I hope I don't find myself in that situation. (Phil, 32, scale 3, PE)

Riseborough (1981) describes how at Phoenix school the majority of male teachers gravitated either towards the clique or the cabal (cf Burns, 1955, pp. 474 and 480). Clique members were deviant, low status teachers, who were anti-institution and who had a negative orientation to work; cabal members were the opposite. As Riseborough suggests, cliques appear to be part of the reality and culture of schools and represent and offer teachers a main line of adjustment to career disappointments. By the time they reach 30 many teachers may suspect that they will qualify for clique membership.

Another reason why promotion may become particularly significant around this time is that domestic and familial commitments are increasing and money becomes more important. Chris (25, scale 1, art) was just finding this out at first hand.

As soon as I heard my wife was pregnant, I thought 'Oh! Money.' Mainly 'cus my wife's working now ... but she won't be able to do that, after a couple more months, so it's going to be pressure, moneywise so I've got to think about that ... so I am looking for a scale 2.

Research shows that money also becomes more important if the job is proving unsatisfactory in other respects, for example, if promotions felt to be deserved are not forthcoming (see Edelwich with Brodsky, 1980, p. 17).

The wish for and assumption of greater responsibility is representative of 'growing up' and moving away from pupils' interests. Some teachers may deliberately make an effort to stay in touch with youth culture, but on the whole, their concerns are no longer similar to those of their pupils. Although like Freema Elbaz's Sarah (1983, especially p. 153) they may retain and even consciously hang on to, an ideal image of themselves as the 'young teacher' on the same side as the pupils, the pupils are less likely to see them in this light. As Peterson notes pupils 'seem to age-grade teachers by age distancing teachers, away from them', and this is experienced as 'a matter of loss ... of some kind of intimate, friendly contact with pupils' (1964, p. 273). Jim (65, retired, biology) put it like this:

When you get a bit older, being familiar with them doesn't work. They know very well they can't be familiar with you ... because the age gap doesn't allow it really, and so they don't appreciate you trying to bridge it'.

In effect pupils can be seen to be forcing teachers to grow up and acknowledge their age. In these circumstances perhaps it becomes easier to be the 'teacher', the mentor who is concerned from above, from a position of greater experience, rather than on the same level. From this time on pastoral jobs begin to seem more appropriate than they previously did. Some who don't want to lose totally the satisfactions they get from informal contact, but who find that because of their increasing formal seniority it becomes difficult to maintain such relationships in school, may incorporate pupils, as friends, into their new family life, involving them in such activities as gardening, decorating, baby-sitting.

For instance:

When we moved into our first house I used to invite kids round at the weekends. We'd do some digging or some painting, sketching as well as house painting. They'd have their teas with us, we'd just have them around. (John, 48, scale 4, art)

It is interesting that if teachers mention having been motivated to enter teaching by a teacher of their own who served as a career model, it was usually someone who gave them an insight into their out-of-school life. This had been so for John (quoted above) who was perhaps reproducing the situation for his pupil-friends, and it had also been Pete's (25, scale 1, biology) experience:

> I think the biggest influence on me when I was coming to career decisions was my own biology teacher ... I used to go round to his house, spent time with him and his wife ... He seemed to have a life style that I would have enjoyed. He didn't seem to be working particularly hard, he had lots and lots of outside interests and he had lots of time in his holidays. And it seemed to be alright moneywise.

Unfortunately there is evidence which indicates that those with such career models are likely to be disillusioned and to become dissatisfied when they find that few pupils are as responsive and cooperative as they were as pupils (Edelwich with Brodsky, 1980, p. 50). Our evidence tends to support this hypothesis, for to some extent John and Pete had both been disappointed in this respect, nor had they found career prospects, working conditions or wages to be as good as they had initially appeared.

By this time, after six or seven years experience, teachers tend to have become more relaxed, and this is reflected in their classroom attitude, for many, like Ann (43, scale 1, art), no longer feel as much need to rely on tight structures:

> I think I was more formal when I first started because I didn't feel secure ... I think if a teacher's not secure if they can stand at the front of a class and dictate and have everybody do as they say it improves their feeling of security ... their feeling that they're in charge.

They have begun to 'develop', to experiment and use their own ideas based on experience rather than relying exclusively upon what they have been taught and advised. Chris (25, scale 1, art) describes this process of working out his own ideas as one of unlearning:

> I'm trying to forget everything (ideas about art in school) I started with because a lot of it was me repeating what I'd read, I mean Herbert Reade and things. I never knew really if that was what I thought or if that was what I'd just read. I know that you do both, gain things from what you're reading but it sounded, to start with, not like me really. I was just picking them up, and I think it sounded like that when I said them to anybody. So as I said, I've tried to forget what I've learnt in a way, and try and formulate something from actual teaching and try and work out something from that. Things like Reade are always pleasant to come back to because they're safe things that somebody else has said and you think, if you agree with them, there's two people who think the same and you're O.K., you know, somebody else thinks like that. It's harder to come up with your own ideas but, I don't know, they feel a bit better.

Some become more interested in curriculum development and innovation. In the early 1970s this was one way of enhancing promotion prospects (cf Whiteside, 1978) but in the 1980s personal satisfaction and maintaining interest when a change of job seems a remote possibility is more likely to be the central motivation.

Teachers of this age often begin to become more interested in pedagogy, rather than their subject. Helen (41, scale 3, art) remembers that she did:

> I think I started teaching as a subject based teacher, where the subject always came first, that was when I started, I think, perhaps until I came here really, when aged 28. I'm not quite sure of the reasons for it. But I think even more so as time has gone on, I've got more of an, yes, O.K., I teach art but I think of myself more as a teacher than artist, so I think it's changed to thinking of art as the motive for it as the fact you're thinking of being a teacher.

Young teachers anticipate this happening. This may partly be because their subject, or rather its culture, as experienced at college or university (cf Lacey, 1977) is becoming increasingly distant. Furthermore, subject knowledge, perhaps especially in the sciences, grows outdated, and there is little time or opportunity to keep up. All the science teachers, except for 25 year old Pete, made a comment similar to the following quote from Margery (45, scale 3, chemistry):

> Of course you very quickly get out of date, within nine or ten years at the most. And though you do try to keep up you don't have the time, or the money, to read the specialist journals. One starts off with good intentions, but it's something that I think you have to accept.

It therefore gets more difficult to maintain an identity as a specialist, particularly in the world outside school, and 'teacher' offers an alternative, perhaps not as prestigious or exclusive an identity but in many respects, a more secure one.

Phase 3: 30–40

Throughout the thirties the conjunction of experience and a relatively high level of physical and intellectual ability mean that in terms of energy, involvement, ambition and self-confidence many teachers are at their peak. Levinson *et al* (1978) characterize this period as the 'settling down' phase, in which a man faces two major tasks: '(a) He tries to establish a niche in society: to anchor his life more firmly, develop competence in a chosen craft, become a valued member of a valued world. (b) He works at making it: striving to advance, to progress on a timetable' (p. 59). It is usually during this period that the male teacher's career is established and, what is likely to be the terminal point is reached, or at least comes into view. People at this stage of life often have to do a lot of adapting to and coping with 'reality'.

Women's experience can be quite different. Many will have chosen to make their occupational career secondary to their career as a wife and mother. This is what is expected of them and those who do not conform may well face social censure. Women who have a family and who continue to work are often under great pressure insofar as they have two jobs. In many schools the attitude towards women teachers is often that they are working for 'pin-money', and in few secondary schools are they equally represented in senior posts.

Those, men in particular, who are following the career path will be working towards a major goal deputy headship, headship. They will probably set themselves deadlines after the expiry of which they expect their chances of success will decrease. These deadlines are frequently extended. The amount of time and energy they devote to their pursuit may be detrimental to other aspects of their life. For instance

> Dave and Ray, they work bloody hard, they drive themselves into the ground, and they're brilliant teachers. But just talking to their wives, ask them what they think about how much work their husbands do and they're not impressed at all. (Pete, 25, scale 1, biology)

Furthermore, the pursuit of rising aspirations can result in 'burn out' (see Edelwich with Brodsky, 1980) and various stress-induced illnesses.

Once again, career concerns and sources of job satisfaction change. Interest in management and organization is common among teachers at this stage. Ray's (39, scale 3, biology) account gives some indication of the network of reasons which contribute to this change in orientation and commitment.

> I'm now prepared to leave teaching, or rather get out of the classroom full-time as it were. Because my interests now are in learning theory and pedagogy and in organizing schools and, managing teachers you might say, in order to get the best out of them — their job satisfaction is crucial of course ... I would really like a Deputy Head curriculum-type role ... to have the time to get into teachers' classrooms and to help them, to influence them perhaps ... It's partly your own career image, I'm not saying that doesn't come into the equation ... in order to get more status, get more influence in schools you've got to go into this area ... and on another level, if we lived in a situation where one's salary as a head of biology just kept on increasing as it were, then the situation might be very different.

On the other hand some teachers say that they are not interested in promotion because it usually means less time in the classroom actually teaching. Professing a strong desire to stay in the classroom and an equally strong dislike of managerial and administrative work may be a contingency-coping strategy used to protect both public and personal self-image in the event of failure to achieve promotion. That some teachers do use such a strategy is suggested by the following quote:

> What I wouldn't like to do is to become an administrator as such, within the usual career structures. I don't think it's because I couldn't be one, so I'm not saying this defensively if you know what I mean, it's sort of conscious. (Roland, 38, scale 3, metalwork)

Those who haven't reached the positions they hoped for have to come to terms with where they are. By this time they will probably have made significant personal investments and accumulated considerable personal valuables, for instance, marriage, children, a home, friends, and these factors may make it very difficult to make a geographical move should promotion seem possible elsewhere. Thus they find they have to make, what are in effect, 'final' decisions and adaptations which take into consideration their long–term future. Some adapt by altering their perception of, and thereby the nature of, their commitment to their job, for example from seeing it as a career in which they can work up to a senior position to viewing it as a worthwhile, interesting job (cf Nias, 1981; Silverman, 1970; Woods, 1979). Within school, a change in commitment can be publicly and personally indicated and confirmed by joining, and being seen to join, a clique. Some decide that the returns are not worth the effort and so cut down on what they do, while others build up an alternative career.

John (48, scale 4, art) for example, set up a small publishing company when, in his late thirties, he felt that his teaching career had reached a dead end. He no longer found his job satisfactory for a number of reasons but neither did he feel that he could move. Once he became involved in his company he found that he was able to 'juggle' his interests (see Pollard, 1980; Woods, 1981a), enjoying those parts of the teaching job he found satisfying and, to a large extent, disregarding the aspects he found frustrating because the satisfaction he obtained from his alternative career more than compensated. Other teachers we met had started shops, restaurants, a market garden, a travel agency, and an antique china repairers.

Not all teachers possess the capital, the marketable skills, or the inclination to start a business, and they may juggle their interests by investing more in their families, homes or hobbies. There is a gender difference here for it tends to be expected that women will make by far their largest investments in their families. It is perhaps significant that Helen (41, scale 3, art) was the only mid–career woman who both had no children and who felt that she had sufficient time to follow her hobbies and interests.

Obviously generational status does not only alter vis a vis pupils, and once they are in their thirties it is no longer appropriate to regard themselves, or to behave as young, inexperienced teachers. Depending on how successful they have been they may see younger teachers who are in relatively senior posts as 'whizz kids' a term generally used in a derogatory sense. Heads of department, faculty, year, house, common positions for those in this age group, have some responsibility for guiding and helping young staff. They often complain that they have no training for this — hence one reason for their growing interest in management. On the whole, those who are concerned about this aspect of their job say that they draw on their own experiences, whether good or bad, as junior teachers.

With respect to pupils the relationship has definitely changed. Teachers in their thirties no longer belong to the same generation as pupils and, even if they should wish to, they can no longer participate as equals in youth culture. Dave remarked on how thirty seems to be a critical age.

> Kids do adopt a different standpoint as you get older. You can't equate with their ideas. I mean I'm long gone and past it, I'm over thirty. I should be buried up to my neck and left there as far as a lot of these kids are concerned, because I don't understand their problems. I'm not in their world, they're quite sure that I don't listen to pop music and to imagine me dancing would be a laugh. The fact I do this every week doesn't matter. (Dave, 45, senior teacher, chemistry)

Around this age, teachers seem to start to make more frequent adverse comments about pupil standards, attitudes, and behaviour. They also compare pupils 'today' unfavourably with those in the past. Peterson (1964, p. 276) reports similar findings, which seems to suggest that this change in perspective of younger people is, to a large extent, a function of ageing and changing generational status. But it is not all negative, for at the same time, teachers all say that discipline becomes easier as they grow into the natural authority of age. By becoming older and maybe more prone to be judgmental and authoritarian they perhaps become more like the 'proper teacher' (and less like an ordinary person — see Chapter 4) as perceived by pupils and some young teachers.

Women who have returned after having children often come back into school as 'mums'.

> You must come back as more of a mother figure, I suppose, than a 'mate' and that has some advantages. (Margery, 45, scale 3, chemistry)

The 'advantage' mentioned by all mid-career women with children was that of greater understanding and sympathy.

> Having your own children must change the way you see children . . . you get an understanding of children but you don't really know where you get it from or how you get it . . . I think having a child of my own helped. And I'm sure I must be more understanding than when I first started to teach. (Ann, 43, scale 1, art)

Teachers who have children of their own often develop a different perception of and attitude towards pupils. The relationship becomes more parental and perhaps, in some ways more relaxed and natural. Mother/father teachers see their own children in the pupils and become more sympathetic.

I think I gradually have come to see pupils differently ... at the beginning really there's a tendency to assert some superiority over them, when you first start teaching, when you're young I suppose but I tend to feel rather sorry for them now, I don't know that that affects my teaching of them very much in some ways, but you know the world is a very hard place for them now. I feel, by and large, rather sorry for them, apart from the rotters ... I suppose inevitably, whether I do it consciously or not I see my own children in them really, and realize that they're having a struggle in some areas, jobs and qualifications and the world generally. It's harder I think than it used to be. (Margery, 45, scale 3, chemistry)

The sheer disregard that many pupils have for themselves in terms of self-respect, respect for others, their general unwillingness to want not just to *learn,* but to want to experience things. They have a very narrow view of life, most of them, far narrower than I had, and my kids have ... And sometimes the sheer disregard that their parents seem to have for them. It makes me more protective and more concerned for my own ... and it makes me want to do right by the kids in school. It's the comparison, I think, between their lives and my kids that's had this effect. (Brian, 45, scale 4, art)

For their part, pupils see older teachers differently. The relationship has changed and, as Margery found, this is reflected in the confidences they entrust and the things they talk about to teachers.

Now they undoubtedly regard me more as a mum and sort of chum up along me. And they tell me incredible things like that they're moving house, or that their granny's ill. You know, things that it's very strange that old pupils would tell you. I'm talking about post-16 pupils. When I was younger I used to hear all about their boyfriends and girlfriends, their romances, but that seemed to stop when I came back ... I was only 33, it made me feel quite old. (Margery, 45, scale 3, chemistry)

Male teachers may find that they are no longer so attractive to young girls, which may be a blow to the ego but means that it is not quite so necessary to be on guard against potentially compromising situations. As Dave explained:

I'm on to the safe area. I think I am the father uncle figure now, and I have been for five or six years. A lot of the worries I had as a younger teacher are no longer there; I'll keep anybody in by themselves, it doesn't worry me. I'll sit and talk to a sixth-form girl, by herself, for an hour-and-a-half, it doesn't worry me any more. I've passed the danger area in that sense ... (Dave, 45, senior teacher, chemistry)

Phase 4: 40–50/55

In terms of the hierarchical career structure the 'successful' teachers of 40+ are in senior management positions and generally have relatively little classroom contact with pupils. This study was not concerned with these people and the teachers in this age group who we talked to were generally in 'middle management', that is head of department, faculty, posts.

For male teachers, promotion after 40 grows increasingly unlikely, although contraction may have had some effect in slowing down promotion rates and altering perceptions of what constitutes an age-appropriate position. By contrast, women whose families are no longer quite so dependent on them may start considering, applying for, and being appointed to, senior pastoral posts.

Kath (retired, chemist) for example became a senior teacher in her early forties and Margery (45, scale 3, chemist) and Sally (41, scale 3, art) were seriously considering applying for deputy headships with responsibility for girls' welfare. Both felt that they stood a reasonable chance of success.

Even so, it seems that the major task for the age group (male and female) is of coming to terms with, and adapting to, what can be seen as a plateau in the life career — it is the time which follows the hurriedly incremental phases culminating in the peak years and prior to the pre-retirement phase.

There is considerable evidence which suggests that between the approximate ages of 37 to 45, individuals experience a phase which can be at least as traumatic as adolescence (see Jung, 1971; Vaillant and McArthur, 1972; Sheehy, 1976; Erikson, 1959; Levinson *et al,* 1978; Bromley, 1974, Dicks, 1965). Crucially it is during this phase that it becomes apparent whether or not the work of establishing occupational career, family and identity begun in the twenties and thirties has been successful; and it tends to involve self-reappraisal, questioning what one has made of one's life and searching for ways of expressing, fulfilling and satisfying oneself in the future. It is the transitional phase from youth to maturity and, according to Jaques (1965) the central issue is accepting and coming to terms with one's own mortality. This task is not made any easier for teachers who are constantly surrounded by young people.

Their relationship with pupils is now definitely parental, indeed they may be closer in age to their pupils' grandparents.

> I do seem ancient to some of these kids. I mean round here they get married early and I'm actually older than some of their grandparents. I mean I go to Toyah concerts with my youngest daughter, I'm a real head banger, more with it than most of them. But they see an older man. like grandpa, and it affects their attitudes. It's bound to. (Brian, 45, scale 4, art)

It may come as a bit of a shock to realize that young teachers are the same age as their own children, as the following quote from a 48 year old teacher suggests:

> As the years go on I realize that I have in my department teachers who in fact are only as young as my own children. This brings me up with a start sometimes but then I think it's all simply a matter of staff relationships. (48, senior teacher, English)

Some are conscious of adopting a parental-type interest in and guidance role vis a vis their younger colleagues. For example:

> I had this young girl from Cambridge as a probationer in my department. I took quite a fatherly interest, I suppose you might say, in her. I helped her out with any problems she might have and so on. And she and her husband came to tea here once or twice and we went to them. She's moved now but we keep contact and meet occasionally. (Mr Count, retired, chemistry)

Peterson (1964, p. 295) found that unmarried older women teachers sometimes sought to extend their services as mothers or aunts to young teachers. And it may be that a role of this type enables them to feel pleased for and proud of 'their' young teachers who are more successful, in promotional terms, than they themselves have been.

Perhaps anticipating, and defending themselves against how they expect young teachers perceive them, those in this age group often mention that they have come to recognize how good the mid-career teachers they criticized when they were young actually were!

Adapting to 'maturity' can mean a new life structure, and new roles. By virtue of their seniority and age within a school, teachers of 40+ are often authority figures, having taken on a role as maintainer of standards and guardian of school tradition (see Lacey, 1970). In some ways they can be regarded as the dependable backbone of the school. They are not 'paid' for this work but it is nevertheless a recognized position within the school's internal, informal status hierarchy. Dave (45, senior teacher, chemistry) sees himself as one of these teachers:

> If I go into the hall with 144 kids to sit an exam, they know what to expect. They know they're not going to be moving around, they're not going to be talking ... now that might not be so with every member of staff. Not every member of staff might want to live that way. But in a community, to get order you need somebody, or a number of people who will do that, otherwise you'd have chaos ... The staff recognize what I'm about ... they recognize the strata, or they recognize the control that is needed.

Those who adopt such roles, whether they say they have done so consciously or unconsciously, often stress that they are not doing anything special and are only behaving as professionals should.

At the same time, some of them may also hope that they are making a point: if they have not had the promotions they think they deserve they aim to show that they can do the job better, and more 'professionally', even without the scale and the salary. Dave, for example, really expected to get a deputy headship at his school. He felt that, over the years, the Head had been coaching and preparing him as his assistant. However, when the post finally became vacant an external candidate, a much younger man, was appointed. Dave was very disappointed and two years after the event said that he knew it was 'sour grapes' and even though it was not good for the school, felt better when he saw the 'newcomer' doing the job very badly and then coming to him for advice.

By and large the teachers who take on authority roles have made relatively successful adaptations and are content to identify with and be identified in terms of their job and their school. Despite the turmoils of the mid-life transition research indicates that many teachers view the period between 35 and 50 as a time during which their morale was high, second only to the first three to five years in teaching in terms of job satisfaction and contentment (Rempel and Bentley, 1970; Peterson, 1964; McLeish, 1969; Lortie, 1975). This is likely to be due to a combination of factors which include relative confidence in their ability to do the job, and declining ambition — when they have accepted that further promotion is unlikely they can stop striving for it and concentrate upon actually doing and enjoying the job.

However, not all adapt so successfully. There are those who find it difficult to accept and come to terms with their position and their age. In some respects these people may be coasting, they are not working towards any goal in their occupational or other aspects of their life. They are, in terms of Erikson's (1959) model, stagnating rather than generating. Those who are cynical and bitter about how things have worked out for them can become central figures in the grumbling cliques which were mentioned earlier.

Phase 5: 50–55 plus

Bearing in mind that as a consequence of contraction many LEAs are offering early retirement, teachers in this age group can be considered to be experiencing a phase in which the major task is that of preparing for retirement.

From around the age of 50 even if their morale is high, energy and enthusiasm for the job often are felt to be declining. Jim's (retired, biology) feelings seem to be typical:

> The kids are always the same age and you gradually get older and older and older, that's very true ... they do. And unfortunately too their capacity for life, their energy remains the same and yours diminishes ...
>
> I think I had some of the best teaching experiences and pleasure when I was round about 35 ... you've got lots and lots of energy

and you're prepared to spend all the time in the world on it, but as you get on you haven't got quite the same amount of energy or time. And it's no good blinking the fact that you're not so eager to take up the challenge of the next trip abroad and so on. Or at least I wasn't and I'm sure it applies to the rest.

Retirement becomes an increasingly attractive prospect (Morse and Weiss, 1955). Those who have ceased to enjoy teaching and who have been 'time serving' now have a goal to look forward to and this, paradoxically, may give them an enthusiasm that they have lacked for some time.

Towards the end of their career, teachers often say that they become freer in their attitude and discipline (Newman, 1979; Rempel and Bentley, 1970; Peterson, 1964; Lortie, 1975). This is partly because they have authority, partly because their experience has led them to the opinion that 'trivialities' are unimportant, that the pupils learn is the main point.

> I became less bothered about things like copying. I thought well, it doesn't really matter where they get the information from, whether from me or their friend, as long as they get it. (Jim, 65, retired, biology)

Arthur (69, retired, art) and Kath (59, retired, chemistry) both said that they came to a similar opinion. Another reason for a more relaxed approach can be because the value of the rewards to be gained by inhibiting their individuality and conforming are now negligible (see Miner, 1962). As Arthur (69, retired, art) pointed out:

> Well, they weren't going to promote me during my last three years or so, well, long before that really, so I had nothing to lose; I did more or less what I wanted to with the kids.

Teachers of 50+ will probably have been at their present school for some time, and may have taught pupils' parents. Thus their reputation precedes them. They may welcome this sense of continuity but can also experience it as a constraint. Jim (65, retired, biology) felt this:

> If you've been at a school for a while you become known. There's a sort of mythology about you that's passed down by pupils you've taught, to their kids. And they come into school with all sorts of ideas about you. In some ways it's nice but people change and things change, courses change and methods, and so on, and it's sometimes very difficult if people have these expectations about you.

Arthur and Mr Bridge just felt old!

> I had kids coming and saying 'Eh, you used to teach my grandma didn't you?' and I thought 'By Heck! I must be getting on'. They married young mind you, but the first time a kid said that to me . . . I nearly dropped bow-legged! (Arthur, 69, retired, art)

> It can be a bit traumatic, the fact that ex-pupils introduce you to their children and you can only remember them when they were in the third year at school and they are introducing you to their children who are probably in the same year ... it makes me feel a bit old. (Mr Bridge, 58, retired, art)

On the other hand, even with such concrete evidence of passing time, working with pupils can keep teachers young; in Arthur's (69, retired, art) opinion:

> This is one of the perks of the job, you are working with kids all the time, and they keep you up to date ... if you can't keep up with them and talk their language, unofficial language, then, you know, the rapport just isn't there, they aren't able to communicate are they? So it's up to you to make sure you are au fait with the music and the telly and so on.

Arthur made a deliberate effort in order to be able to meet pupils on their own grounds. This to him was an obvious and necessary strategy for establishing good relationships. It was in his personality to do this, and indeed, as is the case at any age, pupil:teacher relationships are dependent to a large extent on personalities. However, unless they come to see them in a grand-parental role, it seems that many pupils have a tendency to reject and to distance themselves from the old, and teachers in this age group may find it harder to develop close relationships with pupils. For instance,

> The way in which they treat you changes ... when you get older they treat you with what they believe is respect, but they never really take you into their confidence in a sense. They don't really appreciate it when you've got a few years on your back, over the last five years that I had, if you use their common nickname they used among their friends. Now, twenty or thirty years ago that would have been easy ... with a younger teacher there isn't quite the same gap and they would accept use of nicknames ... you could, or I could, pull their legs, in other sorts of ways but that one didn't seem to go. (Jim, 65, retired, biology)

This account supports Measor and Woods' (1984) observation that 'peer group nicknames (are) for use only by "approved" teachers'. By and large the (relatively) old are not 'approved' by the young.

Young teachers, likewise may regard them as 'past it', outmoded in terms of pedagogy and values. Older teachers tend to be in senior posts as Head of Department or Faculty and, particularly if they exercise a high degree of control, younger teachers can become frustrated and dissatisfied because they are unable to put their own ideas into practice. These feelings are exacerbated if, as they frequently do, they perceive older teachers as having eased up and, unfortunately it seems that the knowledge and experience of older teachers is rarely sought and made use of.

The fault and lack of communication is not only on the side of the young, for, on the whole, older teachers are critical of what they perceive to be the low professional standards of the new generation of teachers, which they also usually add reflect general social attitudes. The following comment is typical:

> I was having this session with probationers or young ones just into the school, on ... I don't know if you'd call it 'successful teaching' or what you'd call it, but, I was trying to give some advice or, the sort of things that I did in certain situations and so on and so on. And I was absolutely floored at a young teacher who turned round and told me that lesson preparation was a waste of time. Well, we were talking about good and bad teachers, how is anyone going to develop if they think lesson preparation is a waste of time? Now, I'm not saying all young teachers are like that, of course not, but that sort of attitude isn't all that uncommon these days. (Kath, 59, retired, chemistry)

Some teachers in their fifties and sixties (and perhaps a few in the preceding age group) started off their careers as class teachers in elementary schools. Without exception, those who did say that they are grateful for this experience and that it made them more capable and more able to adapt to comprehensivization when it came. These teachers often say that they feel that grammar school and younger teachers are very limited in skills and that increasing specialization has not been a good thing for schools, pupils and education in general. As Arthur (69, retired, art) explained:

> When I started I taught everything except music ... specialist teaching in those days — 1935ish — was unknown in an elementary school ... I'd taught all types of ability, others who've never had that experience find they've got problems ... some of them had a terrible time when we went comprehensive ... It happens very often now that somebody's off sick and you're asked to step in if you've got a free period. 'Will you take so and so?' And you walk in this classroom, there's a gang of kids there, 'What should it be now?' 'Oh, we're doing English', or 'we're doing geography' or 'we're doing this', and through all this earlier training you found out that you were able to sort of pick it up from there and carry on, you didn't altogether waste the time of this period you'd got with somebody else's kids in a subject that wasn't yours, cus you can fall back on the experience you'd got, which is something the modern chaps going into the profession can't do. They're highly specialized, they know their own subject p'raps inside out, but stick 'em in front of a class on some other subject or topic and they haven't a clue what to do, so it's 'silent reading for you lot'.

Teachers of all ages often remark that it is difficult to get any indication of how well they are doing their job, and this is perhaps one reason why many teachers are in favour of examinations — results provide some feedback.

Much of the satisfaction that can be obtained from teaching is in a sense vicarious. It arises from seeing what ex-pupils have made of their lives, and, because few people achieve eminence, fame, notoriety and so on, teachers look to being part of the process whereby a child becomes, in Jim's words, 'a responsible, decent citizen'. Even, and perhaps especially, when they retire teachers can continue to meet and hear about how pupils are getting on and thereby get a great deal of satisfaction. All of the retired teachers we talked to had a fund of such stories, and they were an important source of pleasure. The message of stories apparently hold for the older teachers was that, after all, being a teacher had been worthwhile. On this account Jim and Arthur shall have the last words.

Occasionally you pick up little bits from people who've passed through your hands. You hear about what they're doing. And you say, well it wasn't completely lost. Yes we *did* do something worthwhile . . . that sort of thing keeps your flame burning a little bit. (Jim, 65, retired, biology)

I can't go into a bank or building society or any where in town with any privacy, because the old grammar school kids are the ones who went to work in banks and building societies. 'Hello, Sir. How are you?' and I think 'Oh my God, here we go again!'. I like it, I think it's a compliment if a kid'll come and talk to you . . . The other day I met a lass, she's started up a nursing home for old folk, and she said to me 'You needn't worry Sir, I'll look after you, you can come to my place'. And I thought that was great. (Arthur, 69, retired, art)

Pupils are not the only ones who sometimes forget that teachers are human. But teachers are first and foremost people, and like everyone else they are subject to changes which are associated with ageing, and how the process is viewed in this society.

An investigation of the ways in which certain aspects of the occupational culture appear to influence teachers' experiences of growing old contributes to our understanding of schools as social systems, and enables teachers to compare and learn from each others' experiences about a personal, although absolutely central and universal, aspect of their lives. In addition, it gives some indication of the effect that age and experience can have upon motivation and commitment, and therefore of ways in which teachers' job satisfaction and effectiveness are influenced.

Chapter 2

Critical Phases and Incidents

The question is raised, if the teacher career consist of phases, how does one move from one to another? The progress it seems is not always smooth and inevitable. Sometimes there are sharp discontinuities and enormous leaps in such passages. These phenomena are the subject of this chapter.

In the research of life history and sociological biography the issue of 'critical phases' has already emerged as an area of importance. Strauss and Rainwater (1962, p. 105) for example, discussed 'periods of strain' in the lives of the chemists they were researching. During these critical phases, particular events occurred which were important for their careers and identities. Strauss (1959, p. 67) referred to these transformations of identity as 'critical incidents' (see also Walker, 1976). Our research also indicates 'critical incidents' being key events in an individual's life, and around which pivotal decisions revolve. They provoke the individual into selecting particular kinds of actions, which lead in particular directions. Becker wrote of 'these crucial interactive episodes, in which new lines of individual and collective activity are forged ... and new aspects of the self brought into being' (1966, p. xiv); and Strauss (1959, p. 67) of 'turning points' and the 'frequent occurrence of misalignment — surprise, shock, chagrin, anxiety, tension, bafflement, self-questioning — and also the need to try out the new self, to explore and validate the new and often exciting or fearful conceptions'. Critical incidents are a useful area to study, because they reveal, like a flashbulb, the major choice and change times in people's lives. Here, we aim to pinpoint the 'critical incidents' in some teachers' biographies and to give detailed descriptions of them. We can then consider whether there are any common patterns in different biographies, and so work towards 'the developmental, generalized formulation of careers' that Glaser called for (1964, p. xv).

'Critical incidents' are most likely to occur during the 'periods of strain' that Strauss (1962) identified. We term the latter 'critical phases', and we noted among our teachers three particular types: (i) extrinsic; (ii) intrinsic; and (iii) personal. 'Extrinsic' critical phases can be produced by events occurring in society. In the biographies of the older teachers we interviewed, the Second

World War was a prominent example. It had clearly forced decisions on people that had had a profound effect upon career development. At another level, policy innovations, for example comprehensivization, could also have a dramatic effect. We examine these factors in Chapter 3.

'Intrinsic' critical phases occur within the natural progression of a career. Again, the individual is confronted by choices and decisions. We identified the following intrinsic critical phases within the careers of teachers:

1 Choosing to enter the teaching profession.
2 The first teaching practice.
3 The first eighteen months of teaching.
4 Three years after taking the first job.
5 Mid career moves and promotion.
6 Pre-retirement.

Family events, marriage, divorce, the birth or illness of a child, can also provoke 'personal' critical phases, and project an individual in a different career direction from that held formerly. For older, female, unmarried teachers, parental demands and pressures had profoundly influenced their actions and choices.

It is during these periods of changing and choosing that critical incidents are most likely to occur. The incident itself probably represents the culmination of a decision-making process, crystallizing the individual's thinking, rather than being responsible of itself for that decision. We take as our focus in this chapter the kind of 'critical incidents' that occur in one 'critical phase' — the first eighteen months of teaching.

The majority of teachers we interviewed said they had had serious trouble controlling the pupils they taught during their first eighteen months of teaching. This, of course, is nothing unusual (see, for example, Hannam *et al,* 1971; Hanson and Herrington, 1976). Discipline difficulties are one of the defining characteristics of this critical phase. The problems are moreover experienced in the context of an extreme form of exhaustion. Mr Shoe's (63, retired, science) comments were typical:

> I must admit that the first six months of my real teaching was very, very hard.

Mr Quilley (67, retired, art) agreed. He had begun his career in an elementary school in the North of England in the late 1930s, and both times — and pupils — were exceptionally hard:

> I think your worst feelings about discipline were in your first job. I went through hell, for about five or six weeks.

Teachers who taught male pupils seemed to have most difficulty. Women teachers in girls' schools faced comparatively few such problems. Miss Coal (65, retired, science) recalled:

Oh yes, I mean the children were a bit naughty, but it was alright.

The background against which critical incidents occurred revealed the pressures and constraints upon the young teacher entering the profession. The young teacher was usually under the tutelage of a more experienced member of staff. The older teacher exerted pressure to show a 'heavy hand' to pupils. Mr Shoe described the experience of teaching in a small rural school, staffed by himself, and a much older Headmaster. A glass partition was all that separated their classrooms, and Mr Shoe (63, retired, science) remembered the eagle-eyed observation with horror:

> He kept popping in to tell me how to do it . . . he was one of the old school, strong disciplinarian, no nonsense, he was the boss in his school. His advice to me was, if you have any trouble with any of the kiddies, impose your authority. Smack them down. He'd got a very hard, horny hand there.

This graphically portrays the context of the critical incident, which in this case involves a confrontation between teacher and pupils. Quite frequently that confrontation is violent, and leads to the involvement of senior members of staff at the school. One account, from a Glasgow woman teacher, gives a particularly clear view of the character of such episodes.

The woman began her career in a tough elementary school in Glasgow in 1939. During her first year there she experienced considerable discipline difficulties, which culminated in the following incident. One day, the teacher entered the classroom to find that each of her male pupils had displayed their genitals on the desk in front of them. She told the pupils to put them away, and then frog-marched one of the boys out of the classroom. Her classroom was on a first-floor balcony, and somehow she pushed the boy in such a way that he fell over the balcony and on to the floor some distance below. A now carefully buttoned group of boys watched his fall in a hushed and respectful silence. The woman had no further discipline problems. This incident, while perhaps particularly colourful (blue?), is a good example of many of the issues involved. The general properties are that a class is disruptive over quite a long period of time. At some point, a particular potent threat is made by pupils, bringing a response from the teacher, and a violent outcome.

These incidents have long-term effects. The Glasgow teacher reported that as a result of the above event, she established a reputation which enabled her to gain reasonable discipline in the school from then on. It is significant that all the accounts we collected of these kinds of encounters had successful outcomes for the teachers — presumably those who fail such tests give up teaching. Even so, their response to incidents varied considerably, and as a result, the teachers established quite different kinds of reputations. But we can still see some common patterns, as the following two accounts illustrate:

> And I've been bashed by kids about a quarter my size, and one of them got bashed back (laughter) and I ended up on the mat about it . . . It

was near the end of the lesson, and I walked past a child who was working, and he'd take a swing at you. In the tummy, or even further down ... well what do you do? Wop them one then and there? At least I did that, and so I was sent for. Eventually the Head said I mustn't bash them up. I wasn't a bully, but I said, personal violence, foul-mouthed cheek is not on, because most of the staff were wopping them one occasionally, or taking them to be wopped ... Eventually the Head said, 'No more, that's it. The next time and you're going in front of the Director' (Laughs). And I thought, My God, my old man, teaching in town, me in front of the Director, this will be terrible ... This will be ghastly, because my father was running two departments in the local tech (Said in a highly animated way) ... Well I went to see my NUT bloke. Anyway there came a time when a bloke was absolutely terribly disobedient, so I said 'Come out here, I'm gonna cane you in front of all, everybody'. And I rushed into my store room, and I had lots of little sticks in there, and I unfortunately grabbed the first, and it happened to be the black one, and it was about twelve inches long, and I came out, and I said ... (Mr Quilley, 67, retired, art).

We had some difficulty in transcribing Mr Quilley's account from the tape. The problem was in getting down what he had said. This appeared to be because he increased the pace of delivery of his sentences, which were shortened and forceful, piling them up in a staccato fashion. This style of talking, which is difficult to represent in print, emphasized the drama of his narrative:

and I came out and I said 'Hold your hand out lad; now you know what you're getting this for?'
Yes.
'Do you deserve it?'
I don't know.
'Yes you do; hold your hand out'. So he held his hand out and as I struck him, he turned it upward, so I bashed him across the thumb. So I said 'Serve you right. And the other hand, and this one again, and that one'. And I sent him back to his seat.
(Draws a proper breath for the first time and relaxes the pace of the narrative.) And nothing happened, the next day the Head yanked me out and said 'You're as good as fired'. 'Got to go and see — the what's his name, Director — in the town hall, but I'm washing my hands of it, the only hurdle you've got to get past is the boy's father, he's coming to see you. You'd better watch it ... but I've washed my hands of you, I'm speaking against you'. So the father came up, about the boy, and I thought Ughm this is it, and the boy's father came in, and we had quite a nice conversation, we got on quite well, and to cut a long story short, I gave him ten bob — at his request (pause) lots of

money in those days ... I only got paid £14 a month — but, er, he said er, next time Mr Quilley, get him out of school, and knock his head off, I don't want him bashed in school. And that was the end of it.

Mr Tucks (29, scale 2, science) gave an account of a very similar incident. However, his reaction to it was very different:

Mr Tucks: Well ... there was a very significant incident on the ... last day of the first half term ... when I actually came to blows with a student. Yeah, and ... he wasn't a student of mine, but he'd interrupted a lesson and gone out, and slammed the door, and various things (mutters) and, and didn't seem to (mutters, and his voice becomes quiet and indistinct) work at the time (mutters again).

R: Were you teaching him?

Mr Tucks: No, no, no? No — (takes a deep breath in).

R: He just came in and interrupted your lesson?

Mr Tucks: Yeah, yeah, yeah (mutters, sighs). Er mmm! And in fact I was reprimanded by the Head, for that ...

R: What did you do?

Mr Tucks: I chased him and then I clocked him over the head ... yeah ... I completely lost control of myself ... I hesitate to repeat it, I can't, I don't know what ... you know, ... it's difficult to repeat it, don't like it. Well that was crucial. I suddenly got the wrong sort of reputation amongst students who didn't know me, for some time the ones who knew me well, didn't learn anything from it. At least — well not — but it had the effect ... these students could perceive, from afar that I was slightly different style ... they weren't prepared to sort of it ... test it. I was prepared to be very informal with students I was teaching, but I was sufficiently unsure of myself to regard an assumption of students I wasn't teaching, of that informality as a threat.

R: What effects has it had? Do you hit kids now?

Mr Tucks: Noooh! Not at all.

For Mr Tucks the experience had been personally distressing. His facial gestures and tone of voice expressed his discomfort, and he openly stated that he did not like even talking about it. The pace of his delivery slowed down discernibly, and the researcher had to push for the full story. Mr Tucks' response to the critical incident was different from Mr Quilley's. The discovery of such personal anger in himself discomforted Mr Tucks quite considerably and determined his future course of action. He sought to avoid any repetition of such incidents.

Mr Shoe (63, retired, science) gave an account of a similar 'critical incident'. The details were the same — in a moment of exasperation he 'just banged their heads together you know'. He was able to draw out what was crucial in the experience for him:

> I did it once — it was a salutary lesson, so I learned that if I ever wanted to hit out, I never did. I learned from that, and I think one of the things I learned was the fact that one of the worst things you can do is deal with a child in anger, when he's provoked you. I think I learned, too, that if you begin to shout and you begin to rant and rave with the class, you lose your authority anyway.

Mr Shoe gives an indication of one of the elements which make such incidents 'critical'. It is the discovery that a display of real anger in the classroom is genuinely counter-productive, and that teachers need to 'stage manage' a 'front' of anger if they are to cope as 'proper teachers'. Being provoked into a display of real anger by pupils represents not 'coping', but rather a breakdown in classroom interaction rules. Mr King (65, retired, art) recognized this:

> I think you have to pretend to be angry with children, but never to lose your temper. Once you lost it, they sense it, something's transmitted, salt or something is sent across the atmosphere. They know it, just like an animal, a horse will gallop through a wood, if you're frightened of him, and brush you off. If you really hold the reins he won't. So children are like that, they react intuitively or whatever, instinctively is better.

These incidents caused 'trouble' (Furlong, 1977) for the teachers, in which they faced punishment or embarrassment of some kind as a result of their loss of control. The intervention of senior colleagues escalated the affairs beyond the privacy of one's own classroom, so, there is both a public and private loss of face involved.

As a result of the 'critical incident', the teachers involved reached a number of decisions.

> *R:* Did you go on hitting kids?
> *Mr Shoe:* Not really, no ... It wasn't my way really.

The teacher came to a decision about his own teaching style, and about the way he wanted to do things. When the teachers described this process, they usually employed a negative model, to help define their own choices. Mr Shoe, for example, compared himself with the 'horny handed Headmaster':

> I learned by observing him in many ways ... In his lessons there wouldn't be any messing. You hadn't got to think, now how can I make sure I've got their interest. What he did was purely imposing his will on them, that was that really.

Mr Redford (33, scale 4, art) used the same tactic, in reference to his first Head of Department:

I quickly ditched any set rules he was passing on to me, and just taught in my own sort of way.

Hanson and Herrington (1976) discuss the ways that senior members of the teaching profession put pressure on younger teachers to conform. Heads of departments in particular may act as 'critical reality definers' (Riseborough 1981). The 'critical incidents' show how such pressures work, but also how teachers find their way through them. The incidents are 'critical' in that they force a major leap in the process by which new recruits become the kind of teachers they want to be.

We offered this analysis of 'critical incidents' to some of the teachers being interviewed. This was part of an attempt to get respondent validation, but also to involve teachers more fully in the work of analysis. It was suggested to Mr Redford (33, scale 4, art) that a 'critical incident' had set the style of teaching and discipline he had held ever since:

Yes, I think it probably did, although I don't think it came as a great shock to me, do you know what I mean, I think I'd perhaps, I'd actually reached that stage earlier, but my lack of experience had encouraged me to, under the pressure of the situation, to accept the urgings of the Head of Department to take on *his* operations. Plus I was supply at that point. If I'd started in September, perhaps I wouldn't have done that you know, but er … in fact … er

This suggests that the critical incident does not necessarily introduce anything totally new into the practices of the teacher. Rather, it probably acts to crystallize ideas, attitudes and beliefs that the teacher has more generally or less consciously held up to that point.

Teachers gave an account of another kind of incident, which occurred usually soon after the 'critical incident'. We have termed these 'counter incidents'. The 'counter incident', also involved a challenge from the pupils, but brought a different response from teachers which reflected 'their way', and the sort of teacher they wished to be. Mr Shoe (63, retired, science), for example, offered an account of another confrontation situation he had encountered, during his first six months teaching, but this time he had stayed in control, successfully stage-managing the interaction:

I would have felt dreadful, I think, if I felt that I was losing the control and some kiddies wouldn't do what I wanted. I don't think I could live with that, and I think the worst occasion I had, or the best occasion maybe, and that was, with one lad, he had a widowed mother, a very fine lady really, but John, her son, was not particularly able, but tending to be a bit difficult at times and I know one day I had to remove him; I said 'Well if you're going to behave like this, I've had enough of this, it's going to be to the Headmaster'. And we were in a dining room then with a central corridor and this was used as a classroom, and he'd played and played, and he'd been funny and difficult and I thought — well I'd better get rid of him, and he wasn't going to go if I just said 'Go'. So I think one of the best ways, really, you get them at a disadvantage very quickly, to get them by the scruff of the pants and scruff of the neck, and you've got them then and they will go. I got hold of this lad and he was pretty big and heavy, and I said 'Well are you going out?' and he said 'No, I'm not', 'Oh, you are!' and he said 'No, I'm not', 'Oh, you are!' Well, of course, he went down the middle of the passageway, and hitting desks and chairs as he went, there was an almighty crash, bang, wallop, doors open, out he went, and he was seen to go straight through, like that, across the playground and in front of the Headmaster's study. I said, 'Now you can tell the Headmaster what you've seen'. The kiddies had seen all this; heard all the noise and kerfuffle: 'What a tiger we have! But I didn't do that very often, just that one occasion I think. You learn, well I'm not standing any nonsense, so I'm not sure it works on every occasion ... actually end of the day, John Dewhurst and I were the best of pals. He didn't sort of resent me, no; I told him I wanted him out, and certainly I tried to tell the kids that 'Alright you misbehaved, but I assure you that I'm not one to bear grudges, and I would hope that all teachers would, once they've chastized or corrected, are not going to hold it against you — 'I'll remember you in future' — As far as I'm concerned if you accept punishment and it's accepted gracefully, and most of them did, as far as I'm concerned, then it's finished. I'm not going to treat you now any different from anybody else'.

Mr Shoe's 'critical' and 'counter' incident stories were told, closely following each other in the same interview. They were used to highlight the teacher's choices of teaching and discipline style, and indicate the values and attitudes he chose for himself as a teacher. In Mr Shoe's case, his style did not entirely exclude a physical approach. Nevertheless, Mr Shoe learned from his 'critical incident' to pick both his pupil and the form of trouble quite carefully. In the counter incident, the events are staged — to show 'what a tiger we have'. In the second episode, there is noise, excitement, spectacle, and a mass audience. Yet there was no real physical violence or pain. Mr Shoe was in control of the counter incident, unlike the critical one. His comment that John and he were later 'the best of pals' was also significant. No such reconciliation would have been possible after the first incident.

A 'counter incident' in which rather different values were made clear is illustrated in the following story:

I had another quick incident. There was a cupboard, with the stock in, and some of the big fifth years, they were quite toughies, were in the cupboard, and I said 'Come out!' and the whole class went silent. And I said, 'Right, empty your pockets' and this lad said 'No'. [The first 'empty your pockets' was said quite gently]. So I said 'Empty your pockets'. [Mr Redford repeated the order, even more quietly and with real gentleness in his account]. He said 'No', and you know you've got this immediate confrontation, this lad was about six foot tall, and there's me — looking up at him. And he said 'You'll have to make me'. It was an *awful* situation, but I knew I couldn't back down. He walked towards me, and I put my hand out, and he slipped, his feet shot from under him, and he fell flat on his back. He said, 'Right then!' (his tone was very aggressive) and I said 'O.K. come on' (Mr Redford's tone was very gentle). I realized he needed a way out. He said, 'Alright, I'll empty my pockets, but if you don't find anything, I want an apology'. He got up and emptied his pockets, and there was nothing in there, and I apologized, and after that my relationship with the whole group was completely different. (Mr Redford, 33, scale 4, art).

This incident was important to Mr Redford because it showed his preferred way of dealing with discipline difficulties. He attempted to leave violent confrontation completely out of his teaching style. While he could not always avoid confrontation in an all-boys' comprehensive school, he did attempt to meet it when it occurred in a calmly rational way, refusing to allow himself to be influenced by the culture of aggression that, in his view, is current in such schools. He told of a third incident, in which another individual reinforced the identity he was seeking. A pupil approached him:

'Ere Sir', he said, 'Ey, you're all right'. So I said 'Oh, thanks a lot'. 'Yeh' he said, 'Yeh, what I like about you' he said, 'You don't try and be tough like the other guys, some of the other teachers'. And I said, 'Well I'm not', an' you could have heard a pin drop. And he said, 'What did you say?' I said 'Well, I'm not tough', and he said (loudly) 'Did you 'ear what he said', you know. And I was intrigued, and it seemed to me that a lot of teachers, you can get drawn into a situation, where — if you're not careful, where you have to act tough, and you're pushing and pushing and pushing, and you never allow them to see that there's no harm in not being tough, which probably contributes to the tendency for them all to be little tough guys.

Mr Quilley also described a 'counter incident' which reveals some particular features about his teaching style, which were in direct opposition to those of Mr Redford. When Mr Quilley related his 'critical incident' he had shown none of the remorse about his experience of violent confrontation which the other teachers had. He did not suggest that he avoided violent confrontations from then on in his career. Other data gathered in the project supported this conclusion. As noted in Chapter 1, we thought it would make for useful cross-referencing if we chose teachers for interviewing who knew each other, either from working in the same school, even at different times historically, or because they taught the same subject in the same town. Thus Mr Tucks knew Mr Quilley — he had done his student teaching practice at his school. He laughed when Mr Quilley was mentioned, 'Oh he was renowned that guy, everyone knew him'. Mr King declared, 'He was a bully', and Mr Redford told tales of Mr Quilley's monstrous mass canings, that had shocked pupils, parents, and peers alike. Nevertheless, this was not the full picture. Mr Quilley (67, retired, art) did not provide a specific 'counter incident' to reveal his teaching style, but he did make a series of comments which showed there was another side to him. He was anxious to indicate that he did achieve good relationships in some areas, with at least some of the pupils.

> Colliers' sons, wonderful in the playground, great on the football pitch, and in the swimming pool. I had no trouble with them there, but in the classroom, you were a different person, to be got at, if you were gottable at.

In addition, Mr Quilley provided long accounts of the expeditions and trips he had organized, for pupils to go skiing or to visit art galleries abroad, or sailing small boats. Mr Tucks (29, scale 2, science) confirmed this view of a two-sided figure.

> He was extraordinary, such a mixture, he'd organize all these super trips, skiing and painting, the kids loved it, and yet all this violence too. I don't know if the story is apocryphal, but there are tales of him playing games with knives, you know boys had to splay their fingers out, and you dot between them with a big knife.

In all three sets of 'critical' and 'counter' incidents that we have described, the teachers are indicating what choices they took at a particular phase, and trying to show what kind of teacher they became. But the communication of identity is no easy matter. We have considered this elsewhere (Measor and Woods, 1984a), taking Lewis' (1979) argument that values, attitudes, roles and identity are things which are very difficult for people to talk straightforwardly about. Indeed, in Lewis' view, they are precisely the things that people need symbols for. We suggested that adolescents employed myths to signal acceptable role models and identities for themselves. We also documented the ways that adolescent girls personified values into particular people around them, and used them as positive or negative role models.

The same mechanisms appeared to be at work in these teachers' biographies. We have already seen how negative role models were employed. The 'critical' and 'counter' incident accounts were another device, where symbols are used to reveal choice and identity preferences. The 'critical' incident is described, the reaction to it is identified, and the confusion it engendered is emphasized. The choices that resulted from it, are then made clear. The 'counter' incident, when told, acts like a contrastive shadow, reinforcing the choices that resulted from the 'critical' event, and confirming the identity.

Critical incidents set teachers off on a path, looking for a new way — 'their way' — to do things. Mr Shoe (63, retired, science) indicated the importance of discovering positive role models at this phase:

I think one of the teachers that perhaps interested me was a lady, Deputy Headmistress, and I used to admire her in some ways. She always used to seem to have — the kids in her class always seemed to be well occupied, always interested. I used to think, well — I used to see her sometimes coming to school in the morning, she'd get off her bike, and she'd be snatching a sample of this, a flower of that, and she'd come in armed with that, and suddenly you'd see that these were being used in a lesson. She always seemed to, never had discipline problems with the boys that I was having you see. It was just the fact that her lessons were interesting.

As a result, Mr Shoe discarded his old role model, the Headmaster of his first school. He decided he had been wrong, that there was another way and that he was going to follow it!

I think the first thing is that you've got to get the kiddies interested . . . I think bringing in a certain sense of humour, if you can break it up, have a laugh. Involve them . . . (by) . . . talking, even though it wasn't necessarily relevant. Football, if they're a Chelsea supporter, or something. And 'Top of the Pops'. Knowing their interests, whether it be roller skating, or skateboarding or any other interest.

Mr Shoe had, by the time he had been in teaching three or four years, found his own 'way' in school, and it was one that was markedly different from the first role models he had encountered.

There were clear gender differences involved in critical incidents for teachers. All of the incidents we have described here, except for the first, occurred when male teachers confronted male pupils. The women teachers we interviewed who had taught in all girls' schools did not report comparable experiences, although women teachers involved in teaching boys or mixed classes did. The Glasgow woman teacher's story has already been told. Another woman, Mrs Castle (64, retired, art) also had difficulties and experienced violence in her first teaching job. She taught in a selective grammar school in a South Wales mining village. Mrs Castle described the school as 'nicely disciplined'. Nevertheless, there were many challenges to her discipline, and once she cracked.

Mrs Castle: I did hit a pupil once, in a temper, hit a boy of six foot . . . I felt ever so silly afterwards, very upset, I apologized.
R: what had he done?
Mrs Castle: I don't know, he was probably being a bit cheeky or something. I was horrified. I think I apologized almost straight away. He tried to cheer me up then.

Mrs Castle gave further accounts of the challenges she received:

Mrs Castle: As I say the boys did play me up at Christmas. I got chased round with the mistletoe and shut in the art room with some of the sixth form, and they said things like 'Why don't you give in gracefully, or are you going to call for Sir'.

R: Which did you do?

Mrs Castle: I gave in gracefully of course.

There are gender differences, it seems, not only in the ways boys and girls misbehave (Ebbutt, 1981; Measor, 1983; Measor and Woods, 1984a), but also with regard to the teacher's effect on the nature of classroom deviance (Walkerdine, 1980).

One of our teachers felt he had never had any real discipline problems, and could recall no 'critical' experience of violent confrontation. But there were certainly critical incidents elsewhere in his life, and these might hold the key to his comparatively smooth professional development:

> ... Well I was blown up, as I told you and was asked if I would go into a garrison regiment, because that's for downgraded physique. In theory you strut about with a revolver at your hip, and look after a town as opposed to fighting. But no, this garrison unit piled into boats and sailed over to the Channel Islands, we were the liberating force. I remember being in the first landing boat, not a German in sight, but girls galore. I suppose I had been there about three or four weeks, the civic authorities had a big dinner, they invited some officers, I sat next to the Education Officer and he said 'Why don't you come to Jersey, you're just the sort of man we want' ... I said 'I don't care to teach in the Channel Islands'. I saw myself with a good job in a public school. Or painting portraits in a posh studio of posh people. (Mr King, 65, retired, art).

However, Mr King agreed to take the job. His military background was to have a profound effect on his career and identity as a teacher:

> The Channel Islands, public schools had suffered like hell, because the Germans had imprisoned a lot of the teachers that hadn't escaped, so it was more less run by the locals and senior boys. I remember being shown around by the HM and the first room he opened, he, not me, was hit in the face with a book, and he spread it around that I was an ex-commando, which I wasn't, and of course boys immediately moved to the other side of the corridor and said 'Morning Sir', and that was what I was really enrolled for, to impose discipline, there was none. I never hit a boy. I would grab him by the scruff of the neck and the trousers and pick him up, and say 'Now what are you going to do?' It didn't matter if he was eighteen years of age, because I was very strong then, I would put him down and say, 'Now, *behave yourself*'. I never needed to hit the boys.

Mr King had finished up as the senior tutor at his school, in charge of discipline. He had a reputation in the school and wider community, for excellent discipline. He felt that these early incidents were crucial in enabling him to build a confident front. They had set his image and given him his teacher style.

What is it then which makes these incidents critical for the teacher telling the story? The account involves a set of claims about the self. For the individual particular claims are made about their ability to maintain discipline, and their authoritative image. It represents a claim to the identity of being 'a proper teacher' (see Chapter 4). The critical incident involves a challenge to this identity. As a result some of the claims are dropped, others are made real. Some parts of the identity are confirmed, others renounced. In addition, the critical incident can involve a discovery about parts of the self hitherto unknown, about, for example, one's capacity for anger, and this can be difficult to cope with. The incident provokes a series of choices, as the individual sorts out which kind of behaviour, and which parts of the self are appropriate for display in the teacher role. Strauss (1959) discussed the way a particular event can change the things an individual wants, or sees as important, thus changing the trajectory of a career. The critical incident works in this way. It involves a reassessment of priorities. By examining such incidents, therefore, we gain an insight into the processes by which identities are built by individuals at particular points in their life cycle. Hankiss wrote of the way 'people endow certain fundamental episodes with a symbolic meaning, by locating them at a focal point of the explanatory system of the self' (Bertaux, 1981, p. 205). The individual chooses 'a way' and by so doing, makes a self.

It is open to question whether these changes remain permanent. Hankiss felt that 'key events' were important because 'they constantly lead or force that person to select new models or a new strategy of life' (*Ibid*, p. 206). However, coping with such 'critical incidents' 'constantly', or even quite often, would be extremely exhausting, probably destructive. Critical incidents occur at fairly lengthy intervals, probably during critical phases, and they have momentous consequences for the self.

Critical incidents then have a far-reaching effect upon teachers careers, but there are a number of critical phases in any biography. Teachers, if they survive this kind of test, find others later on in their careers. They have to negotiate their way through promotion hurdles once they are established in their role, and this calls for increasingly sophisticated strategies in the current economic situation. They always have to cope with senior colleagues, and have to set their own ambitions and career interests alongside those of their family. They may experience a 'mid-life crisis'. Finally, as the teacher comes up to retiring age, another critical period ensues. More adjustments are made as the teachers look forward to retirement, and back over what they have and have not achieved.

Chapter 3

Coping with Constraints

Critical incidents are occasioned by the conjuncture of particular sets of constraints. We now change the focus of the analysis to concentrate on these constraints, and how they are 'managed' or 'coped' with by a teacher in the course of a career. A certain amount has already been written about coping strategies, and their theoretical attraction in requiring consideration of both structurally generated constraints and teacher creativity in handling them (Woods, 1979, 1981a and 1984; Hargreaves, 1977, 1978 and 1979; Pollard, 1982). Curiously, however, we know very little as yet of the teacher's own perspective on this matter. The life history approach enabled us to gain some insight into this, encompassing the whole span of a career, and affording both the teachers' views of constraints and how they felt they dealt with them. Our conversations with the teachers in our sample indicated they experienced constraints at three levels — societal, institutional, and personal. The major ones for our teachers were as follows:

1 *Societal*
These include (a) large-scale socio-economic conditions, general, political and cultural climate, nature of the educational system; and (b) more specific aspects of educational policy. Teachers in our sample were particularly concerned with:
  (a)   The economic depression of the 1930s.
        The 1939–45 war.
  (b)   Comprehensivization.
        The cuts.
        External examinations.

2 *Institutional*
  (a)   The teacher role.
  (b)   The management context (what Pollard, (1982), refers to as 'institutional bias').
  (c)   Pupils.
  (d)   The subject.

(e)   Managing the hierarchy.

(f)   Work context, equipment and resources.

3   *Personal*

(a)   Personal biography and early life influences.

(b)   Family.

(c) · Private interests.

The influence of teacher role, management context, pupils and subject on teachers' careers and identities is considered in the following four chapters. We discuss the other constraints here, in turn. At the same time, we look at how the problem of coping with them was defined by our teachers, the criteria teachers used to judge degrees of coping, and the goals that they brought to the interaction (Pollard, 1982). We found it useful to distinguish between 'private' and 'public' strategies for reasons that will become clear by the end of the chapter.

Private strategies are employed by individual teachers to gain their own ends or cope with whatever is in front of them. Public strategies involve groups of teachers in collective and public actions to gain certain advantages for the group or even the profession as a whole. The majority of the strategies discussed in this chapter are private ones.

Wider Influences

Economic Circumstances

In the current economic situation, there is a lot of discussion of the difficulties teachers face in getting jobs, and in getting promotion; and also in working with limited resources and cut-back budgets. The situation was different in the 1960s and 1970s, but it does have close parallels with the situation in the 1930s, when many of the retired teachers began their careers. It was the time of the depression in England, and world-wide economic and political events had a hand to play also. For them teaching represented a resource and a safe refuge, a way of coping with the rapid economic and political changes.

> *R:*   What got you into teaching really then?
>
> *Mr King:*   It was an escape route. I was born in China and came to this country at 13, in 1929, after having been around the world two and a half times. Later, my father went bankrupt — it was the situation in China, and I realized then that I had to think in terms of a real job. I think the insecurity was a shock. (65, retired, art)
>
> *Arthur:*   Originally I wanted to be an architect, my father was a miner in the 1930s, and the mining set up was very poorly paid. Going to grammar school was a bit of a struggle. Father went to see the Head, 'He wants to be an architect'. The old Head said 'Well you

know it's a four-year university course'. My father said, 'That's out, I can't do it'. So I went to college on a two-year teacher training course. (69, retired, art)

Miss Nott (66, retired, art), told a similar story, of limited opportunities in her family background at that period, but gender had made a difference too. She had left school in 1931.

> *R:* I'd like to begin at the beginning and ask you what made you want to teach.
> *Miss Nott:* Well that's odd, because I didn't. I would have liked to have done something in the mechanical line, I was very interested, but of course at that time girls didn't do anything. I got thoroughly interested in science, but my mother was a widow, she was having quite a struggle, so I just shut up about science and research, when I found out that exams are frightfully expensive. Suddenly I discovered that my mother had been to see the Head, and they had decided I would teach. But that was the last thing in the world that I wanted to do.

It is worth emphasizing the tremendous difficulties, which teachers beginning their careers in the 1930s had in getting their first job.

> When I came to get a job it was very depressed, and I did supply work all over the place for about twelve months. I went everywhere ... Blackpool, Croydon, Winchester, Sedburgh, anywhere where there's a job going. I used to fill about twenty applications in a week. (Arthur, 69, retired, art)

Newly-qualified teachers had to be prepared to move around the country, and to take jobs at whatever level they were offered them.

> I left college about 1935, really it was very difficult. I started applying for jobs, and everybody wanted experience, it was absolutely hopeless. I got offered a job in a senior school, it was not a grammar school, it was not a secondary school, it was a senior school, and I said to the Principal of the college, 'But everybody says you can't get out of them, once you get in.' We were grammar school trained. He said, 'nonsense, what you need is experience, you can't get jobs, because you haven't got experience. Get experience and you can do what you like.' (Miss Nott, 66, retired, art)

Mr Quilley (67, retired, art) wanted a job in a private or direct grant school, where his own education had taken place. He ended up in an elementary school in a small mining village. He found it tremendously difficult to move.

> *R:* You took the first job you were offered then?
> *Mr Quilley:* I don't know if your other North country folk have said

this, but one was so fearful of losing one's job in those days, that you made the best of what you'd got, or if you moved, you made sure there was a good prospect that you were going to stay in that job, there was no use taking a chance on it, that was the end of the thirties.

Miss Nott (66, retired, art) described her feelings, which resulted from her situation.

R: So, you got pushed into teaching rather against your will?

Miss Nott: Oh very reluctantly, yes, at the time it was just a case of necessity, to earn a living, but er, I didn't, all the time, there was a bit of me, wanting to escape, and I'd never done anything else, and it was more than anything, because I wanted a practical job. All the way through teaching I found it frustrating. I had a terrible feeling of wanting to jump out of the window sometimes, just because I felt . . . it's not a feeling, you can describe, unless anybody else feels that same. There were times, when after kids are gone, I just get a piece of chalk and draw on the blackboard, big drawings all over it, until I've felt better.

The 1939–45 War

The Second World War was probably the major historical event which impinged upon the lives and careers of the older teachers in our research group. All the teachers interviewed said it had meant an interruption to their careers, and most saw it as reducing their mobility and flexibility. This was true for both men and women teachers.

You see I had only been teaching for three years when the war came, and I don't know what I would have done, if war hadn't come. I think I might well have gone off somewhere else, but you did not feel you wanted to start uprooting yourself. (Miss Coal, 68, retired, science)

Other male teachers had opted for teaching when they left army service, because of the uncertainty the war had created.

It (teaching) was an escape route. When I came out of the army I had married. Teaching seemed the only thing after the war, there was no doubt about it — faced with the uncertainties of coming out of the army, I took teaching. (Mr King, 65, retired, art)

Many male teachers felt that the years in the army had put their careers back.

On teaching practice, many of us wondered if we had made the right choice in taking up teaching, but decided to soldier on, as one couldn't go back to square one. Because of the war, speaking personally, I started teaching when I was 31, (Mr Ladyhill, 67, retired, science)

Mr Shoe agreed, he felt he could not contemplate starting on any new training when he left the RAF. He was already in his late twenties, and had a family to support. Nevertheless, for some individuals the war offered opportunities in teaching careers. We had no emergency trained teachers it happened in our sample. The war offered an entrance into teaching for such people.

There was another point. The years in war service had put careers back, but it had also provided useful expertise in handling people. Teachers had been in positions of responsibility and in situations of real danger during the war. It meant that the discipline problems presented by children was very little threat.

I was a strong chap. I'd spent the war teaching blokes to blow up submarines, and get themselves out safely. The boys in the school knew that, I didn't have much trouble with discipline, no. (Mr King, 65, retired, art)

Educational Policy Changes: Comprehensivization

There have been a number of major changes in educational policy in Britain, during the careers of the teachers in this study. Perhaps the most significant is comprehensivization. It affected different teachers, for example, those in grammar schools, and those in secondary moderns, and men and women teachers, in very different ways.

Other research has indicated that grammar school teachers experienced greater role change and stress than secondary modern ones (Dodd, 1974), although the latter also faced problems of status in the new institutions (Riseborough, 1981). For the grammar school teachers in our sample, it was perhaps the prospect of losing their most 'academic' pupils and the academic work that dismayed them most. Without doubt there were social class sensibilities at work here too. Many of the teachers interviewed conflated their 'brightest' children, with the 'nicest' children. This was not true, needless to say, of all grammar school teachers. Mrs Castle (64, retired, art) herself had been in favour of comprehensivization, but she was aware that her views were not commonly shared in the staffroom at Valley School for Girls.

When we went into the comprehensive situation, there were a fair number of mostly older teachers on the staff who regretted the change very much, one or two did retire, one or two said 'No way' and disappeared from the scene. But I had always approved of comprehensive education, I thought it was to the good, so one has to accept that it is more difficult to teach in a comprehensive situation. I think you have got to be a better teacher. Working in a grammar school is a piece of cake really. You have got all those nice, clever kids, who on the whole come from nice homes.

Despite her favourable orientation, Mrs Castle encountered problems when it came to teaching in a co-educational comprehensive. She had almost thirty years teaching experience, and reckoned herself a successful teacher. Nevertheless, there were one or two classes she was unable to cope with. This represented a serious blow to Mrs Castle's self-esteem and self-image. It was one of the factors which made her opt for a particular strategy — early retirement.

Some teachers in grammar schools in the Southern England area found the path laid easily for them. When the schools became comprehensive they lost their sixth-forms. Some of the grammar schools became sixth-form colleges. This was true for Valley Boys' School, and for Mr Quilley's grammar school. Valley Girls, where Mrs Castle taught, became one of the town's comprehensives. For others, who had a particularly academic orientation, other strategies had to be found. Mr Shark (45, scale 4, Head of Department, art), found his own way of coping.

> *Mr Shark:* My own degree was in a very specialist and narrow field.
> Zoomorphics in Celtic illumination. I did an unusual course in
> calligraphy and the history of writing, that gave me an interest in
> academic things, which I hope I have followed throughout my life.
> *R:* In what ways?
> *Mr Shark:* Well, I have always been fascinated by history. I have
> written a couple of books myself on the history of painting.

With this background and interests, Mr Shark had found a post in a small highly academic rural grammar school, which had some boarding pupils too. It had been to his taste, and had allowed him to pursue his interests:

> I only met highly intelligent children. We had an elitist elite, and the
> grammar school only took fifty-two people a year. We had superb
> results in the old grammar school, in terms of the number of state
> scholarships we got a year. We felt it was a bad year if we didn't get
> five or six. We managed to brainwash them into highly academic
> creatures. We always felt that the grammar school achieved really
> quite outstanding things.

In addition, the school was well ordered and rigorously disciplined.

> When I came into the profession, there was a set code of behaviour.
> Teachers wore gowns, all classes were expected to stand quietly out-
> side the room. The prefects really did make certain that the areas of
> the school where they were on duty were quiet. There was a House-
> master you should send boys to who were a nuisance, and a Head-
> master. The Head was a ferocious old man, he would cane people for
> no reason at all.

This had all changed when the school became comprehensive. Mr Shark commented 'I realized I knew nothing about children at all'. He adopted a number of strategies to create a space in the school, which was congenial to him. When the school went comprehensive he was offered the job of Head of the Second Year. He rapidly left it, and became Head of the Art Department. He commented 'I was finding my main interest was always with the senior pupils'. Later he gained the position of Sixth-Form Tutor, which meant he had restricted contact with the comprehensive intake lower down the school. Once he had established this position he created specialist sixth-form courses that he could teach:

> I do art history to what we call the subsidiary level, and I try to encourage as many scientists and mathematicians to study it in their first year sixth. I usually have about a hundred candidates.

In addition, he developed the interest and work in examinations, that has already been discussed. He referred to it as 'the work I do at the University'. He also created the time to write academic books on art history. Thus Mr Shark made a personal escape route from the comprehensive for himself.

For teachers in the secondary modern schools, the position and problems were different, and usually were ones of status (see Riseborough, 1981). Miss Nott (66, retired, art) described the problem:

> They discussed comprehensivization, and the Director gave a talk to us in the staff room about it, and I do remember him saying, of course there is going to be one difficulty. There are heads of department in both schools, and there won't be the need for two heads of department in the future, but I'm sure we shall find something for you to do around the place. Which I thought was not a very tactful thing to say to people with University degrees, that they were going to be found something to do around the place.

The majority of secondary school teachers had fewer paper qualifications than their grammar school colleagues. Comprehensivization, therefore, threatened demotion. One alternative, however, was the pastoral channel. Mr Shoe had been Head of the Science Department in his secondary modern. He was made a year tutor in the new comprehensive, and this preserved his status (Sikes, 1984a). In recent years, however, as promotion prospects decrease and pastoral posts have the coveted scale 4 status, competition for them has increased dramatically. Promotion has become more of a problem for the older teachers as qualifications have escalated (Dore, 1976). Mr Shaw (45, scale 3, Head of Department, rural science) explained:

> I did a two-year course at training college. I was the last of the two-year trained people, and I decided to do an extra year. I was advised by the Principal and everyone to do that extra year. And the indication was that if we did that we would be sufficiently well qualified to get Headships in secondary moderns.

Events had entirely overtaken Mr Shaw, He had found it advisable to take an

Open University degree, a further diploma and an MEd but was unable, despite this inflation in his qualifications, to gain promotion from his scale 3 Head of Department's position (see Goodson, 1983a for the special case of rural science teachers).

Miss Nott (66, retired, art) identified another gender problem arising from the comprehensives. She was certain it made it harder for women to get promotion:

> I think one thing is true, that since they started so many mixed and comprehensive schools, there have been fewer and fewer chances for women to be head teachers and in my experience the women were always the better head teachers, because they not only paid attention to discipline, and paid attention to the staff but they set a high standard for the children.

In her view, it also made it more difficult for women to become heads of department in her own subject area, art. She cited her own experience:

> There were three of us doing art and I was in charge of the subject, but not head of department, they'd done an economy trick and called the department a craft department, it was a crafty way of making sure a man had the job. He had all the sections, art, metalwork, woodwork and technical drawing — not that he ever knew anything we were ever doing.

Another change, which went along with comprehensivization, was the development of much larger schools. Without exception, teachers opposed larger schools.

> We have created this great monster we have now. It's a huge school, and most of our problems are associated with administration and transport (Mr Shoe, 63, retired, science)

Mr Shark taught in the same school.

> Teaching is a job I find I get less enjoyment out of today than I did in the past, because while children are pleasant, and I enjoy their company, the opportunity to get to know them any more doesn't exist, as it did in the smaller unit. In a school our size, well I know my own teaching groups, but I see every day hundreds of people I have never seen before in my life; this is the problem you meet in a big school. (Mr Shark, 45, scale 4, Head of Department, art)

We have identified the teachers' relationships with children as one of the rewards of their job, in their own view. Educational changes which threaten this are viewed with some hostility. The opportunities offered by large schools were dismissed by the teachers. They did not regard the compensations as valid educationally.

This idea that you need enormous great schools, so that you can offer them Russian and goodness knows what else is ridiculous. It's important that you get the child right, then they will learn what they need. (Mr Shaw, 45, scale 3, Head of Department)

In recent years there has been an increasing fragmentation of the pupils' career (for a fuller discussion see Measor and Woods, 1984a). Teachers had strong views on this. They objected to losing their 11–12 year old pupils. In addition they missed the sixth-form work, when that was separately institutionalized into sixth-form colleges. For many teachers, it diminished their work satisfaction. They could survive a double period with 3Z if they knew there was the sixth-form next. It was one of their coping strategies. There could be other problems too, for example, when the philosophy of a teacher or a department was in contradiction to that of the sixth-form college. Mr Redford (33, scale 4, Head of Department, art) experienced this when he attempted to introduce new work which he thought pupils would find more relevant. The sixth-form college art teacher had very different views:

He is a very traditional art teacher, and he gets good results. But I've sent pupils down there who had tremendous talent and ability and good 'O' level results. But he wanted them to change. He sees art in a particular way, rather than encourage them from where they were. I always thought the important thing was to get kids motivated, and let them develop, I hadn't realized that you had to impose this high culture thing on them. He insists, he has made it very difficult for some of my former pupils, to the extent that they had to go along with him, and do their own work, in their own time.

Such comments mediate the view that has sometimes been taken of the teacher as having virtual autonomy in their own classroom.

The Cuts

Educational research, and the educational press, have been claiming for some time that a crisis of morale and motivation exists within the teaching profession today. It has arisen because of the economic cutbacks in education which have stilted promotion opportunities for teachers, and left them with diminished material resources (Spooner, 1979; Dennison, 1979; Kyriacou and Sutcliffe, 1979). We had many examples of teachers unable to gain promotion and move. Mr Shaw, for example, felt stuck at scale 3. Mr Indus had been teaching for seven years, but was unable to move from a scale 2 post, even to another school. Miss Lavalle was on scale 2 after the same number of years. She had been on scale 1 until she retrained. Miss Judd and Mrs Richards were on scale 1 and 2 respectively and found it impossible to move. Some of their cases will be discussed in more detail, but it is interesting to contrast their experience with that of the older teachers. In Mrs Castle's (64, retired, art) career, promotion to Head of Department had been a simple matter, and almost automatic.

> *Mrs Castle:* I left art college at 21. Went to a South Wales grammar school. Spent three years there, got a Head of Department at Valley Girls — age 24.
>
> *R:* You were quite young to get a Head of Department's job, weren't you!
>
> *Mrs Castle:* Not then, anyway they were very short of art teachers in those days. I sent my application in at the last minute, I got a telegram asking me to go for interview.

Mr Shark (45, scale 4, Head of Department, art) gave an account of a career which began in the mid-1950s and had a steady rate of progress. As the school changed and grew, so did his opportunities, this was probably a very common experience and career pattern for this time.

In January 1956 I took my present job, and I have been there ever since. (Mr Shark, 45, scale 4, Head of Department, art)

> *R:* That's a long time in one school, does that mean you are happy there?
>
> *Mr Shark:* It means that education is changing so much. I think everytime I have gone to change my job, something has turned up within the school itself. I have had four different jobs in the school. At first I was the only art teacher in a staff of fourteen. In 1960, I was about to look elsewhere, and the Head offered me the housemastership. So I stayed on as Housemaster, I enjoyed that, it was a very rewarding job. The school was divided into four houses, I literally ran a quarter of the school. It was like being mini-Headmaster, we literally ran our section as we saw fit. The Head was a very liberal man, he leant heavily on his housemasters. Then of course in the mid-60s they started talking comprehensivization, and I reasoned that to be a new boy in a new establishment was not the best opportunity, so I waited to see what happened. I was offered a Head of Year job, and the allowance was a considerable one, so I stayed. But at the end of the year I told the Headmaster that I wasn't very happy and he offered me the Head of the Art Department on the same scale. I took over as Head of the Art Department, which rose to five of us, from three of us, then to six of us, and seven of us. It grows remorselessly as the numbers in the school grow. When comprehenzivation had obviously settled down, I decided to go into private education, but I discovered I didn't really like the set-up. Now the night before I went the Head said 'Why are you going?' and I said 'Really it is basically money', and he said 'Whatever they offer you I will offer you to stay'.

It is the younger teachers in our sample, who had the biggest problems getting promotion, and whose frustration levels were highest.

> I've been teaching for about ten years now, I was very lucky at first, mind you, in those days you got a scale 2 for surviving the probationary year. Anyway it all worked out that after five terms of teaching I was made a Head of Department on a scale 4. I was encouraged to be ambitious. I got on CSE panels, in the 1970s there were lots of opportunities around. I could have gone for an Assistant Adviser. At that point I moved down here, my family wanted to live in the South. Having said that, I still find myself hankering after some kind of promotional ambition. I got involved down here with so many things, an MEd, the Arts' Teachers Association, CSE panel work too. The ambitiousness is something I've had to learn to live with in an area of reduced opportunity. I've also had to come to terms with what I can cope with, I was definitely doing too much for a while. But I still can't not be ambitious, no matter what I say. (Mr Redford, 33, scale 4, Head of Department, art)

Mr Redford is one example of a teacher stuck at scale 4, but many teachers would count themselves very lucky to get so far. Mr Shaw taught rural science. Goodson (1983) has documented the constraints that having an unfashionable subject specialism like this one place upon career opportunities. Mr Shaw told a similar story. Judy Lavalle, a young teacher of art, had been stuck on a scale 1 for a long time, and had finally retrained in craft, design and technology in order to have any chance of getting promotion. Each of these teachers are individual cases, but their stories can be reproduced countless times. They illustrate the fact that there are blockages at every level of the system.

Again, such stories could have been repeated endlessly. We have seen from the data from the retired teachers that austerity is not new to teaching. Those teachers who began their careers in the 1930s had coped with very limited resources. However, things were different in the 1960s and 1970s, as we have noted, and teachers beginning then have found it difficult to adjust to the cutbacks of the 1980s.

How do teachers handle these constraints? We have already discussed Mr Indus. He had tried unsuccessfully, but repeatedly to change jobs. He had tried gaining an extra qualification, and had done an MEd. This is an increasingly important safety valve for teachers. It does provide real hope that the new qualification will open new doors. In addition, teachers value the intrinsic qualities and benefits of the course itself, which gives opportunities for discussion of educational problems — opportunities which are not usually present in the daily school routine. Teachers also employ a number of private, emotional responses. Mr Indus, for example, had in part tuned out, but it was only partially successful. He still felt frustrated.

Mr Redford (33, scale 4, Head of Department, art) had also done an MA, and then had turned his attention back to teaching, but it was only partially successful, as he recognized:

> I'm very definitely getting myself sorted out in the classroom, and I've got lots of new ideas, but having said all that —having said all that, I don't quite know how long you can go on remotivating yourself like that, and I suspect that much as though I don't want to it, it's going to raise its ugly head, I mean, am I going to be here for thirty years, because that's what it looks like at the moment.

Mr Shaw (45, scale 3, Head of Department, rural sciences) too had done an MA in an attempt to improve his promotion prospects, but by the end of his MA year, he had failed to get another job. In a follow-up interview done a year later, he still had failed to gain any promotion. He found the situation very difficult:

> The kids enjoy it, they really do get a lot out of it, that's been my reward. But now I'm doing this MA trying to get some status. I'm saying to myself, do I really want the money that much, promotion means losing touch with rural studies, but I'm 45, I've got twelve years or seventeen, what's rural studies going to be doing in seventeen years time? There's the personal satisfaction, there's the status we all seek in some way or another. Am I going to find it, or am I going to become one of those grouchers of the staffroom corner who complain about everything, and become bitter and twisted? I'm having a crisis of conscience at the moment. I believe in rural studies, and yet I'm trying to get out of it for financial gain.

Strategies employed by the individual teacher caught in these promotion blockages thus are only partially successful, and a high level of frustration remains.

Examinations

Our teachers identified a number of ways in which the external examinations affect them. Examination syllabuses set what teachers teach, and patterns of examination papers influence the amounts of time they spend on particular subject areas. At the same time, however, examinations are seen by teachers as a resource. For example, they can help motivate pupils, although some teachers felt that particular point of declining importance in the current economic situation.

Miss Nott (66, retired, art), took a typical middle of the road position. She acknowledged that examinations affected her work in the classroom, although it was always tempered by other ideas of what was important:

> I would never let art work be governed by a GCE, but I have it in the

back of my mind, that they built up skills towards that end, and there was always praise and encouragement.

Mr King (65, retired, art) took a similar line:

> One cannot ignore the fact that if you are a teacher there is an examination at the end of it, and what you do must be tempered with some recognition towards that end. I mean it's no good going all long haired and saying 'Oh, I'm an artist'. It doesn't work. You've got to look at life sensibly. It's no good being long haired about it. You have to teach, you can't say 'Oh — self expression, let yourself go'.

Mrs Castle (64, retired, art) found more difficulty with examinations, for she had more radical ideas of what she wanted to teach anyway:

> At the end of the sausage machine, there was the examination, you couldn't ignore it.

Nevertheless, she accepted the limitations of the examination system, and took steps to change her own practices, because of it:

> One year we had very poor results — at 'O' level, we had a lot of 'O' level failures, and they were things I didn't expect to fail. I went to see the Chief Examiner, he made me feel quite ill. It was clear that their expectations were changing, what the examiners wanted was changing.

Mrs Castle objected strongly to the situation, but she acted to overcome the problem:

> The chief examiner advised me to go and see the work in other schools ... anyway I realized they were going all academic, they didn't want the bright colours and strong design they had in the early days. So I went back, and I thought, right, we'll give them what they want.

Mr Redford (33, scale 4, Head of Department, art) also objected to the examination system. He felt it constrained curriculum reform and limited what he could do in the classroom. Like Mrs Castle, he had radical ideas of what he should be teaching:

> The best way forward, curriculum wise, would probably be outside of the confines of the exam system. But we can't ditch it of course. But, teachers should be saying: 'Yes, you've got a picture, a second cover — a picture from a magazine, that you are impressed with, bring it in here, this is the place where it should be'. But art education has said no, we don't want those in here, come in here and we will teach you about Impressionism, or about art with a capital A. Now the other side to that is, that I can welcome them in, but when it comes the exam system, you run into problems. I think we're on a path that's good, but I'm not getting the exam results.

Like Mrs Castle, he had to accept the confines of the examination system, and adjust his own aspirations to it.

Other teachers had made a different adjustment. They had tried to get inside the examinations' system to refine it and affect it in the light of their own ideas. Mr King (65, retired, art) had done this. He had begun teaching when he returned from overseas, after the war. He was totally out of touch with what the examiners wanted, but

> . . . I hustled into linkup with examinations, boards, because I thought it was an important part of learning how to teach.

But it did not change his basic methods:

> I would say I incorporated what I learned from marking. But I didn't change my way. No. I couldn't change my attitude to teaching art.

Mr Shark (45, scale 4, Head of Department, art) went further and attempted to enter into the policy making areas of the examination system to get his ideas included:

> I have always been associated with examining, I used to work as an 'O' level local examiner for one board, then for the last fifteen years I have been the Assistant Chief Examiner for 'O' level for a second, and for the last five years I have been Chief Examiner for a third.

Mr Shark had made the examination system work for him. He had incorporated exams into his career. They had become a resource to him.

While few teachers went so far as Mr Shark, they acknowledged that examinations were a resource in the classroom. They have been one of the carrots, one of the ways of motivating pupils.

> With the comprehensive situation, the examinations were certainly very helpful, they helped engender a feeling of hard work. I think the examination system has a lot to answer for, but my goodness, it would be difficult to motivate children if there wasn't some kind of structure. (Mrs Castle, 64, retired, art)

Mrs Armitage (35, scale 2, art) was in agreement with this view, but she was also aware that in the current economic situation, it was losing its motivating bite:

> We're living under the fact that examination results have to be published, so you have to keep coming up with the exam results, despite the fact that we know in our own minds, that the fourth and fifth years aren't rising to the challenge of exams, because they don't see its immediate benefits in job terms.

This trend has itself led to a further strategy. One science teacher, Mr Hardy, had been instrumental in introducing new examinations and new courses into the secondary school to attempt to improve pupil motivation. He had got City and Guilds' courses to replace the more traditional GCE and CSE ones. The school had local authority approval to introduce and experiment with a variety of youth training schemes, and has been awarded the only local TVEI allocation. Mr Hardy felt that such vocationally-oriented courses and syllabuses and examination qualifications were valued more highly by pupils and had a good motivating effect.

The Institution

'Gatekeepers' and 'Critical Reality Definers'

At the level of the institution, headteachers and heads of departments play a significant role in the teacher's career. In the early stages, it is heads of department who have the critical position. Later it is headteachers and their deputies. Chapter 5 deals with the organizational issues involved in some more detail. Here, we consider the relationships.

We have already discussed in Chapter 2 the kinds of pressure that heads of department and other senior teachers bring to bear on young teachers beginning their career. They seek to induct them into the routines of school, and the 'taken for granted recipe knowledge of school' (Hanson and Herrington, 1976). We have seen the problems that this causes for some young teachers. Frequently, heads of department set up a style of teaching, as well as a syllabus and a timetable for the new teacher.

> One is most influenced by the sort of head of department of the school you go to first really. In a way they give you the sort of pattern you had to follow. I mean I didn't agree with all of it, but you had to do it to start off with. It was rather rigid. (Miss Judd, 25, scale 1, art)

Mr Ray (38, scale 4, science) had found himself more at odds with his first Head of Department than had Miss Vicar:

> I was introduced to the Head of Biology. I didn't like him at all. It was easy for me to dislike him, because he used the belt, and because he used to spend quite long periods out of the classroom on the telephone, and I resented his bourgeois background, sort of tweed jackets and so on, and great thick brogue shoes and things. It used to irritate me.

In other words, the Head of Department was seen as a 'proper teacher' (see chapter 4). Mr Ray was concerned to establish himself as something rather different. He found a range of ways of coping:

> I was lucky though, because there were three Heads of Science Subjects, and they rotated the Head of Department. That made it

slightly easier for me to be slightly more deviant, because you know, I didn't have to answer to the biology man, because I could give my allegiance to the Head of Science, rather than the Head of Biology.

In addition, Mr Ray had discovered an external resource in the science adviser — someone outside the school who could be relied upon:

> The science adviser was also taking a great interest. He became a sort of patron, he was a man you could relate to. It meant I did not feel unduly constrained by the Head of Biology. I think he resented that.

Miss Nott (66, retired, art) had experienced a particularly difficult situation with her first Head of Department. She had begun teaching in the early 1930s, and in a small village school had found the Head of the Art Department had ideas which seemed Victorian to her. For example, the Head of Department insisted that the pupils paint and draw only on small sheets of paper, which could fit into exercise book size loose covers. In addition, the work she set was to Miss Nott's eyes very out of date:

> I had to do what she had arranged at first. She gave me small sheets of paper — ready cut, and these set exercises. She was friendly, but I didn't quite know how to get away from her tight little stereotyped thing. (66, retired, art)

Miss Nott also recognized that improving the position partly required time. She had to wait until her confidence grew sufficiently:

> The HMI came to see me, and I'd got a very backward class, and they were painting freely on ... well, I'd managed to get hold of a packet of duplicating paper, and they were just painting freely on it, enjoying it, not making any particular guided pattern, and I thought, well at least they're getting away from the tightness, and the HMI liked it.

As a result of this backing, Miss Nott gained the confidence to approach the Headmistress:

> Finally, I went to the headmistress, and said, I'd like to work on larger paper, and do more modern things ... and all the rest of it. And she was a great help, and let me go ahead.

Miss Nott also recognized that improving the position partly required time. She had to wait until her confidence grew sufficiently:

> Gradually I got more what I wanted. I think, um, well, I wasn't sufficiently experienced to know what to do about it. In later years I would have just had it out with her.

Mrs Castle (64, retired, art) had the same Victorian legacy in her first job, but the constraints were solidly material:

> The previous art man had given them all books to work in, little

painting books, well! I soon got rid of those, and got them paper to work on, but they couldn't work on very big pieces of paper, because the desks weren't big enough. (64, retired, art)

With the exception of Miss Judd, these teachers were retired or mid-career teachers. All had gained promotion to Head of Department rapidly and without any real problems. This meant that they did not have to cope for very long with heads of department with whom they were in disagreement. They went on to their second job as a Head of Department, and could try out their own ideas. The situation is, however, very different for young teachers in the current situation, where promotion opportunities are so much fewer. They find themselves stuck with a Head of Department. In addition they frequently cannot even move sideways and take a job in another school to avoid the problem. This was Mr Indus' (25, scale 2, art) situation. He had a number of problems and disagreements with his Head of Department. They disagreed about the way to treat pupils:

> Young people with new ideas are seen as frightening in that department. The head of department comes from the old school, where you tell kids to sit down and do as they're told. Well kids aren't like that any longer.

Mr Indus also disagreed with his Head of Department on the issues of curriculum change and development:

> He doesn't understand all the new ideas, photography and graphic design and things, and that's a real problem, because that is where all the career opportunities are these days, not in painting and drawing.

In addition, Mr Indus found his Head of Department was not a particularly efficient filler of his role:

> My Head of Department used to be in the colonies, he got really out of date, he didn't understand anything about CSE for example, he didn't even know what all the abbreviations meant. I had to carry him for years. For years I had to show him things.

Finally, there was also a hint that the Head of Department came closer to the 'proper teacher' stereotype than Mr Indus wanted to:

> He's booted and suited, he looks the part, he looks stable, he looks good for the governors. Appearances seem to matter, so much in schools.

There was one further source of Mr Indus' resentment. He had been at the school longer than his Head of Department, and had applied for his job. This clearly illustrates one of the perennial managerial problems which face schools, when they have to decide on choosing internal or external candidates for promotion. Mr Indus' own promotion hopes within the school had been crushed with this man's appointment. His next attempt to cope with the situation had been to apply for other jobs in other schools, at first on a higher scale, and then at his present scale (2). He had been entirely unsuccessful in his attempts. It had made him bitter, but he blamed the current economic situation, rather than himself:

> In the sixties, teaching was a good career, things were a lot easier then. You could expect to be a Head of Department in two years. It used to be a good career. That's all gone by the board, there is no innovation now, no movement, people don't even move sideways.

Mr Indus had begun an MA in Art Education in an attempt to improve his promotion prospects, and also to provide an external interest and stimulus. These courses increasingly provide an important safety valve for teachers who cannot escape the promotion trap.

Mr Indus had also evolved some strategies for improving his lot within the school. He used his expertise in photography and graphics to run extra courses:

> I have to run all kinds of courses for the sixth-form to keep any sixth-form work, otherwise my Head of Department would just cream off all the interesting sixth-form work for himself.

He justified running these courses by an appeal to the outside employment situation, where it was those skills which employers wanted more than the fine art ones. Mr Indus had also adopted another strategy:

> So what can you do in this sort of situation?' I just pretend to do what they say, then I do what I want. There are all kinds of ways I can do that, things I can hide behind, to get away with it. Cultural things, for example, they say 'He's an Indian, he doesn't understand'.

This is an interesting example of using ethnic origins, usually seen as a constraint, in a creative way for one's own benefit. Nevertheless, there are limits to what Mr Indus can achieve with this resource.

Later in a teacher's career, headteachers come to exert more influence in these areas, although that is not to suggest headteachers do not influence younger teachers too. Nevertheless, if a teacher gets promoted to Head of Department, then they have to deal more directly with the headteacher. All the teachers interviewed acknowledged the importance of headteachers as 'critical reality definers'.

> I stayed in the same school, but of course at Valley Girls you had three different Heads. Now having a different Head alters the school, doesn't it — really. (Miss Coal, 65, retired, science)

> The last few years at school were happier, because we got a new Headmistress, who was much more relaxed, and smiled and said

'Thank you', and didn't try to frighten me. (Mrs Castle, 64, retired, art)

Mr King (65, retired, art) discussed the disorganization that had arisen when the school experienced a series of rapid changes of Headmaster:

There was an unfortunate phase when we changed Headmasters. There were three Headmasters in three years. One died, one came then went to Australia, and then another one, he should never have been a Headmaster. He had the education, but he just didn't know how to handle people. Not the variety of things that come into a Headmaster's study. If he was in the right mood he would consult the right person, but not always.

Teachers had very clear views on what they wanted and needed head-teachers to be. Foremost amongst their concerns was discipline.

My last Head — he was a *rotten* Head, you need discipline right throughout the school, he just stayed in his room — office wise. That's no good, it meant everybody had to fight their own little battles. We had a few very bad types who needed tackling by everybody, and especially the Head. But he didn't do it. You don't want one of those office boys who just stay there. You need to feel a Head's presence right through the school. (Miss Nott, 66, retired, art)

Mr Shaw (45, scale 3, Head of Department, rural science) had been made uncomfortably aware of how dependent a teacher is on a headteacher for discipline. In his first school, he felt that both the Head and his deputy were tremendously weak. For example, they failed to construct timetables until the second week of the school term, and the Head was frequently absent from the school:

Of course in that situation, you had no discipline, except what you could construct yourself, and young teachers had a rough time getting started.

Some teachers voiced the opinion that heads did not simply have to be strong disciplinarians, they needed to understand ways of motivating pupils too.

You could send a child, with a note to the right sort of Head and that Head would know that there was a chance to praise somebody who needed praise. You would send them with some work they had done, something. When I first went to a school with a Headmaster I tried it, and he didn't know what the child had come for, so I stopped doing that. I always used to send good work to the Head, otherwise they became nothing more than smacking machines — they always get children sent to them, who have done wrong. It gives them a chance for themselves as well as for the children. (Miss Nott, 66, retired, art)

Most teachers accepted the situation of the power of the headteacher, and negotiated within that, for what they could get. Mr Redford (33, scale 4, Head of Department, art), for example, sought always to maximize his own position, and he enjoyed the process of minimizing the constraints:

> The Head is a bloody good strategist, and I've never met anyone it is so difficult to outwit. I would never deny that I'm a manipulator and a political animal ... but I like to think that if I benefit so does art education, and I don't think I'd like to be exposed, that I did it just for myself. But this Head is good.

Contexts of Work, and Resources

Teachers found the cutbacks in resources, equipment and staffing very difficult to deal with, and it led to frustration. Teachers who had begun their careers in the 1960s and 1970s were particularly aware of the ways levels of resourcing had dropped. It is interesting though to compare the experiences of teachers who had begun their work in the 1930s, with those who began in the 1980s. Both generations found difficulty in getting their first job, in a way we have discussed, and found the resources they had to work with limited. Although few teachers today shared Miss Nott's (66, retired, art) experiences, she taught in one of the poorest areas of England, and she began in 1936:

> It was a very poor area, they were closing the terribly old and inadequate schools, so we had 700 girls in the school intended for 600, and very big classes. I had a corrugated iron hut in the playground, and only a cold water tap over a little wash bowl out in the corridor. And the corrugated iron hut was divided in half, and the other half was used by the infants. I used to try and finish talking before they arrived, because the hut was built on brick piles with a hollow floor, and the infants came storming in, and their teacher sat down at the piano, and that was the end of that, you certainly couldn't do any talking. We had a coke stove in the corner to warm us, and in the winter we used to take turns to sit round the stove and thaw out. Nevertheless, it made quite a chummy atmosphere somehow. But the kids were very very poor. There was 60 per cent unemployment in that fishing village then.

The school had few resources, and the pupils did not come from families which could make up the differences.

> The children were so poor, in the village, my first job that I couldn't do any craft work, that they would be expected to buy. There was a Senior Art Mistress, and she had lived all her life in that place, and she had quite a lot of art work going on for people, who gave her commissions. She used some of it for class work, they all made door

curtains for people. Every child did a square, that went all the way around the edges. Well I don't think that was very creative. I wasn't very happy with that sort of thing.

Miss Nott described how she went about tackling this problem. She had gone to local firms and factories and begged and borrowed waste materials from them. They were different strategies from those used by her Head of Department:

> I did all sorts of things, used waste materials, cartons and cardboard, and bits of string, anything, just to make fun things with children, it is all exciting for them. I scavenged shops and factories, I improvised all the time.

Her resourceful keenness paid off. She stimulated children to take on individual projects — which carried a high emotional reward for her!

> Gradually I got more what I wanted. The children wanted to do things you see. I had a group all from one orphanage. They were beautifully cared for, they were thoroughly happy and well organized. A few children came to me one day and said 'It's matron's birthday, we'd like to give her a present. She's just got a new tea service, and we like to make her a cloth, and would you help us'. And I said I certainly would, and they said, we can only give you about a penny a week. They all did their little bit of it, when we got to art class. That was lovely. It's something you remember all your life as being something really worth while.

Mr Redford (33, scale 4, Head of Department, art) had begun teaching in 1974, and at first resources had been fairly free. Then cutbacks started. Mr Redford decided to fight, as best he could:

> I very consciously thought that I could either give in to the cutbacks, which meant accepting a very restricted vision of the job, or I could make it what I wanted to, and it seemed to me that the field was open to some manipulation — if you wanted to make the effort to do it.

All of the strategies discussed so far have been private ones. Mr Redford himself did an MA in Art, and he was very aware of the credibility this gave him with the Headmaster, for it made him the best qualified member of staff in the school. He also, however, employed a public, collective strategy:

> I got the local art teachers' association going strong. It was with one eye on the need to get art teachers involved as a unity to survive the onslaught I saw was coming on art education.

This teacher was resolute in his determination to fight to the best of his ability. In a situation, which is objectively increasingly constrained and restricted, Mr Redford sought opportunities and saw ways through:

Because we're all accountable at the moment, it seems to me, there's a slight area for manipulation here. Headmaster and the hierarchy, if you like, are also out for things that can be held up as being different from other schools. You would think that there's a reactionary turn, and there is — no doubt of that — but it also makes a gap, because we're all out to come up with something special, which makes us stand out from the school down the road. You need to be forceful enough to mine the space.

He was not the only teacher who saw things in this way. Miss Judd (25, scale 4, Head of Department, art) was aware of the constraints, but equally, she was impatient of the ways they were used as an excuse:

Every excuse is 'because of the cuts'. If you want to do something, they say 'no, no, you can't do it, because of the cuts'. There should be more money in education anyway — of course, but, things *can* be done, even with less money. You just have to try.

The problem of cuts in staffing was seen as very serious by all teachers we talked to. Most teachers felt it placed headteachers in an intolerable situation.

Heads are in an invidious position. They carry the can from below and above, and they're being pushed from both sides and staying on the tightrope is not easy, certainly at the moment. (Mrs Boyd, 26, scale 2, science)

Mr Redford (33, scale 4, Head of Department, art) agreed:

The Head in a school is told he has to lose six staff, and the Head has to decide how to do it. The subject survives, or doesn't survive, according to the relationship they have to the Headmaster. But it puts heads in an unenviable position. They are dealing with people's lives and careers.

He also felt that it placed him in a position of responsibility too. He felt the cuts made it imperative for him to have a good relationship with the Head, in order to protect the members of staff in his department.

Personal factors

The third category of influences are those that arise from the private life, family and personal biography of the individual teacher. Clearly there is enormous variation, and it is difficult to draw generalizations. Nevertheless, some structured similarities occur. One interesting factor to emerge is that a great many teachers had a kind of academic hiccough in their academic biography. At one point in their school or university life, they did substantially less well than they had hoped or expected. This led them to opt for teaching, as opposed to something they viewed as more difficult to be successful in. Mr Tucks, for example, gained a third class degree at university. He felt it limited his options. Mr Ray's (38, scale 4, Head of Department, science) case is given in detail:

> *Mr Ray:* Looking back now, I wish I'd worked harder. I never really embraced the whole thing, the zoology curriculum, I was always off reading fat art books somewhere, so as a result I ended up with a 2.2 which was a critical factor in deciding to become a teacher. If I'd got a 2.1 I wouldn't have become a teacher, it's as simple as that.
>
> *R:* Why didn't you do better?
>
> *Mr Ray:* I didn't really get on with the faculty there, they weren't what I considered intellectual, they would listen to the *Sound of Music* and things. I just wasn't aware enough, and I didn't have good study skills. I had an absence of an 'au faitness' with the university world, and knowing what degrees mean.

He had a personal sense of academic failure, which remained with him, and which was only really redeemed later by successfully completing an MA course in Education:

> I do have a sort of Kafkaesque notion about this ... which I have perhaps mentioned before ... the idea that ... well ... perhaps I don't really measure up to what is required. And that's something which goes back all the way through my education, and it's only on this course ... it's quite strange, that I feel I've ever really done my best, and that I can cope.

Many of the retired women grammar school teachers had no such hiccoughs in their record. Miss Coal and Miss Sale, both had outstanding academic records in the early 1930s. Both won scholarships to university. Miss Sale gained the only scholarship offered by the whole county she lived in. This could be contrasted with Mr Ladyhill who failed to gain a scholarship. For both women there were few other options of career opportunities for women, and they chose teaching.

Family pressures also have an effect on teachers. Two case studies are chosen as representative, one from a retired woman teacher, another from a mid-career male teacher. Miss Nott (66, retired, art) had already described how the straightened financial circumstances of her family made it impossible for her to complete the technical training she wanted. She was pushed into teaching. She accepted the responsibility of looking after her mother who was ill. Although she was well established in the North in a job she liked, she had to give it up, and she returned South. Why did she have to do this?

> Oh dear, my mother was so miserable in the North basically. After three years there, I had made friends with the staff, and was really getting along quite happily. I was getting on well with the Head, she

was a good strong Head. But my mother was getting into this very low state. She hated that town, so in the end reluctantly I decided I'd have to think about it. My brother had bought a piece of land down here, and rather suddenly we came down here, and I was two years trying to find a job down here. And the school I finally got was a slum area one.

Several of the retired women teachers told similar stories, indicating the sorts of family pressures that bore heavily on women earlier this century. There was not a social climate in which there was much support to resist such pressures. Miss Nott had clearly carried resentment for her mother's actions throughout her life. Her mother had intervened in her personal life too.

Miss Nott: I was engaged, making things for my bottom drawer, but the war upset that.

R: Did the war upset a lot of things? Was he killed in the war?

Miss Nott: No, my mother, I realized, wanted to cling on to me, and his mother I realized wanted to cling on to him, and the battle got into the state where I couldn't stand the strain any longer. The best thing of course would have been if we had buzzed off and got married. Instead of that, I was very nice, and said perhaps we can be friends until we can see our way to getting married, and then the war came. I am sorry about it. I think if we had torn free and gone up to London, but ... But I thought, if you push someone into it, and that mother commits suicide, how do you start life?

This illustrates the way family pressures can affect men too.

For the mid-career teacher, family pressures can change pursuit of promotion and advancement. It had forced Mr Redford (33, scale 4, Head of Department, art), for example, to reassess his priorities and change his approach:

I realized I had totally missed the early part of my daughter growing up as a result of commuting. The job down here wasn't anything like as good a job, but I wanted the commuting to stop. Also all the friends I was making were in the other town, it stopped us having a social life.

Mr Redford had taken a job on a lower scale nearer home, in order to give his family some priority. However, he felt he had to undertake a number of extra activities in order to gain promotion, and this had again caused problems for himself and his family:

I was doing the MEd and I was Chairman of the local art education group, and I was playing a lot of football, and taking the school team, here there and everywhere. I was out a lot, and my wife was starting to resent being left at home with the kids, and was rethinking her career, and personally I think I'd have been all right if it had been OK at home, but I'd get home and there were a lot of traumas there, and my wife got to the point of saying I wish you'd never done that MEd. And then I went ... I just suddenly — well I wouldn't say I broke down, but I had to start having some time off school, because I was getting the shakes ... and this ... From that point I've had to decide what's most important to me, like I've given up all the football, resigned lots of committees, I've finished the MEd. I'm taking my time, I'm choosing not to get uptight about things, I'll walk away from it. I've really learned to cope with it.

Such data reveals one of the social trends today, where women are more concerned with their own rights and career opportunities. This must have an impact upon the careers of men.

There are numerous other examples of family affecting career. Male teachers found their commitment to their job increased when they had families to support. Women teachers found it more difficult to return to teaching after they had families in recent years. Mr Ladyhill described refusing promotion, because it meant moving to another town and disrupting his children's established education. Mr Quilley had missed out on getting an art college job in the North of England, because his children were ill and needed to move South.

Trends in Coping Strategies

We have discussed in Chapter 1 the sense teachers have of the declining status of their profession. Teachers are resentful of these changes, and of the worsening position in respect of salary, promotion and resources. We detected a possible change in teachers' approach to handling these problems. They appear to employ two types of strategy, public and private. By public strategies we mean those that involve a group of teachers acting together to gain their aims. This would include union activity, involving various types of pressure, including working to rule, strikes and guerilla tactics. It also includes teachers within a school, acting together for example to defeat some timetable reorganization, as was described by one of our teachers. Private strategies are those engaged in by individual teachers to gain their own individual objectives, for example, as discussed earlier, Mr Shark's finding an escape route from the comprehensive situation through concentrating on sixth-form work.

It seems that teachers may be increasingly willing to engage in public strategies to gain their aims with respect to status and salary, though many of the older teachers stated their hostility to union and strike action. Their objections stemmed from their long-held notions of what teaching was all about. Strike action carried identity implications for them. It implied a loss of standards and status, and it just was not right.

Mr King (65, retired, art) had very strong feelings on the subject:

Mr King: The REAM, which was the graduate section of the Union, asked on one or two occasions, I think, if we were prepared to strike, and on both occasions I said no . . . Just like a nurse, I felt we were there for the kids. And there were so many broken homes in (. . .), that I felt if the kids had nowhere to go, there would be more crime, more this, more that. That sounds very morally smug, but it's true . . . I couldn't judge it from any other profession, and I couldn't judge it from any other school. I probably would have gone on strike more readily in London, where the teachers were oppressed so terribly. Grammar school life wasn't all that bad. We were on a very cushy number in the grammar school . . . I supplemented my income, driving lorries, collecting tomatoes, I did all kinds of catering work at a weekend. I could make more money than I could for a whole week on a regular salary as a schoolmaster.

R: And you didn't have feelings about this?

Mr King: No . . . I don't know, I didn't ever feel bitter about the salary side.

R: You said you felt it was wrong to strike as a teacher. That wasn't what you thought being a teacher was all about. Well, that suggests that teaching wasn't just a job.

Mr King: Oh no, I loved it. I used to go to Union meetings. Teachers look a rabble, and the way that they behave at meetings is I think unforgivable. In their appearance, the way they shout and swear at meetings.

Miss Nott (66, retired, art) was in full agreement with Mr King. Union activity and strikes deeply offended her sense of propriety for teachers:

I was disgusted. It was an unprofessional thing to do, and I said so. I was not going to strike. And of course at the local NUT meeting I was the only one who put up my hand to vote against a strike . . . I nearly fainted because it was such an effort, but I thought I have to or I shall never forgive myself. I felt so sick, and my legs were shaking afterwards.

Why did she feel so strongly that striking was wrong?

Well, because I felt that intelligent people should be able to settle their differences without taking any violent action, or any other kind of action. And I thought we had a duty to set a standard for children whose fathers were always going on strike for nothing. And I thought if we behaved no better than they did, we weren't setting any sort of example. We couldn't preach to them about anything.

It was not only age that was significant here. Mr Shaw (45, scale 3, Head of Department, rural science) was a mid-career teacher, but he had always taught in rural schools. He also had strong religious views. He was in agreement with the older teachers.

> I was a member of the NAS and I left it when a strike was called by the leadership of the NAS without consulting the membership in an inter-union battle, and I refused to strike against the kids, when my dispute is not even with the employer. Since then I've not been in a union. I don't think a trade union can do something on remuneration. I don't think a trade union can do anything to raise the status of teaching within a community, it goes the opposite way. My thinking now is that if you want to raise the status of your profession, and your position with the children, then you don't go on strike, therefore I would go for a professional status, rather than a trade union one. Now the only union at the moment bound not to strike is the PAT. I think they're a bit weak on educational problems.

All of these teachers were prepared to resist Headteachers and examination boards and pupils with a wide and effective range of private strategies. They all employed strategies to cope with their situation, and to improve their own situations. However they were unwilling to use public and collective strategies. It conflicted with their sense of what a proper teacher should do.

Younger teachers may not share their views. Pollard (1982, p. 24) has commented

> The particular level and type of professionalism has varied historically in response to such factors as the social esteem in which 'education' has been held, and levels of demand for staff. There is therefore a link between teacher perceptions of professionalism, and their macro-structural conditions.

Miss Nott (66, retired, art) recognized this:

> But it is very difficult to say what I would do now, if I had been teaching for the last ten years, because the conditions have got steadily worse and worse, and by now I might have been driven to taking some action.

Such a change in teacher's attitudes would match the pattern in other 'white collar' occupations. There have been over a million new white collar members of trade unions since the 1960s. White collar workers as a whole have been willing to move into public and collective strategies to improve their own positions, in a way they were not in the first half of this century. Bain (1979) points out that as white collar workers find themselves in larger work groups their tendency to join trade unions increases. He also analyzes their perceptions of their own power positions in the pre-war years, suggesting that white collar workers saw themselves on the same side as management, therefore they used private strategies with managerial figures, whom they saw as colleagues. Bain (1970, p. 20) writes 'The older reluctance to join a trade union was based in a strong sense of individualism. They felt that their best chance of getting ahead was through their own efforts, and not through collective union activity'. Since the 1960s, Bain suggests that it has been much more difficult for such people to perceive themselves as having the same power position as their management. As individuals, they no longer feel they can achieve what they want, and so they act as a group.

Teachers do work under a number of given structural constraints, but they perceive them differently, and they react to them differently on the basis of their personality, biography, and their work context. Our data supports Pollard's contention that individual actors make meaningful action for themselves to deal with the situations in which they find themselves. One of the advantages of a life history approach is that the long time span it provides enables us to see not only the ways that the structural constraints vary over time, but also the way the coping strategies, too, vary during the life cycle of the teacher, and according to the historical conditions in which they find themselves.

Chapter 4

Managing the Teacher Role

As we have noted earlier, the task facing teachers in their first two or three years in post is not only managing classrooms and pupils, but also accommodating to the teacher role. There have been several studies of this (for example Hoyle, 1969; Shipman, 1975), but our method again enabled more of a teacher's eye view of the process. We have seen, in Chapter 2, in the 'critical incident', one of the essential elements in the general structure of adaptation. In this chapter we consider the full nature of the role and teachers' relationship to it, as perceived by them. How, then, did they see it?

During our talks with them, a notion of being a 'proper teacher' kept emerging in their accounts. At first it seemed as if they were describing individual teachers that they knew or had worked with. A 'proper teacher' was someone who fully engaged with the teacher role, and who accepted the conventional wisdom current in schools (Hanson and Herrington, 1976). Some teachers, however, appear to resist that role, despite all the pressures from senior staff, who act as 'gatekeepers' and 'critical reality definers' (Lyons, 1981). As with the constraints of the previous chapter, they 'manage' the role, taking on some of its aspects, rejecting others, and being changed themselves in the process. This view of teacher adaptation has important parallels with the pupil's. Both respond to expectations by producing differentiated groups, some of whom are more conformist than others (Hammersley and Turner, 1980).

As the talks went on, it became clear that our group were, in fact, posing an ideal type figure. No one actually knew a person who was a 'proper teacher', nor did any appear in our sample. The 'proper teacher' was an artefact, a composite of elements derived from common expectations for a particular purpose, not one of the teacher's colleagues, sitting with them in the staffroom.

The purpose, we would argue, is to do with identity construction. It is useful for teachers to have such an image to measure themselves against. Depending on personal predilections, some will approximate more closely than others to the image. Thus, the proper teacher is one who has engaged completely with the teacher role. Being a teacher has become their whole identity. Significantly, they may be viewed by some as not 'proper persons' (Blackie, 1977). Some teachers become more proper than others. It is, therefore, a dimension with teachers situated at points along it according to how many elements of the role they have adopted, and to what degree. There may be conflict between teachers who have taken up different positions, but not inevitably so. Much depends on other factors, for example the kind of school they work in. Also when we look at a whole career, it appears that some teachers take on more dimensions of the proper teacher identity at certain points in their life cycle. The adaptation is thus affected by age factors. We were at pains, therefore, to show the shifting adaptations that an individual teacher makes through a career.

What were the characteristics of teacher propriety as described by our sample? They fall into four main areas: appearance, attitude to pupils, relationships with colleagues, and teaching.

We shall examine each in turn.

Appearance

The appearance of the teacher is crucial, as is the teacher's attitude toward the appearance of pupils. Proper teachers were described as dressing in a 'teacher uniform'. We gained a clear picture of this from teachers who did not consider themselves proper at all, though here, Mr Tucks (29, scale 2, science and maths) came close to recognizing the 'straw man' nature of the concept:

> I've never worn teacher uniform. I teach in what I'm wearing now . . . often criticized by colleagues, but then I nucleated a group of non-teacher uniform wearers, they were all a bit younger than me . . . (proper teachers) wear suits and ties. Yes, or tweed jackets, with leather elbows, cherry blossom boots and cavalry twills (laughs) . . . Now I have to admit that few colleagues of mine have ever fitted into that category, but they were essentially tie wearers and I was essentially not a tie wearer . . . Shoes can be important too. That's all very 1960s, but they're not as critical as ties. I think if you're all right from the waist up, although . . . well, preferably trousers with a crease.

Mr Ray (35, scale 4, Head of Department, biology) agreed with Mr Tucks' perception, but added details about personal appearance that were not only to do with clothes:

> I think if you wear a sports jacket, if you've got a sports jacket on, and you're going a bit bald, and you're a bit overweight, that somehow carries the image of proper teacher to me, you know.

Women teachers also acknowledged the same issues as important:

The way we went about it mainly, the younger ones, was with what we wore. The Head, the old Head, did comment once that, something about open sandals ... so, we all went to great pains, all the younger ones, to wear our sandals as minimal as we could, with the most violent scarlet nail varnish on our toe nails. And I mean I once heard — a teacher — she was a very nice lady, who was Head of English — thought black was so unsuitable for school. Ermm! ... and a lot of us took great delight in wearing black. There was a whole little brigade of us. When fashion was that skirts were straight, black, slim-line skirts, with slits up the side, longer or shorter according to how you were feeling and how much you wanted to shock. And black jumpers with plunging necklines some of them ... and high heeled shoes if you could bear the strain on your toes. And there was quite a little brigade of us in classy black outfits and little stilletos, and in the summer, low necked dresses, with the backs scraped out ... and sleeveless, because arm-pits aren't nice you know. I was very blonde, and I kept up with fashion quite a bit. I never wore stockings, except in the winter for warmth. I did varnish my toe nails. (Mrs Castle, 64, retired, art)

From Mr Tucks and Mrs Castle, we gain a sense that there is pressure put on young teachers to conform to a particular dress code. Sarah (25, scale 1, art) agreed with this:

The school I'm at now, I mean if I went in jeans and my hair more scruffy than it is now, generally expressed my artiness, then I think it would be frowned on. I'm not the type to dress wildly. I've changed my dress quite considerably, I mean I never used to be out of trousers, I usually wear a lot of rings and jewellery, and I wear me mam's 1950ish dresses.

Sarah had experienced pressure, and had modified her appearance accordingly. Mrs Castle had the same experience. Things changed for her as she got older:

But I never did succumb, though I think I did ... er ... go out of my way eventually, not to flaunt my bare toes, and I tended to buy rather more covered-in sandals, or shoes that were open at the sides, but not so much at the front ... so the head didn't feel I was ... except the last week of the summer term, then I used to wear my sandals, I used to think 'what the hell'.

The generation faction is clearly important. Mr Tucks commented that the group of 'non-teacher uniform wearers' was 'younger than him', and Mrs Castle certainly felt pressure on her to change as she got older. We shall consider this in more detail later.

One teacher (Mrs Think, 38, Head of Department, art) in the sample had a particularly unusual appearance — for a teacher. The data which follows is taken from field notes.

> I met Mrs Think at her house. She was wearing tight blue jeans, a black roll-neck jumper, very bright pink socks and white lace-up shoes. She had long, peroxided blond hair, and huge ear-rings. At the end of the interview, she offered me a ride to the station, and put on a leopard skin (artificial) short coat. She made a point out of her appearance, for example, she indicated the coat, and said in an imitation cockney accent 'It's a bit of all right this, isn't it! Really attention-seeking, in' it'?

The researcher made no comment on Mrs Think's appearance. It was Mrs Think herself who brought it up, and it was obviously an issue of paramount importance to her:

> I have six pairs of these socks now, I always wear them now. I did it first to see how many people would ask me why I was wearing cerise coloured socks . . . I wear jeans most of the time. I'm occasionally asked by pupils 'is my hair natural?' and I say 'of course not', and their mouths fall open, which I encourage, that process of questioning. And I'm very into media stuff, Bowie, etc. and I structure English lessons so that questions of appearance come up, and mine, and I encourage that . . . I was talking to a pupil, she said she thought it was incredible that someone who wore pink socks, could teach English.

For Mrs Think, her appearance was an important factor in a set of strategies for challenging traditional schooling practices, and it has a key role to play in her whole political philosophy, which will become apparent throughout the chapter. She had probably accepted fewer, and pointedly opposed more of the dimensions of proper teacher than any of the other teachers. But she had not done these things from the beginning. Rather, it had developed 'in practice' and 'with my history'.

There were teachers at the opposite end of the line, whose attitudes on appearance contrasted sharply with those just expressed. Not only did they see appearance as a key factor in their identity as teachers, they were also sharply critical of teachers whose appearance they did not consider proper:

> I do think you have got to be prepared to set standards, and I think the way you dress, the way in which you appear, if you are sloppy in any way, kids will quickly catch on to it. (Mr Shoe, 63, retired, science)

> Young art teachers who came to me, clueless wonders some of them, drab girls who came looking as though they were selling off jewellery, and wiggly hair and long woollen things, and skirts that come down to their ankles, and toenails that could have been cleaner. (Mr King, 65, retired, art)

I had this chap in my department, I was glad when he went. He was the bees knees, god's gift to the art world, he came to school the first morning in a policeman's cape and wellingtons, bearded too, and he walked into the staffroom and everybody said 'Good God!'. And they used to pull his leg. Do you have to wear a beard to kid yourself you're an art teacher? He wore corderoys and sandals without socks on. They used to rib him unmercifully. (Arthur, 69, retired, art)

Not only do senior members of staff have strong views on the subject of teacher's appearance, but 'staffroom culture' can exert considerable pressure, going by Arthur's account.

Appearance is a key factor in the preservation of general standards in the view of many teachers:

I do think the standards that I can expect are going. Young teachers come in and feel they are unnecessary, they want a more free and easy kind of association, which I could never go along with. The way you dress, the way you appear in class, the way that the kiddies sit in class all seems more casual really. I always appear reasonably turned out, I think. I try to insist on this, but maybe this is a bit dated now. I saw a laddie the other day, sitting on the radiator, taking his class (one year out of college) sitting on the radiator, with his feet on the desk, with a book, reading to the class. That's not the way I would go about things. I couldn't agree with that. (Mr Shoe, 63, retired, science)

Mr King was not a conformist in many respects, as data throughout this book would show, but he had strong views on this issue:

The standards of appearance and behaviour started to slacken when I was senior master, and I found I was more in aggression with staff because they'd wear a polo neck jumper, and they'd complain about the behaviour of children, and they would have hair falling out, and dandruff on a black pullover, couldn't understand why the children didn't respect them. I always wore a suit, not because I liked to, but because I wanted them to say 'Sir'.

Women teachers agreed on this issue:

Young teachers who so often came in in faded blue jeans and tatty clothes, and they didn't want to look like what they thought was a traditional teacher, they wanted to look like teenagers, and this was very detrimental, because on the whole children really prefer to look up to somebody. They just didn't like the teacher who came to teach them and looked just like their elder brothers and sisters. And those who came looking like adults, and were clean and tidy, got on much better. (Miss Nott, 67, retired, art)

It is perhaps significant that these attitudes spread across the subject divide. Mr Tucks, Mr Shoe, and Mr Ray were science teachers. Mrs Castle, Mr King and Miss Nott were all art teachers.

Attitudes to pupils' appearance were also important in this context. The 'proper teacher' was seen to be very concerned with the details of school uniform, and with keeping pupils' appearance in it neat to every detail. Mr Tucks (29, scale 2, science and maths) contrasted his own attitudes with those of Bill, one colleague who came close to being a proper teacher:

> And also, the school has always been fairly easy-going about dress, about the dress of pupils, and although there is a uniform for fifth form and below, it was never considered. Most staff like to cherish their relationships with pupils, so that they would think twice about threatening it by pointing out pupils had yellow socks on or something. I mean it's not something you do with your best friend is it to censure them for wearing a particular style of socks, so ... again Bill broke the rules here, I think Bill really typified a different sort of teacher culture, which he tried to supplant on this laissez-faire, rather more enlightened sort of teacher culture, and in fact he alienated himself from a lot of staff by trying to do so. But that school is not a typical teacher culture. But the laissez-faire thing is not consciously worked out. If people said, look I don't think it's worth fighting with pupils over long hair or details of uniform, because we do think it's destructive to relationships with pupils.

Women teachers saw it in the same way:

> I don't like looking to see if they've got the right colour socks on, I don't care if they come in a wet suit. (Sarah, 25, scale 1, art)

> It's this pettiness that I think you've probably got to have and be, or it seems that you've got to have and be, you know, to pick up things like uniform in particular irritates me and I feel that professionals shouldn't always be looking out to see if they've got the wrong colour socks on, you know it's part of the job and I find that very hard to do or to notice or to be bothered by and I think really I'm probably not a proper teacher because I don't ... A proper teacher should be interested in all that and I'm not. (Ann, 43, scale 1, art)

However, not everyone agreed. Teachers who accepted more dimensions of 'proper culture' felt quite differently about school uniform. Bill was one example in Mr Tucks' account. Mr King (65, retired, art) also felt it incumbent on him to enforce school uniform rules:

> I've always assumed that. And I noticed that 80 per cent of the staff would look the other way. That was apparent from the day I went into teaching, and was even more apparent when I left. More apparent.

Attitudes to Pupils

There were three sub-categories here, relating to pupil deviance, discipline, and relationships with pupils.

Pupil Deviance

Proper teachers had an unsympathetic attitude to what Mr Tucks (29, scale 2, science and maths) listed as 'the factors of smoking, swearing and drinking'. Pupils drinking are a perennial problem for schoolteachers. Mr Tucks, as usual, took a 'radical' line:

> In the upper sixth, you know, you often see them in pubs . . . well, that's another area, where I'm completely laissez-faire, and I don't bother at all, and often get drinks bought for me, or . . . reciprocally by pupils, but Bill, if he came to the pub, and saw someone he knew was lower sixth or he knew was under 18, would go to the barman and say 'this boy is under age', and he might actually teach this bloke, and it might completely, I mean, I still have anecdotes poured out to me about these kinds of things, and the ill feeling they engender is amazing'.

Another teacher, Arthur (69, retired, art), had witnessed the attitude of younger teachers toward drinking, and found himself very uncomfortable with it:

> We'd quite a few younger members of staff, and somebody said 'Let's go down to the pub for a Christmas booze up at dinner time'. All right, fair enough, but damn it, half the sixth form was there. The younger ones on the staff just took it in their stride, they were buying the kids pints and the kids were buying them drinks, but that didn't quite ring a bell with me somehow. Maybe I was just too old fashioned by then . . . I didn't fancy drinking with the kids. I don't drink a lot anyway.

Mr Shoe (63, retired, science) also disapproved, and found the situation very difficult to cope with:

> Nowadays you meet the kids in pubs at a very early age, which I always find a bit of an embarrassment.

Most teachers, however, worked out a solution to the problem. They would not have intervened directly as Bill was prepared to do, neither were they happy to drink sociably along with pupils. A number of strategies were employed. Mrs Castle (64, retired, art) made sure she knew enough of her pupils informal culture to be able to avoid the problem. These teachers 'knife edged' quite successfully, that is to say, trod a very thin line between two desirable, but mutually incompatible alternatives (Measor and Woods, 1984a).

> When we had a sixth form, you could come across pupils in the lunchtimes in the pub. You had to make sure you didn't go to the wrong one on the wrong day.

Other teachers took up a half-way position, for example, employing distinctions between 'school' and extra-curricular time, different rules applying in each.

> I take sixth-formers to Paris, have done for the last ten years. They are on holiday and can smoke if they wish. I ask them not to drink anything alcoholic on the coach — they get sick, but I tell them there is plenty of opportunity on the ferry, and in Paris. But, when I take them to London on a school expedition I tell them they will not smoke and they will not drink, and I usually take the precaution of telling them which pub I am going to, so they won't inadvertently wander in there (Mr Shark, 45, scale 4, Head of Department, art).

This is not an entirely new problem, as it is sometimes thought to be:

> It was thirty-six years ago when I went to that school. The boys used to be reprimanded for spending too much time in the miners' welfare hall, where they played snooker and things like that — and drank beer. I used to go out with the other young teachers, and we had to stop drinking in the neighbourhood at all, because we went a little way into the country, because women weren't allowed at pubs in the village, and we went up into the country and in the other bar were all the sixth-form boys. (Mrs Castle, 64, retired, art)

Pupils smoking is also a problem that most schools face, and towards which individual teachers take different attitudes. Mr Tucks (29, scale 2, science and maths) discussed Bill's — the proper teacher's — attitude again:

> Smoking — Bill went round looking for people smoking, most people know that smoking goes on, it goes on in certain illegal places, but there has never been any policing of those territories, but Bill would sort of break this rule, this non-policing rule and go and find people. He was actually disruptive to the system.

Other teachers accepted the need to keep schools policed for smokers:

> There you are, forever chasing fifth-year girls out of loos. There they are sitting in a circle in the girls' toilets, passing fags around. This is the way it is going, becoming more difficult all the time. (Mr Shoe, 63, retired, science)

Another teacher was not having any nonsense on the subject:

They tried all sorts including smoking in the garden. One youngster pulled out a packet of fags, and lit one up, and I wiped him across the face hard with my hand, cigarette and all went flying. I didn't take him into the boss like I was supposed to do, I just took my chance when it was offered to me. But I never had that kind of problem again, I just waded in. (Mr Shaw, 45, scale 3, Head of Department, rural science)

Some teachers who had accepted more of the 'proper teacher' role, refused to relax the no smoking rules even for older pupils on an extra curricular activity. Mr Ladyhill's (67, retired, science) attitude to smoking contrasts directly with Mr Shark's to drinking here:

At that time, we were very keen on not allowing any smoking in the school. We used to take boys on educational tours of industrial areas. I wouldn't have the boys smoking in any of the halls of residence we went to, and I got a signed statement from their parents, saying that they accepted this.

It is always possible for a teacher to take up a half-way position, for a teacher who 'cherishes' his relationships with pupils to quote Mr Tucks' term. The teacher recognizes the importance of smoking in pupil culture, and avoids pressing the issue; nevertheless, he has a canny eye on the formal culture of the school, on the demands it makes, and on his well-being and prospects. He walks the 'knife edge'.

I don't ever look for trouble, but I don't ignore it if I see it. I say to the sixth-formers not 'You shall not smoke' but 'You will not be seen smoking', it's as simple as that, and I tell them if I see them smoking they're in trouble. But if they want to smoke and they are discreet, if I saw them walking into the woods, I wouldn't dream of creeping after them to see what they were up to. I might get an incredible surprise. (Mr Shark, 45, scale 4, Head of Department, art)

This kind of attitude is reminiscent of the 'smoking truce' in Reynolds (1976) (see also Woods, 1979).

Again, teachers adopted a number of attitudes towards swearing. Mr Tucks' (29, scale 2, science and maths) was one of flexibility:

There are all kinds of things, for example if kids swear I just ignore it. I don't respond. I don't respond unfavourably.

Mr King (65, retired, art) had a 'conformist' attitude on appearance, but a much more radical one on this issue:

If I can possibly deny hearing a swear word at school, I will, because they often say it's not dirty to them.

More 'proper' teachers had different views:

If a four letter word is used, and I look up in amazement, they say, 'Well what did I say'? 'You don't know what you said'. 'Oh everybody says that'. They think it's nothing, and here is me, with ideas that go back a few years, I am amazed, the kids aren't shocked at all. (Mr Shoe, 63, retired, science)

The use of swear words in school raises a more general issue of language. We have suggested elsewhere that some teachers make a conscious effort to avoid 'teacher language' which they felt could alienate some children in the school (Measor and Woods, 1984b). They introduce colloquial language into their lessons, and prime their discourse with frequent references to the world of advertisements and the mass media. Teachers in this sample thought language use was important.

I mean my own language in . . . my teacher language and my day to day language are very similar. (Mr Tucks, 29, scale 2, science and maths)

Mr Ray (35, scale 4, Head of Department, science) agreed:

I try and be colloquial, when I can, and I enjoy it. I celebrate it, especially in the area I live in. And I write little documents on the use of language in the science department, you know, don't use 'verify' things like that.

Other teachers did not agree at all. They viewed themselves as upholding another, better culture and language in school, for pupils to look up to and aspire towards:

It is important to have traditions of good behaviour and standards of tidiness, appearance and good order. If we don't show them some standards, for many of them, no-one else will. I remember we did a 'minstrel' show one year. It swamped the whole school for a year. They had hundreds of kids marching round to the 'saints go marching in'. All the time they said 'chin in' and the music teacher never even heard their bad diction. I thought there was so much they could have learned, if they'd been learning to shape their words properly, because 'chin in' couldn't be right — if they'd been learning to hold themselves upright, not slouching, they'd have been learning something, and so on. (Miss Nott, 66, retired, art)

Discipline

Again teachers had different approaches to the issue of discipline. Mr Ray (38, scale 4, Head of Department, science) described his first Head of Department, who came close to the stereotype of a proper teacher. He was overweight and wore tweeds.

My first Head of Department seemed to be an unreflective man about his own practice. He accepted many things about class teaching that I wouldn't, class recitation, corporal punishment.

Mrs Castle (64, retired, art), too, disliked corporal punishment, and acted to protect her pupils from it. She refrained, for example, from sending boys to the Head in her school because:

> they'd have got beaten. I just didn't want the boys to be hit. The Head came into my room once, and one boy was just walking across the room to empty a water pot, and the Headmaster gave him a great big clout across the face, for being out of his place.

Some teachers objected very strongly to the way they saw their colleagues behaving, when they were disciplining pupils:

> You can feel an awfully important person in a school, by shouting at the poor little brats, I've seen it, so much bullying going on. (Mr King, 65, retired, art)

Mr Shoe, (63, retired, science) who accepted much 'proper teacher' culture, drew the line here:

> You hear it so often, teachers will bark and snap and snarl 'Pick that up!' 'Do that!' and I think kids react in the same way. I think it is important to communicate, and courteously. If I snap and snarl, then kids will react in the same way.

For him, it was improper teacher behaviour to 'snap, bark and snarl'.
Mr King found himself getting very angry with his colleagues, certainly toward the end of his career:

> That was one of the most harrowing parts of my job toward the end. To walk past a room, and see things going on, like a child bending over a desk, being hit by a gym shoe. I thought that was unforgivable. The teachers were losing.

Mr King had taken a much more open view of discipline right from the beginning in his school career, and had attempted some innovative tactics, which he believed were now more widely accepted:

> Parents are important to work with, but not that easy to work with, and the ones that never come are the most difficult. I need to organize religiously parents' meetings for each form, that's twenty years ago, which now I believe is spreading more and more, but it wasn't done all that much.

This can be contrasted with Mr Shaw, (45, scale 3, Head of Department, rural science), who had a much more rough and ready approach:

> I'll put a kid across my knee quite happily, I did so with a fourth year

about twelve months ago, I said 'look, if you're cheeky to me, I'm going to put you across my knee in front of the class and spank your bottom, like a little boy, because that's how you're behaving'. And he tried it once again, so I did it. And that was the end of it. It's a question of what works. But I was prepared to lose the job over it, rather than having children I can't control.

Relationships with Pupils

Some of the teachers interviewed, who saw themselves as very far away from the stereotype of a proper teacher, considered they had particularly close relationships with pupils. They hinted also that their relationships with pupils were far better than those of 'proper teachers':

> I think you have to have a certain view of pupils as beings with restricted rights, thereby you respond differently to them than to other people ... You have special things that kind of correspond to Christmas day on the front, you know little end-of-term discos, where you slot in to a different mode of responding. But immediately you are in the classroom, bell rings, you are instantly back in the teacher role. But my whole teacher style, it emerges has been grounded in strong relationships really. (Mr Tucks, 29, scale 2, science and maths)

Mrs Castle (64, retired, art) did not state her view so theoretically, but she had a sense of the same issues. For example, she liked to teach art, because 'there's a little time to show a human face'. Both teachers told anecdotes, which gave details of close relationships they had with pupils. In both cases, breaking the formal rules of the school seemed to be crucial to these relationships, as was a mutual pleasure in doing so (Woods, 1979):

> At Christmas they had marvellous Christmas parties, the male staff really went to town, did song and dance routines. Do you remember the Much Binding song? They made up verses about all the staff. They made up a nice one about me. 'Why do all the eligible boys drop French for Art?' It was the boys who were the most forthcoming all the time, I think because I was female. There was just the two young ones on the staff, me and the new biology teacher, whom they called Betty Biol. So we got all the attention of the boys and so on, because we were the youngest on the staff. The boys got me up to the youth club, to talk about something to do with painting, and in this church youth club, about half a dozen of these lads got me sitting down and said we'll have a cup of tea afterwards, in this little room, and told me some of the filthiest jokes I've ever heard, some of which I only vaguely understood.

Mr Tucks also told similar tales (Measor, 1984), in which he drank too many bottles of cheap wine at lunchtime with pupils, raced through the home counties countryside in an open sports car, and made them all late for an afternoon exam.

All of these stories involve the teacher trying to escape from the conventional teacher role. Mr King (65, retired, art) felt relationships with children to be of paramount importance.

> I like children, I taught very much through my relationship with them ... I never find children too immature, they're as good as you treat them. They'll discuss the most profound things, because they haven't got this sequence of barriers that we put up.

Mr Redford (33, scale 4, Head of Department, art) also felt it made for good teaching:

> I think somewhere along the line you can get through to these kids on a personal level, if they respect you as an individual. If they know that you don't necessarily shirk the issues, but you are fair, and you will apologize if you're wrong, and you will hold open a door for them. I think that last thing is a very interesting thing, because a lot of teachers in this school, and in other schools, will accuse kids of being rude and whatever, and yet would never dream of holding a door open for a boy, I think you teach more by example. An awful lot of teachers will just push through a door in front of kids — yes — I think that's to do with the conflict between the values that were evident in schools, twenty years ago, and the values that are current now.

Other teachers felt differently about the right way to relate to pupils. They discussed the need they felt to 'cultivate a distance' from pupils, and the strategies they employed to do so:

> I suppose you have got to learn to keep kiddies at a distance, you can get on well with them, but you have got to recognize the signs whereby they'll get familiar. (Mr Shoe, 63, retired, science)

> You have to cultivate a kind of distance, I won't say detached, but I have tried to be professional. You have to cultivate a distance. I see some of the younger teachers making difficulties for themselves, difficulties which need never have existed ... By getting a special relationship with the children, which is temporarily to their advantage, but which if things change — and children are volatile, they do change — then suddenly things which they have built up become weaknesses in their defence. You can't really complain when somebody empties a bowl of custard over your head, if you have been on knock-about terms with them. I find it difficult to be sympathetic if a teacher goes out drinking with kids in the evening, then he must

expect that if horseplay comes his way, that it might not be the way he likes it. (Mr Shark, 45, scale 4, Head of Department, art)

One of the practices which most clearly signals this distancing process, is when surnames only are used. Most of the teachers were not prepared to have pupils use their first names. The more 'proper teachers' objected strongly to the practice. Nobody, for instance, ever called Mr Shark anything but Mr Shark, though he said a number of the younger teachers in his school allowed pupils to use their first names.

Some teachers were only prepared to use pupils' surnames.

It has always been surname terms for me. I certainly never let them call me by my Christian name. rightly or wrongly, I always tended to call girls by their Christian names, boys I used surnames. Once I start calling them Peter or Jimmy, I just don't feel happy with that. (Mr Shoe, 63, retired, science)

Relationships with Colleagues

The data presented so far suggests there are quite strongly differentiated attitudes within teacher culture. We might then expect to find different groups emerging within it, and within individual schools. From the work on pupil cultures we know that the two broad groups of conformists and deviants take oppositional stances to each other (see, for example, Hargreaves, 1967; Lacey, 1970; Ball, 1981) and it is interesting to explore whether the pattern holds true for teachers. There is a connected issue that relates to generation, and to the way senior staff act to socialize younger teachers (Measor, 1984).

Teachers who stood opposed to the 'proper teacher' stereotype usually saw themselves as 'outsiders', they did not see themselves as able or willing to fit into teacher culture as they found it.

Mrs Think (38, scale 4, Head of Department, art) told us:

I'm very much aware that I'm seen as a bit of a character, it doesn't displease me, I must be honest.

Mrs Castle (64, retired, art) had been aware of being an outsider ever since her first teaching practice experience:

I think you did come to grips with handling a class, but they didn't do anything about integrating you with the school, you were not encouraged to go into the staffroom ... Well I think I went in once or twice, and found that I didn't like it. Well I think it was so full of people anyway and people were busy and didn't notice you. It was easier to stay in the art room and get the pencils out for the next lesson, something of that sort.

This teacher, like Mr King, sensed that she 'was not popular in the staffroom'.

There was always that sort of slight implied criticism, I was getting a bit too avant-garde . . . Also, they knew I was the left wing kind. I did join the Communist Party when I was in South Wales, I'd resisted joining it when I was still at college. I had a feeling it could get in the way of getting decent references and things. Though my father was quite a well-known Communist at the time, so people assumed I was anyway.

But if Mrs Castle did not feel she was approved of, equally she did not approve of her colleagues:

Yes, I enjoyed shocking them. A staffroom full of thirty, almost all maiden ladies with the old university tradition of addressing you by your surname, we thought it was awful. We laughed at them.

Mrs Castle went on to describe the 'we'. It was a group of younger women teachers, already mentioned earlier as wearing tight black skirts with slits up the sides. No doubt these formed a peer group support system, which helped them to maintain 'outsider' positions (Nias, 1985).

Nevertheless, schools do aid the task of managing the role. Mr Tucks (29, scale 2, science and maths), for example, said he had experienced criticism for his refusal to wear a tie, but he found his particular school displayed a latitude which stimulated his own attitudes, and allowed them to grow:

I had a commitment to doing things differently and breaking the rules. At my school, when I first went there, it was an *amazing* collection of people on the staff, very very lively, very young, very stimulating, very opinionated, not at all stuffy. OK, there were some gowns on the wall hardly ever worn. But, there seemed to be a continuing dialogue between staff about educational issues, and even a very lively extra curricular side. So one was able to be oneself, you could make your role, you didn't have to step into a ready-made role. Course this was the late 1960s, and it was a role-making time. I think it's not true now. Anything — well not anything went, but it was the shifting sands of values. You know you had the hair problem — do we bother about hair, or do we not. Sixth-form uniform went, and they went around in all sorts of weird gear, which was great. So, insofar as I was starting in that era, it was easy to make your own role.

Pedagogy

There are 'proper' and 'improper' approaches to teaching. Mrs Castle (64, retired, art) had rebelled against the teaching situation she found herself in at the beginning of her career, and experimented with some very different practices:

My first job was in a small grammar school in Wales, it didn't have a proper art room, and they painted in little books. Well, I did away with all that. The first Christmas I was there, we painted a mural up on the art room wall, directly onto the wall, not on paper that was stuck up. Before that they had exercise books to paint in.

Miss Nott (66, retired, art) had found a very similar situation in her first job:

We had to do book covers, loose leaf covers, all quarter imperial size, and all my Head of Department's exercises went in there and mine were supposed to, too, so all the work was supposed to be quarter imperial. And she went through a series of exercises in colour mixing and all that sort of thing, which was very Victorian you see. And I was in some difficulty, having to do her tight, stereotyped thing.

Clearly this is all connected with generational change. New teachers bring in new ideas and values to the school classroom. Miss Nott never went as far as Mrs Castle though. She got the children painting on large pieces of paper, never onto walls. She nevertheless broke away from the stereotyped ways of doing art, and the account is dealt with in full in Chapter 7.

Another individualistic approach was expressed by Mr King (65, retired, art)

You have to teach people how to look, it's getting them interested, and once they're interested, I come home from the lesson, what's the word — revitalized. I want to come home and paint sometimes. When you're teaching young children, don't put them at a desk, try and break down the classroom formality. It's like, helping — you can throw a bundle of acorns on to a table, or a bundle of cones from a fir tree, one each, or better one between two, they're sharing, they discuss about the fir cone, and then you discuss it, and if you've got a few slides you can — oh you can win them in so many ways. You can talk about colour, come on — you want to say that he's a rude, crude person — what are the lines, jagged, why? — is he going to be red faced? It's tremendous fun and the work sparkles, it becomes vital. Teaching is showing somebody how to use the facilities they have, not telling them what to do, I think ... I was after another thing, what was my job was, er, to stimulate, to open eyes, to er, make them think as well, to live in an art room, is to be alive, think, do, make, if your other senses aren't working, use feel, touch, it's a beautiful sense. I was nearly arrested in Spain for putting my fingers on a Goya painting, but the paint was — so — and I *had* to.

Mr Shoe, (63, retired, science), on the other hand, was more proper in his approach:

Mr Shoe: You have got to set standards I think, good standards of teaching, that your lessons are well prepared, and your marking up to date.

R: What about all that child-centred stuff that became so popular in the 1960s?

Mr Shoe: I am sorry, I was always rather too traditional I'm afraid, and I never went along with it. There was a lot of project work around, but I was never convinced.

There was interesting corroboration of Mr King's account, from Mr Shark. Mr Shark (45, scale 4, Head of Department, art) had been a pupil of Tom King's, and then had gone on to be an art teacher himself, and a Head of a large Art Department at a local school. He discussed Mr King's influence:

I was enabled to develop my own abilities at secondary school. Tom King was a real reforming influence. The previous generations of art teachers had been very limited and stereotyped involving the setting of set exercises, and the repetition of the sort of work I consider moribund, where everybody is trained to do something in exactly the same sort of way.

Similar issues applied in the teaching of science. Mr Ladyhill (67, retired, science) had particularly conservative views about what ought to be taught:

I was a very firm believer in Latin, I still am, it is a good thing for medics and pharmicists to have, but more than that, it's a good subject to study.

He also had some views on the right and best ways of teaching things:

One learned the value of precise, painstaking methods, it gave one a good technique. In mathematics, I was fortunate in being able to go through at a time when the separate branches were treated separately. We had to learn about fifty theorems, which I can remember to this day, twenty years later. This sort of thing is very good, I was a great believer in geometry. It's a pity that so much of it has dropped out of the curriculum. There was a tendency to overdo it, I think you could cut down to thirty the number of theorems you need. I think it's a great pity that we didn't keep more geometry. Of course syllabuses can't stay static, but too much of what was good has gone.

This can be contrasted with some of the newer methods of teaching science that Mr Tucks (29, scale 2, science and maths), for one, espoused. He criticized his first Head of Department, who had similar views to Mr Ladyhill.

We had a very chequered career, he was a very pernickety, old fashioned type of schoolmaster, had a first from a red brick university in 1932 or something, knew nothing about modern physics actually. I don't think he had any inkling about quantum mechanics or anything, but knew ... you know ... seventeen different ways of finding the thermal conductivity of cardboard, and things like this. But ... he was a lovely old time teacher you know, but very formal, and everything was just so and of course at this time we were just introducing Nuffield, and Nuffield was sort of a different world to him and we had the oil film experiment, which always left the lab looking as if a bomb had hit it you know — looking like they'd been having water fights or something. And ripple tanks, and all this sort of thing. And I was a new teacher and obviously my classroom ... laboratory organization wouldn't be perfect and he tended, because he had very much a sit up and beg, talk and chalk teacher style, associated Nuffield ... He did teach Nuffield in the first year, but not in the Nuffield spirit. So there was tension there.

Teachers who did not consider themselves 'proper' had another principle they held dear. They were very keen that pupils should somehow find their 'own way' to approach the subject. This was true for Mr King (65, retired, art):

I would do demonstration lessons at Valley, quite a lot. Not for 'How clever I am', but 'this is one way of how to go about it. Now, you do it your way'.

This could be contrasted with Mr Quilley (67, retired, art):

These were fifteen or twenty years after the war, and I was still saying to pupils 'Stand to attention, and pick up your brush and paint to the left. I never fully got rid of this. 'Do as I tell you, I'll get you there. Do what I lay in front of you. Knock it off by heart, obey me implicitly, treat yourself as if you are a Roman Catholic, obeying the Pope, no questions, and I will guarantee on my part, however nasty a person I am, to get you the prize you want, that examination result you want'.

Mrs Castle supported this view, but doubted Mr Quilley had ever really got rid of the attitude.

He was the sort of teacher, where you had to do what he wanted, and not what you wanted, and if you didn't do what he wanted, he wasn't very nice to you.

In the teaching of art today, one of the important issues appears to be the attitude to the culture which derives from the mass media. Mr Shark (45, scale 4, Head of Department, art) took a conservative line. He was opposed to visual references from the 'ad-mass' world in art education.

I think you only get genuine experience from children with things they understand. I try to get children to look at their own lives, and draw from things they know, rather than from the world of fantasy, because the world of fantasy is almost always dominated by comics, or television, or second-hand images.

Mr Redford (33, scale 4, Head of Department, art) was in profound disagreement with this view:

> Art education has cut itself off from contemporary visual culture. Popular culture is seen as invalid by art education right back to an NUT conference in the 1960s where popular culture was seen as impoverished, and something education should work to overcome. Schools have generally followed the plane of disavowal. I regard popular culture as quite proper for art education, I mean if art education isn't about seeing, previously I never questioned the role art had in larger culture, I now question its position, and its place in the school curriculum. You can criticize art's role in school in terms of higher and lower culture. Art has taken on a role of counteracting cultural impoverishment, and that implies the pupils' daily cultural experience is of a lesser standard than what we do here, and I don't think that holds water. You've got to accept that it is a fact of their culture, so I don't think it's right to confront that culture and say I don't think it's valid, because it's not like Raphael. That's the first step, to say 'Yes that's a valid culture, come in'.

This had led Mr Redford to introduce new subject areas into the art department:

> I teach something called visual education which deals mainly with advertising and things. And I feel probably happier teaching that now, than I do fine art, and my enthusiasms are for talking about ways in which, well ways of seeing if you like, and I've found kids very receptive.

Nevertheless, Mr Redford was very conscious of the problems he was facing in taking this direction in school.

> Taking art education forward in that way, means a kind of critical studies approach, and that's what our lords and masters certainly don't want. Also, at this point in time, you've got to justify art being included in the curriculum, and you can only really justify it giving the arguments they want to hear. And now there is retrenchment, they've gone back to an emphasis on the three Rs. Obviously they're not going to be impressed by arguments that take art education into a totally new arena. So ironically you are arguing on grounds you don't necessarily agree with. But you've got to — it's real politic. The government doesn't want questioning curriculum, but it's a bad time to get art education into that area, I get very divided, because my heart is with the popular culture side, but the resources are in the fine art side. So I'm trying to find my way through it.

Teachers who did not think of themselves as 'proper' also questioned the traditional 'transmission' mode of pedagogy. Mrs Think (38, scale 4, Head of Department, art) had worked out a theoretical position on this:

> What I think tends to happen, and it is justified by teacher training courses, is this idea that knowledge is a monolithic thing, and that the teacher holds the key so far, and the pupils are lucky if they get some feed-back.

She linked teacher practices to a whole notion of hegemony.

> I think that educational practice implies a measure of control, in the sense of imparting this mysterious knowledge. Educational practice is one of many practices, such as literature, art, music, science, which operate, whereby people make sense of the world ... Most teachers operate under this taken-for-granted thing. I am as much a learner as a teacher.

For Mrs Think it was important for her as a teacher to question recipe knowledge:

> I'm interested in taking apart things that are taken for granted, things that are perpetuated. As I got older, I discovered that certain things were contradictory, and should not be taken for granted, but it took me a while to get the articulation I've got now. I questioned things, my God I questioned things, and I want the kids to do that too.

Such views were not confined to the art teachers. Mr Ray (38, scale 4, Head of Department, science), a science teacher, held similar views on the role of education, of teachers and of his subject in maintaining a hegemony that he was unhappy with:

> I have always had a political aim in my teaching, that is the demystifying of science as an aid for working class pupils to become critical and competent in being able to change society. I read Kuhn's science revolutions book, and presented science as a revolutionary activity. *Teaching as a Subversive Activity* was quite an influential book on me in the early days. Teaching science, certainly I had a missionary activity in the early days. I wanted to teach working class kids, in a comprehensive. I wanted to teach them science, I was fairly clear, it was to do with things like science has revolutions and change, and if you can teach them that science has revolutions, and revolutions and change are implicit in science, then revolution and change might be implicit in their own lives.

Both teachers had a number of strategies which derived from their theoretical stance. They involved a deliberate side-stepping of the teacher role. Mr Ray said:

Mr Ray: I would do things like show films and disagree with them, or say oh, the book's got it wrong, or say 'rubbish'! if the commentator on a film said something. I think authority is a central issue in all my lessons, and that is useful, to play around with notions of authority, and I therefore didn't see myself as the chief definer of reality in the classroom, nor did I see the book, nor the film, not even the experiment, although that had priority.

R: How did you play around with notions of authority?

Mr Ray: By never coming down to final judgments, never really committing myself to one side of a question, saying things like 'Well that's one way of doing it' or 'Well you could look at it like that'. I'm talking about a consistent hidden curriculum, it involved a pretty heavy presentation of self.

This had implications for his whole teacher style and behaviour in the classroom.

I don't completely neglect class teaching, but I tend to avoid it, it's one to one interactions or small groups, I feel guilty when I'm doing it, is what I'm trying to say ... because it's inappropriate I think. It's OK for, like, a demonstration, or introducing a film, or on a safety incident, but I don't think it's very good for learning.

Mrs Think had basically the same strategies. She insisted 'How I teach is by continually listening and exchanging'. She was pleased when one pupil paid her the compliment of saying 'You really listen to us, and you always ask for our opinion'. In addition of course, Mrs Think's rather bizarre, non–teacher appearance stood as a systematic challenge to conventional notions of teacher behaviour. Mr King (65, retired, art) did not go as far as the other two teachers, but he recognized the importance of pupils' learning to challenge, as an aid to his general aim of encouraging their creativity. He also criticized other teachers who did not have any such views:

I would often ask kids questions too, about my teaching. 'How would you like this lesson to have been given?' And they would come up with suggestions. Davy Quilley sometimes had more discipline in his art room than in himself. He would swear at kids and throw blackboard dusters at them.

Teachers are often represented as being politically and theoretically unaware, as in fact being unseeing and unquestioning dupes of the system. But several of our teachers not only lived school lives which challenged many traditional practices, but also had very well worked out theories of the way education fitted into society structures. They had accordingly tried to develop strategies for change. There were some differences in opinion on the best way to go about this. Mrs Think and Mr Ray believed in challenging and questioning school realities. Mrs Think and Mr Tucks additionally believed that their own personality and appearance helped in this process. All of these teachers became identified within their school as wanting change, and of being outsiders. They were categorized as different. Mr Redford (33, scale 4, Head of Department, art) counted himself as wanting change too, but he was worried that making himself identifiable in this way was counter-productive.

> The more involved I've become in reading the messages of society, the more I've realized that art plays quite a considerable part in subjugation, if you like, maintaining hegemony. I now question all that. I think teachers have an opportunity to be considerably subversive, but I think they usually aren't, because teachers who are inclined that way are so easily categorized as subversives, and I think that kids can so easily disregard them. You need to be a good reader of the situation in school. I do want a kind of cultural studies in school, where kids are encouraged to question what goes on, but you do need to sell it right.

Factors Associated with Different Degrees of Propriety

We noticed two prominent factors associated with approaches to the 'proper teacher' role — political background and age.

Political Background

Many of the teachers who reacted against proper teacher culture had left wing political commitments. This supports the work of Klein and Smith (1985). They found that such teachers had a prior commitment, either political or religious, which they surmized enabled them to resist socialization into traditional teacher culture. Several of our non-conformist teachers came from a left-wing background. They had parents, or more accurately fathers, who had been Communist party members. This was the case for Mr Tucks and Mrs Castle. Mrs Castle (64, retired, art) had also become a Communist Party member, although she left the party in 1956. It had created some problems for her. In her folio of paintings and drawings there was

> A drawing of my father who was sporting a little red star and hammer and sickle thing in his buttonhole and this Headmistress promptly said to the art adviser, 'Oh dear, I do hope she's not a Communist'. He said, 'Oh, I shouldn't worry'. He told me this afterwards because he was all for me, there were lots of nice pictures of coal mines, slag heaps and things amongst the work, which was a great recommendation to him and she liked it as well that there was something a bit down-to-earth. Again, that was much more important in coming to Southern England. Communism was much more a dirty word than it was in South Wales. I did get ticked off in

my first years down here for selling *Daily Workers* in the streets and things like that.

R: Told off ? By whom?

Mrs Castle: By the Senior Mistress. Very nicely, though, you have to give people their due. Most people weren't as prejudiced as you thought they were. One tended to think that just because they had different political opinions that they were rather stupid and bigoted and all sorts of things, but this woman took me on one side and just said 'Oh, it's ghastly, this thing, you must have to more or less volunteer to do and get up early', and we sold Daily Workers once a week outside the station yard, where the men were going to work. I think it was a child's parents who'd seen me doing this, who worked there and he'd told her. All she said was 'that's all right, only I didn't think it worth your sticking your neck out if you were just in it for kicks.' Which just shows what a civilized woman she was. I think, looking back at myself, I always rose to bait and I tended to ram my ideas down people's throats a bit.

Mr Ray (38, scale 4, Head of Department, science), too, had a clear set of political commitments, which he related more directly to his teaching practices than Mrs Castle did:

My political stance, has always been socialist left, I don't like communism. I was reasonably politically aware when I went to university, and I think it was the notion of doing missionary work amongst the masses in my last year, that led into teaching. Teaching in a comprehensive was a real political commitment for me. I did believe schools could change society and make it a better place and I still do.

We wondered if teachers who distanced themselves from the proper teacher role might be less interested in the normal career routes within their profession; or, if they were, whether they felt it was more difficult to get promotion. Further research might investigate this.

Age Factors

Among our sample the pressure to become a proper teacher increased as the teacher got older, became more established in the schools, and took on more senior positions within them. However, different teachers responded differently to the pressure. Mr Tucks (29, scale 2, science and maths), for example, recognized it but refused to conform to it.

I suppose it was thought, that my rather different style, I would grow out of it, which I never did. I started a school newspaper, we have a pretty free editorial policy, and we published some articles that were critical of the school, and this caused a great rumpus. The Head said —

Well ... almost tantamount to 'we don't expect this from senior members of staff'. I had the impression that it might have been better tolerated, if it had come from a less senior member of staff ... What we're really saying is that I have resisted complete socialization into their value system. But ... in fact ... they see it as what is common sense.

(Mr Tucks was later to leave school teaching, and take up a post in teacher training, as was Mr Ray).

Mr Redford (38, scale 4, Head of Department, art) was also aware of such pressures. They derived mostly from his sense of responsibility for the members of his Department:

The Deputy Head said that the Headmaster had asked him to see me, because he liked his teachers to wear ties, and I didn't wear a tie. I've always fought against this kind of hypocrisy, but the next day I came in wearing a tie, not because I wanted to just bow down to it, but because if I didn't, I would have had to challenge the head over an issue that basically didn't have very much significance. And if I ended up having a bad working relationship with the head, then it wouldn't be just me who suffered, it would be the department, and the department had to be more important than a petty issue like ties. Now Jim, the pottery teacher, refused to wear a tie.

The responsibility for other people's welfare in a school where there were cut backs and threats of redeployment influenced Mr Redford's behaviour. He described the way his attitudes had changed as the environment in which education operates had changed. When he went for interview for his first teaching job, there were five candidates. He was the only qualified art teacher among them, and he had some supply teaching experience. He knew his chances of getting the job were high.

When I went for my first job, I was a student, and I'd got long hair. At the interview, they called me in, and said they were going to offer me the job. They said, 'there's just one thing. We have found that teachers with long hair have discipline problems, and would you be prepared to have your hair cut, to accept the job?'. So I said 'I don't know if I would say it now. As a matter of fact I was going to have it cut last week, because I wanted it short, but if your comment is indicative of the kind of constraints you place on personality in the post, then I will have to turn down the post'. And the Headmaster said 'Oh, no, no!' (laughs). But the point was you see, I'd given him room for manoeuvre, so I didn't lose face, and he didn't need to, because it wasn't worth losing the teacher you wanted, because I'd already said, I'd have my hair cut. I think you'd be pretty foolish to say that now, because there would be twenty other people ready to jump over you. Then, teachers were few and far between.

Mrs Castle was also aware of such pressures, and she also chose to adapt to them. Again, appearance was a prominent issue. As she got older Mrs Castle (64, retired, art) dressed more conventionally:

> I think that if you tried too hard to look like the kids, like trendy lecturers in college, they try too hard to look like students, I think the kids think they are a bit weird, it is them that are allowed to look like that and not the staff. I think if there wasn't a generation gap, one ought to create one, because it is part of life, and children want there to be a generation gap, they miss it if it isn't there.

Her attitude to discipline and pupil deviance had also changed:

> When you are younger, you don't notice if children aren't wearing the uniform. I think young teachers really don't notice. Then I think there is a stage where you do notice but you don't really know what to do about it, and you don't want to do anything about it, you don't see why you should, then there will come a stage where you realize that if you do notice, and it is agin the law, or the rules, that the kid thinks you are a bit soppy if you don't actually do something about it, so that if there are rules, you have to be seen to implement them, and to be willing to say, if they say 'why?', you have got to say 'because it is the rule, and because I say so', and in fact, that is a good enough reason about things being for the good of the community.

Mrs Castle basically accepted that as she got older, she became absorbed into the bureaucracy of the school, and personally responsible for making it work. It indicates the effect an organization can have upon personal development (Merton, 1957).

Again as she got older, Mrs Castle (64, retired, art) found her relationship with pupils had to change:

> They want to be friendly with you, but they want to know that you are older than them. They don't want any nonsense about you thinking you are the same as they are, so I think that a lot of young teachers about student age try a bit too hard to be too much like the children. The children, I suspect, think they are rather foolish, so a bit of a rift is quite desirable perhaps. I don't think it hinders the learning process.

Much of what Mrs Castle was saying here went against the image of herself she put forward in her early teaching career. She explained the change in attitude in terms of generational change.

> As you go on teaching, I mean you do adopt different attitudes. Certainly as I went on I think I became a lot more committed and I

accepted myself as a teacher. I think when I first started I did not want to be a teacher either: I don't think I did want to be part of the establishment. I wanted to be me. I wanted to be a bit of a tearaway, and so on. But I think at some stage or other, probably in my thirties, I realized that actually, if you accepted what you were, you enjoyed it a bit better. Like, if you stopped apologizing to non-teachers for being a teacher, you actually found non-teachers who felt it was quite nice to be a teacher; you didn't have to apologize; and also, if you were part of the establishment you might just as well be a part of it and get on and do it properly instead of pretending not to be.

Mrs Castle thought it was specifically a result of 'getting older':

I think it was just that you got older; your attitudes change and also, seeing younger teachers perhaps doing precisely what you did and being a bit irresponsible, feckless, and not pulling their weight in the teaching situation, in the community, in the staff room; seeing them sort of 'scamping their duties', being late to register. Yes, I think it is seeing other people committing faults that were your own a year or two ago that make you get a bit pious. It is just a process of getting older.

There was for her a specific sense of development, from a first stage adaptation into something rather different. It involved giving some things up, but Mrs Castle felt she had gained things in compensation:

Yes, but also, I realized if I put my back into it a bit, it was easier — that if you worked hard, the lessons went better and so on.

Others, however, like Mr Ray felt unable to give some things up:

As a teacher, I like education, and children a lot more than I like schools and teachers. I have a daydream from time to time of an HMI coming to my lesson, and saying, 'I'm sorry Mr Ray, but you're not a real teacher, are you? You'll have to go'. (Mr Ray, 38, Head of Biology).

Chapter 5

Managerial Contexts

The Headteacher's Influence

Each school has a different atmosphere and it stems from higher up. I mean Roman Girls Grammar School was such a marvellous place to work in because of Miss Jersey, she was a tremendous presence and she had 'em, the girls, and us just like that. She was the school. (Arthur, 69, retired, art)

The Headmaster was very keen on fulfilling the destiny of the school as a technical school, a Technical High School, and he set about turning his school into a first class technical school. Eventually we were, without any shadow of doubt, one of the leading technical schools in the country. (Mr Count, 54, retired, science)

Headteachers generally enjoy a high degree of freedom to organize and administer their schools as they wish. In doing so, they exhibit considerable variation in natures, philosophies, values, and consequently their management styles. This becomes particularly apparent when teachers describe their experiences of working at different schools, or at the same school under different heads. For example:

Atmospheres change through all sorts of factors really don't they? They change, obviously through the staff in the school; they change through a different head having a different emphasis and a different approach and so his or her approach is reflected in the staff in the school ... (Brian, 44, scale 4, Head of Art)

The teachers who were there in Mr Welch's day found that he was interested in them as people, he went out of his way to get to know them. They knew that he'd got standards that he expected them to meet. He made that clear to them, not in any formal sense but in his process of getting to know anybody it would be quite clear to them what Mr Welch's educational principles were and what he was expecting them to do and what standards he expected them to meet ... When Mrs Brown turned up, well, she'd got a different sort of personality altogether. She was concerned, I think, more with the situation of the school than with anything else. The future of the school had been questioned, but it was to continue and she was concerned with building it up ... and consequently she didn't put quite as much pressure on her members of staff as regards the philosophy of education; that, she wasn't particularly concerned with, she was concerned with the development of the place; and building up a sixth-form. Her concerns were more academic you might say, whereas Mr Welch was interested in working towards a 'true comprehensive' ... To some extent she lost touch with the teachers. (Jim, 65, retired, science)

Because they have so much influence it is all the more significant that headteachers determine a substantial part, not only of teachers' occupational careers, but inevitably of other aspects of their lives as well. It is not surprising, then, that research shows teacher morale, motivation, commitment, job satisfaction and career plans to depend, to a large extent, upon the managerial context in which they work (see Hunter and Heighway, 1980; Nias, 1980; Sikes, 1984a).

How, therefore, does a head's influence as the main immediate determinant of that context potentially extend over a teacher's life?

Appointments and Promotions

The most important influence is over appointments and promotions — and hence over teachers' salaries and life styles. This is perhaps the major reason why some teachers feel that the promotion system is unfair (Sikes, 1984), for, in many schools teachers suspect that heads develop latent status hierarchies which reflect and support their own orientations. At the same time, however, it is important to consider that it is perhaps part of the head's role to be a focus for dissatisfaction of all kinds.

Appointments and promotions are, of course, an extremely sensitive issue. Material rewards and status are at stake, and it is possible that people 'account' for their failures to progress in ways that do not reflect on their own possible inadequacies (Lyman and Scott, 1970). On the other hand, it is generally accepted that the system in teaching is open to abuse, and teacher unions have made recommendations as to how this might be avoided (NAS, 1979; NUT, 1981). And yet, teaching is not alone among occupations in having a 'seamy' side to promotion (Dreeben, 1970, p. 178). Bearing these points in mind, the following quotes should be read as opinions and perceptions rather than as factual, objective statements. They do illustrate, however, some of the more common areas of concern that have a relevance for subjective appraisals of career. Formal qualifications are often believed to be regarded as more important than relevant experience:

> I don't think in this school a person without a degree would be appointed to a senior position. And I think that's a sad thing. (John, 44, scale 4, Head of Art)

and teachers of certain subjects may receive preferential treatment (see also Chapter 7).

Sometimes candidates for posts discover that particular attributes, unrelated to the job they are applying for, are an advantage.

> It was only after I started at Sylvan that I found out from another member of staff what the score was, I didn't even understand why I was asked about rugby when I was in the interview ... It's an old local joke, he had a staff who had to be interested in rugby because he wouldn't play football you see. I went through the interview being very naive about all this, didn't know a thing about it and the first thing he said to me when I'd been appointed was, 'I think you'll like the set up down here', and I thought he meant the chemistry, 'because', he said, 'we've got county players in the PE Department'. And that really shook me in a way you know, I was a rugby player, yes! And it made me wonder why I'd got the job. (Dave, 44, senior teacher, Head of Science)

Discrimination on grounds of race and sex is believed to occur. People who suspect that they are perceived to be a threat to the Head's authority also feel that they are likely to be disadvantaged:

> I'll never get on in this school ... for a start I think the Head likes conformists and I don't think he would consider that I was and also I sometimes say things perhaps I ought not to say if I don't agree with something. (Ann, 43, scale 1, art)

Similarly, Keith felt there was no promotion for him at his present school 'for a number of reasons, partly because I don't get on with the Head'.

> I have applied for jobs and I have been stopped, yes, to be honest, because I am a union executive man. I discovered on one occasion that the Headmaster stopped me from getting the job. You know, you get this business of the private phone call. I discovered this from one of my referees when he retired, who was also a Head as it happens. There was nothing I could do about it, nothing I could say about it. Well, I mean you accept it to a certain extent. I also discovered that after the Headteacher had died, that on one particular occasion that the NUT girl and myself had had to go and present the staff views to him, that he had made a note in his own private notebook that neither of us should receive any further promotion. Now it may have been pure

coincidence but it just so happened it was dated the day after we'd been. I discovered that two years later. So what? It's just one of those things, I mean, it doesn't really bother me ... It did at the time ... I was blazing mad. (Brian, 44, scale 4, Head of Art)

On an (unsuccessful) interview for a deputy headship Ray (39, scale 3, Head of Biology) said that he got what was to him the surprising impression that his MEd and his ideas and interests in education disturbed the interviewing head.

For heads to say that people are a threat to them strikes me, it's obviously psychological, there are obviously status things involved in headships which I have no perception of. I would have thought, from a head's point of view, that they get people with ideas round them and milk them if you like.

On the other hand, there are stories of heads giving glowing references to teachers they didn't want in their schools. Jim (65, retired, science) tells one:

I remember there was one member of staff who didn't who couldn't, meet the Head's standards, who left. He wasn't thrown out or anything like that, but it was quite obviously the situation was such that, the individual found it much better to apply to another school for another job, and he had no difficulty in getting it. I don't know whether that had got anything to say about it, the nature of the reports that were made about him, but he left quite easily.

Timetabling

Blau and Schoenherr (1973) argue that allocation of personnel, which Conway (1980) points out is the essence of timetabling, is the ultimate mechanism of organizational power and control. If the Head does not do the timetable himself he usually delegates it to a deputy, whose job may be defined in terms of this responsibility. Managerial decisions about timetabling, the content of the curriculum and pupil academic and pastoral organization, determine the teachers' job content.

It's no good saying, as the management people will ... say that you're not a good scientist if you can't teach at least the third year in the sciences. I'll resist integration but I know I'm under pressure to go into integration, not from the science staff, but from what is called 'rationalization in the curriculum'. In other words, 'We can't fit separate sciences into the curriculum'. (Dave, 44, senior teacher, Head of Science)

Headteachers also have control over capitation which again can have a crucial effect on job content and working conditions. Jim (65, retired, science) hypothesizes about how heads might use capitation as a 'control mechanism'.

> This business of capitation, and how much money's available. In the past it was something heads used to play very close to their chest, nobody really knew how much was available, or how it was split up and so on and many heads were very careful to make sure people didn't know. Matters have now come to a stage where everybody wants to know and does know and it becomes a matter of argument about whether such a department is justified in having this, that or the other and are they advised to put up for it. Of course that might be a way of control, it's one way of controlling the heads of department, give them something to fight over and work about. Particularly if you sit at the top there saying 'well, you've all had your say and now I think for the benefit of the school, for this reason, it'd better be this way'. And after everybody's spent all their passions arguing they're left with what they're given. I think the history teachers are the people who come out of it best because they've really studied how societies have operated. They know the strategies.

Influences on Management

Contraction

Contraction has reduced the number of promotions and appointments Heads are able to make, and the amount and the nature of the resources they can allocate, but this does not mean that their power has been diminished. Indeed the scarcity value of what they do have to distribute has actually increased it. Hunter and Heighway (1980), for example, hypothesize that 'given the resulting constraints and possibilities of falling rolls and economic cuts ... the prime (but not only) source of higher (teacher) morale and motivation lies initially within the school itself rather than central government or local authority centres' (p. 484). The onus of maintaining and finding ways of increasing teachers' motivation, morale and job satisfaction, would, therefore, seem to fall on the Head and management team who are, after all, appointed to oversee the running of the school. (cf Kelsall and Kelsall, 1969, p. 31; Watts, 1980). The teachers themselves were quite clear on this.

> Well as I see it, it is within the brief of the Head, and senior management staff, to monitor staff morale and motivation. This, I think, is a large and an important part of their job. Crucial these days really. (Ray, 39, scale 3, Head of Biology)

Comprehensivization

The jobs of the Head and management team are perhaps more difficult in a comprehensive than in a selective school. This is because the selective schools were characterized by more exclusive functions and philosophies. Generally the grammar schools and technical grammar schools were oriented to achieving success, in terms of exam passes in academic subjects.

> In the grammar school where I first worked I don't think that there were many influences other than hard graft, that kids had to work hard. The Headmaster's philosophy was, 'it doesn't matter what you teach them as long as it's hard'. He was a mathematician, and he believed that you really had to push them, which grammar schools were, weren't they, you push kids along. (Dave, 44, senior teacher, Head of Science)

> The school was originally known as the Technical High School for Boys and then it became known as the Technical Grammar School for Boys. They incorporated 'Grammar' purely to indicate to people that we did 'A' levels ... at one time we were getting six or seven a year into Oxbridge'. (Mr Count, 54, retired, science)

In the secondary moderns, the emphasis tended to be on social relationships and social control (Reynolds and Sullivan, 1981, p. 124) — although there were those which attempted to ape the grammar schools.

> Relationships were most important. And schools (secondary moderns) were known for things like their band, or for the fact they went to a camp each year. Social things like that. (John, 44, scale 4, Head of Art)

Comprehensive schools do not serve such relatively homogeneous clienteles. They have to cater for the different needs, abilities and expectations, of pupils, teachers, parents, employers, government, the public. The expressed aims of the comprehensive have, therefore, tended to be in terms of general principles, such as 'equality of opportunity' and the 'development of the full potential of the child' (see Ross, Bunton, Evison and Robertson, 1972).

Daunt (1975) suggests that the 'successful comprehensive' is characterized by innovation, and initiative for 'both pupils and teachers'. The unsuccessful comprehensive by comparison lacks, Hargreaves (1982) hypothesizes, a sense of community. Central to both of these definitions is the notion of a sense of shared understandings, a shared sense of purpose and central, clearly defined, generally accepted aims. From the point of view of teachers especially those who initially worked in selective schools, these have often not been developed.

As an illustration, it is interesting to consider what four teachers had to say about the same comprehensive school. Sally and Margery were, respectively, previously from a secondary modern and a grammar school which had amalgamated, and both were reasonably content. Mr Count and John were not. Mr Count was originally at the same grammar school as Margery, and John from a secondary modern — not Sally's. Both men had had extremely satisfying careers up until comprehensivization but from then on things had gone wrong for them; for Mr Count, because pupils could not cope with, or did not respond positively to, the 'grammar school' ethos which the Head wanted for the comprehensive; and for John, because the grammar school ethos and the problems of working on a split site made it difficult to develop the relationships he values and because he felt that so many pupils were 'doomed' to failure.

> The atmosphere, or the ethos that the head wants for the school is that of a grammar school. There's the banding, the house system, the academic gowns and the emphasis on 'academic' success. There's quite a lot of teachers who think that all this means that the kids in the lower band get rather a rough deal. There isn't really anything for them. (Sally, 40, scale 3, art, Head of Year)

> It isn't a grammar school, unfortunately, and I think one of the problems is keeping what should be the grammar school stream afloat as it were. There are lots of interesting little options going for the less academic, like courses on life skills and different modular teaching and various things. I think what it boils down to is the difficulty of keeping a tight academic top. We haven't done too badly yet, there are still pupils who do get excellent results at the top, but I think too many of them look rather enviously at the easier life a bit further down. (Margery, 45, scale 3, Head of Chemistry)

> I retired when the school went comprehensive . . . when there was the addition of people further and further down the academic scale . . . the academic ethos had been considerably diluted and I didn't like this . . . I wasn't happy there any longer; it wasn't a school I knew, and I couldn't see any alteration taking place, any betterment. (Mr Count, 64, retired, science)

> I don't like coming to school any more, I used to look forward to it . . . The role of the teacher as I see it, should be building some sort of relationship with pupils, but you can't do that any more . . . it's partly to do with the split site, and partly to do with the way the school's been organized, and the things that seem to be seen as important now. (John, 44, scale 4, Head of Art)

All of these teachers are critical of basic characteristics of their school. Taken together, their opinions suggest that management, the Head in particular, has failed to organize the full ability intake in a way that accommodates their different perspectives. To please everyone on all accounts is probably an impossible task. However, if it is accepted that it is management's role to strengthen and build up a school's character then it is important to work towards certain goals and a sense of unity. How can this be done? How do heads manage schools?

Management Styles

While we did not set out with the intention of classifying headteachers or their management styles our evidence suggests that Weber's typology of legal authority offers a valuable frame of reference. Of course the types Weber describes are 'ideal', that is they are unlikely to be exactly reflected in the real world. Rather, it is on the basis of the characteristics of the style, the way in which heads approach and perform their managerial role, that they have been classified.

The Charismatic Head

Charisma is rare, circumstantial and precarious for, as Weber noted, the success of the charismatic leader depends on those to whom the mission is addressed recognizing the charismatic claim (see Weber 1948, pp. 244–7). Charismatic heads can communicate their ideas and enthusiasms to their staff who are impressed and influenced and who are then prepared to work together and to work hard because they become fired by the same vision.

> It took us about five or six years to achieve a good school, but we made it. We definitely made it ... it was all inspired by the headmaster. He had a very clear idea of where he wanted his school to go and the standards he wanted, and we had meeting after meeting, maybe during break, say in the morning, and he would come down and he would address the whole staff, setting out the sort of standards that he wanted to achieve and he wanted us to achieve, and it may sound corny, but he was an absolute inspiration this fellow, he was an absolute dynamo and he would just talk for about half an hour and at the end of that time you were almost on your feet shouting 'Yes, let's get at it', he had that sort of effect. His personality wasn't all that impressive: he couldn't come into a room and everybody would stop talking. He was very quiet, almost diffident, but when he was fired with his ideas of the way he wanted his school to go he could communicate these to people and, the longer he went on the more his personality grew, as it were, and the greater effect he had on the staff, and so in the end we were all virtually on our feet cheering 'Let's get at it'. This is where it was built up, through his enthusiasm which he communicated to the staff. (Mr Count, 54, retired, science)

> The Head, he was something very, very special. He was a man with a

drive, he turned that school into something ... He wanted a youngster to come out of his school capable of standing on their own two feet and talk, this was more important to him than academic results. He had people who worked with him who were prepared to assist him on these sorts of lines. He was a man with a vision and he shared it. (Jim, 65, retired, science)

It seems that working for a charismatic Head is a very special experience, one by which teachers measure their job satisfaction and commitment under other heads. Usually nothing ever meets the same standards. They will never again have such an intense and rewarding experience, and they find it difficult to come to terms with this.

Changes in the composition and nature of staff and/or pupils, circumstantial changes within or outside the school, can mean that the organization breaks down, that there is a weakening of commitment to what were the central aims, with the result that charisma is no longer recognized.

The process is described by Mr Count (54, retired, science), whose description of a charismatic Head has already been quoted.

The original ethos of the boys' Technical Grammar School was to do with technical and applied science, it was academic. Then we amalgamated with the girls' school. The two heads were to be joint heads which they were for a while. Then the boys' school Headmaster left, he went to work in a Polytechnic and the lady who was Headmistress of the girls' school she stayed on for an extra year and then she retired and the chap who was Deputy Head became Head, and still is. But by then of course the school had lost this technical excellence and its original ethos; it became just a straight down the middle grammar school, and then later a comprehensive.

The Traditional Authoritarian Head

... the Head at Relfield was, I suppose, best described in the nicest possible way, as one of the old school.... He was never a pressurizing chap, but he was a very traditional sort of Head. He ran his school along traditional lines ... it was a reasonably tough, boys' secondary modern. He ran it very efficiently. (Brian, 44, scale 4, Head of Art)

Some heads favour the traditional authoritarian approach. They rely on the authority traditionally associated with their position as Headteacher, and their belief in the legitimacy of this authority lends conviction and strength to what is frequently a comparatively strong personality. Others also believe in and therefore validate this authority. Older and retired teachers in particular say that an authoritarian, matriarchal or patriarchal Head was what they expected and accepted as a taken-for-granted aspect of school life. The elementary school Head Arthur (69, retired, art) describes is archetypal:

> The headmaster sat at his desk in the middle of the hall on a raised platform. You weren't allowed to put illustrations on the inside windows of the classroom because that stopped him having a look in. He was a real whip cracker and every three-quarters of an hour a bell went. He rang the bell. That meant finish whatever you're doing, finish your English, put your English books away, get out your History books. As soon as that bell rings you weren't allowed to overflow.

Although such a strict regime would probably meet opposition today, there is evidence to suggest that many teachers do appreciate and prefer a relatively authoritarian Head (cf Banks, 1976; Dreeben, 1970; Richardson, 1973; Watts, 1980).

> Mrs Brown, who was really the typical sort of hierarchical figure, but good at that, left and the next Head was Mr England who, in some ways has the sort of approach, 'What are we going to do about this? It's not just me who's responsible' people don't like it, they like to be told what to do. (Jim, 65, retired, science)

Similarly pupils prefer 'strict' teachers (cf Musgrove and Taylor, 1969; Woods, 1979) — partly because it decreases personal responsibility and can provide a sense of security. Margery's (45, scale 3, Head of Chemistry) opinion would seem to be fairly common.

> I think all the heads I've worked for have been fairly authoritarian really ... the only exception was one lady I had ... who just wasn't up to it and she wasn't authoritarian, and it was a muddle really, but the others I've worked for have all been authoritarian first, with a little bit of paternalism and goodwill thrown in ... I think this is probably an inevitable role for an efficient Head because everyone's got to take ultimate direction from somebody and it's no good sort of squabbling among yourselves as far as departments and resources are concerned. Someone has got to say something! Yes, I think almost all the heads I've worked for have found it impossible to delegate, and that's not a good thing always.

Arthur's Head would probably have been taken aback had anyone even suggested that he might delegate some of his responsibilities, but now attitudes are different. Teachers frequently complain that pupils are less inclined to accept authority. Yet their own perceptions of authority have also changed. Authoritarian heads recognize this but while they may be willing to delegate, they do so very much on their own terms.

In their schools, there tends to be little ambiguity, especially from the Head's perspective. Aims and rules are clearly defined, pupils and teachers know what is and is not required of them. They attract certain teachers, those who are not prepared to comply are not made welcome: and it may be made clear that if they stay at the school they will be unlikely to get promotion!

> I wouldn't complain or criticize any aspect of school organization, not when I'm on scale 1, I might not get promoted ... It would be treading on very dangerous ground if you did anything like that in school, dangerous insofar as you wouldn't get promoted afterwards if you ever overstepped the mark. (Jan, 24, scale 1, art)

However, there has to be a balance of power because a too authoritarian approach can lead to alienation of the 'weaker' side. Jan describes what might be regarded as a threshold situation where it would seem that some teachers, or Jan at least, obey partly because they are ever mindful of management's powers. Pupils have a similar attitude:

> There is a strong ethos here but it's imposed. It's a rigid place, you've *got* to have discipline in the classroom and the staff are disciplined as well. Teachers accept this because we don't have a choice because ... they (head and deputies) can make life infinitely more unpleasant for you than you can for them. Most of it (management's rulings and control) particularly on discipline, I'm 100 per cent behind the powers that be, but there are other niggling little things and I mean no one's going to agree with everything all the time ... We put forward ideas but the ideas are either taken or rejected and if they're rejected, nothing more can be said. OK, you can keep taking the ideas back but as regards the kids, pupils either have a healthy respect or total contempt for the Head, and if they've got total contempt for him they'll show it. (Jan, 24, scale 1, art)

It may be that more pupils, those who for whatever reason are not conventionally successful, those who do not work hard for and pass exams or do not belong to or support the culture that the school represents, have less to lose than most teachers and are therefore more prepared to make their feelings known.

But there can be valuable advantages in working for an authoritarian Head which helps to explain why teachers put up with the less attractive aspects. For instance:

> Here, the standards set by the senior staff are very high so it makes it easier to teach in a school like this, behavioural standards, so you know that any decision you make about discipline will always meet with the Head's approval. This support perhaps means that you're more prepared to go along with other things he does. (Christine, 35, scale 3, Head of Physics)

> People do go along with his rulings because it makes life easy and also particularly on the discipline it does make it easier because quite honestly I'm in agreement with it ... We'll put up with things we don't agree with for the discipline, it's a bargain ... We do talk about

> it, say 'Oh he's been at it again' or something like that, or 'what're we
> going to do now?' On the whole we do anything for an easy life. I
> mean you've gotta work here, there's no point in making it un-
> pleasant. (Jan, 24, scale 1, art)

As a new teacher Jan feels it particularly important to 'fit in' in order to
establish a secure basis for getting on and advancing her career (cf Hanson and
Herrington, 1976, pp. 5–6) but what she says about going for an easy life
reflects the views of teachers at all levels and also of pupils (Measor and
Woods, 1984a) — and perhaps of the majority of people in most social
situations. This is another reason why authoritative heads are able to continue
to be authoritarian.

Yet they don't always get it all their own way. Arthur (69, retired, art),
for example, had discovered that a strategy of suggesting an idea and then
allowing the Head to think it was her own usually got the results he wanted:

> She told me once in a corridor, she said, eight members of the staff
> were men then, and she said 'Do you know Mr Borough, there are
> men on this staff that are afraid of me?' she said, 'there's one there, just
> now, look'. He was going to go right round and come round the
> square and us in this corridor and he saw us talking and he turned
> around and went back, right round the quadrangle. 'He's afraid to
> come by'. I thought, well, you'll never say that about me. So I went
> straight into her with this timetable. I said 'can I remind you about this
> RK business', and she sort of smiles, I said 'we did say it wasn't on . . .
> I'm very cynical and sceptical, I'm not religious, I'll take it but the
> Head of RK doesn't like it'. I didn't have to teach it, she was just
> trying it on, just a bluff. . . . When you stood your ground, and if
> you'd got a logical reason for standing your ground and going against
> her, she wouldn't agree with you there and then, but the next day an
> edict would come out. The very things you'd been arguing were set
> down with her name on the bottom. *She* had decided so and so.
> Everybody was happy. If you could talk sense to her she was very
> good.

The Bureaucratic Head

Charismatic and traditional authoritarian heads rely on themselves, in particular upon being able to project and inculcate in their subordinates an almost
omnipresent sense of themselves. Their authority depends on their continuing
ability to convince subordinates that they have that authority and that they are
a suitable person to have it. Some of the problems associated with these
management styles have already been mentioned, and in any case not every
Head has the inclination or the ability to use them, so, what are they to do?

In recent years, as schools, comprehensives in particular, have become larger and more complex organizations, and managing them has become more complicated, school management has become a growth industry; numerous books on the subject have been written, often by practising heads (for example, Poster, 1976; Marland, 1980) and courses and conferences have been staged, again often with senior school staff playing a prominent part. Within teacher culture school management courses seem to have come to be regarded as 'promotion enhancers' in much the same way as curriculum innovation was during the years of expansion (cf Whiteside, 1978) — and so, many ambitious teachers have taken them.

These courses, and the books, have often extrapolated from business management theory and techniques and favour an approach to 'effective and efficient' school management via bureaucratic systems run by bureaucratic heads.

Even so, substantial authority is traditionally associated with, and is there by definition, in the position and role of headteacher. Thus, the authority of the 'bureaucratic' head is in fact likely to be based on an amalgam of traditional and rational authority. Bearing this in mind, in the interests of clarity we will continue to refer to the 'bureaucratic' head.

Hierarchies, statuses, specialization, the separation of the role from the individual and authority based on rational grounds are characteristics of bureaucracies. Ideally the responsibilities attached to a bureaucratic post are clearly defined (as Weber puts it there is a specified sphere of competence) as is the post's relative position within the hierarchy and the status associated with it. The incumbents of a post can feel secure, knowing their place and what is expected from them. They can also do what is required of them without necessarily agreeing or identifying with it — they can role distance themselves (cf Goffman, 1961) because the post is independent of whoever fills it.

However, it has been suggested that bureaucratic systems are inappropriate in schools (see Lacey, 1983; Lavelle, 1982; Poster, 1976) and, for that matter, in industrial and governmental settings (cf Blau, 1955; Gouldner, 1965). Criticisms tend to focus on two fundamental problems; (i) that because bureaucracies use hierarchical lines of communication they are cumbersome and slow. This may not matter in a stable environment when, according to Burns and Stalker (1961), they tend to emerge, but it may cause problems when changes are taking place, and (ii) that because bureaucratic structures fail to take account of human needs, they easily lead to alienation. With particular regard to schools, and especially schools which are experiencing contraction, bureaucratization can lead to institutional fragmentation and individualized commitment. Examples of what this can mean include:

(i) Traditional systems of communication and sharing ideas can atrophy when peoples' concerns and commitments come to centre only on the areas their job definition and/or the system assigns them to (cf Selznick, 1948 and 1949, on the concept of recalcitrance). For example, when a formalized pastoral care structure was first introduced at Kath's school, teachers were expected to officially report any 'significant' pupils' problems they became aware of to the pupil's Head of Year, who would then decide what action to take and who else to inform. Previously the teachers had used their own discretion based on knowledge of the pupil and the circumstances, about who they told. The new system was supposed to protect the pupil's confidentiality and to ensure they got the maximum help and support. According to Kath it didn't work like this. It took a long time and the Head of Year didn't always know who were the most appropriate people to inform.

(ii)   If an individual wants to advance their career in a bureaucracy, it is usually important for them to conform to rules and regulations, which can mean that innovation and initiative are stifled (see also Merton, 1961, p. 148). Some teachers were of the opinion that the scarcity of promotion posts had led to greater conservatism among their colleagues because fewer people were prepared to innovate and experiment in case they failed and thereby perhaps jeopardized their prospects (Sikes, unpublished work).

(iii) Bureaucratization can encourage boundary maintenance and militate against an integrative and cooperative atmosphere. Members of subject departments can become very insular and protective of their resources and knowledge. This can have a negative influence on relationships and can also be wasteful of resources and time:

> We had a smashing science staff ... and we all very much worked together and we had a Science Department in which we taught physics, chemistry and biology but we really had a Science Department. But at another school I worked at I can always remember asking for discharge tubes ... and I got 'Oh no, we don't have those, no, no, we don't have any'. And it took me six months to find they were in the lab next door, locked in a cupboard. But, they went, 'Oh no, those belong to physics' ... This, to me, was so ridiculous, 'that belongs to physics, that belongs to chemistry, that belongs to biology' and you might only use it twice a year and so on. (Kath, 59, retired, science)

Faculties and departments can also develop and set their own standards and criteria of acceptable behaviour and work levels and requirements for pupils and for staff, as the accounts of three teachers in the same science faculty illustrate.

Dave (44, senior teacher, Head of Science) felt that he made his expectations quite clear to the teachers working in the faculty:

> One of the demands I make on my staff, you see, I say to them 'You will take thirty-six kids in the first year and you'll teach them practical work, and they will do things, and you will mark their books once a week'. You know, I'm a swine ... I have a style of teaching, a

way of going on which I don't like people to come under, come
below. I am told by my Headmaster I set too high standards ... now
he's being very kind there but I am well aware of the fact that, since I
mark every kid's book every week I don't miss out on that, I don't like
to be late for lessons and things of that nature, I am that sort of person,
but that to me is good teaching, its good managerial teaching as well.
It's this getting back to I won't ask my staff to do something that I'm
not doing myself, in that sense, so if I see somebody leaving the, well
if you look at my lab you will see it is neat and tidy, if you look
elsewhere you'll see perhaps it isn't, and er, it's that sort of style. I try
to treat them on the same ground. I don't wear my stripes on my
sleeve, some heads of department do, don't they? You know, you've
been in schools, the Head of Department is obviously Head of
Department and I try not to do that. Anyway, ask the others if I do.

Some members of the faculty did consider the workload to be somewhat
excessive, especially when compared with other faculties within the school:

I really love teaching kids but I'm getting ever so fed up with all the
marking I have to do which is a special feature of this department
because lots of subjects have small groups, because lots of subjects
might teach a class for five or six periods a week and only give one
homework, whereas if we teach a class for two periods a week there's
a homework to that which needs marking. Which means for an hour's
lesson you're gonna have thirty-six books to mark, because we have
big group sizes and try marking thirty-six books in an hour, you
know, that's how long it takes. So for every hour I spend in front of
kids I spend another hour marking books, and that's just to keep my
head above water, that's putting no effort into preparing lessons,
organizing apparatus, preparing courses, preparing syllabuses, preparing exams, writing reports, you know, it gets pretty tedious. (Pete,
25, scale 1, biology)

There is a problem within a school that if you're in a department
where the expectations are high ... and you look outside your
department and you see other areas of the school where the pressure is
considerably less, because the expectations aren't so high and the
instrumental (marking) aspect of the job isn't taken quite so seriously,
you get another problem with motivation that is, if you like bitterness
and cynicism that, you know, the other beggers get away with it and
we're tanning our backsides off! (Ray, 39, scale 3, Head of Biology)

(iv) In a bureaucratically organized school, where strong departmental
      boundaries are maintained, teachers who want to widen the scope of
      their experience, responsibility and influence must seek promotion, or
      move to another school. For instance:

In order to be able to change things, to have any real influence in a school I think you've got to be in a senior position, which is why I'm looking for deputy headships. I mean, I've been on loads of courses since I've been at this school and made reports and this sort of thing, submitted them to curriculum committee and they've discussed them and this sort of thing ... and the impact I have had is zero outside the science department. And you know, it's not all that great outside biology really ... Whereas the language and learning and science course which, I would say was the most critical experience I have had, I produced a very long report for that and tried to circulate it amongst all departments and I tried to get a language across the curriculum movement going and it met with very little success. Now I feel that had I been at, and this might be pie in the sky, I don't know, I mean I have to find that out, but had I been at a more senior level within the school, deputy head level, then I could have had some effect. ... in an ideal world it would be nice to be teaching in a department and have a much freer interchange of ideas and so on between departments, you know, in a Bernstein thing ... to get into a much less structured situation would, I'd say be the ideal, and promotion wouldn't be as important either. (Ray, 39, scale 3, Head of Biology)

Ray's last point is important. It seems that without realistic opportunities to develop their careers, not only in terms of promotion but also by taking on more responsibility and by being in a position to implement change, many teachers say they alter the nature of their commitment to their job, generally by becoming more involved in other areas of their lives, for example with their family, or a hobby.

(v)   If management and organizational decisions and policies differentiate staff, a situation of cliques and cabals can develop (cf Riseborough, 1981) and this is perhaps particularly problematic when there is little or no turnover of staff. As Watts (1974) notes, 'a most unpleasant atmosphere develops in a staffroom divided into cliques'. Such an atmosphere can spread from the staffroom and become a characteristic of a school's character and atmosphere. And if they are 'grumbling' cliques their influence is likely to be negative (cf Sikes, 1984a). Cliques are not necessarily destructive, nor are they exclusive to bureaucracies. Even so bureaucracies do provide a structure in which an 'us v them', 'management v workers' mentality can easily come to prevail and be characteristic of relationships between, for example, the Head, or the Head and deputies, and the rest of the staff; the heads of department, Head of Pastoral Division and members of the department and pastoral division, teachers and pupils. For instance:

There's very little group feeling in the school. Well, I suppose what group feeling there is 'us against them'. 'Them' are the hierarchy. It's just, 'They're gonna try and make us work and we're gonna sit here and not do anything' ... I think that some people will say, I mean there are, in our particular school, two of the hierarchs, two of the deputy heads are an absolute waste of space. So that cheeses people off no end. Now, if they could see the deputy heads setting an example and really making things buzz and working hard themselves, I think they would be a bit more responsive, but the fact that all the deputy heads seem to do is ask them to do more work, that could be one of the causes. (Pete, 25, scale 1, biology)

The 'hierarchy' are all old cows and boots!! (Laughs) Well, I mean, they've got their job to do but, I mean, sometimes they can be, appear insensitive, but then I suppose they've got to. They've got to maintain their position like we've got to maintain our position with the kids. (Sarah, 25, scale 1, art)

I think an 'us and them' situation is quite tragic, especially when young people see it that way, because how does a school develop? ... I remember in the really early days during the first year of the comprehensive school, and it became apparent that a couple of young men in the Science Department, they hadn't been there long enough to have a view, they weren't allowed to speak ... this was in the Science Department meeting. There were two young women from the girls school who had views just as I, as Head of Department, had views, but these two young men, oh no.... that's what the men in the first year of the comprehensive thought. These two young men hadn't been there long enough to have views and thoughts. This was a real eye-opener to me. (Kath, 59, retired, science)

Such attitudes are likely to be maintained as newcomers, of whom there are likely to be few in any case, are 'encultured' and, perhaps co-opted into cliques. Some teachers, perhaps especially those who see themselves as 'workers', rather than 'professionals' (see Lawn and Ozga, 1981) seem to see the conflict between management and staff as natural and irreconcilable, and their strategies are accordingly based on this philosophy, which pre-empts mutual trust.

Roy (1983), for instance, writes about 'bridging the gap between management and shop floor, that is the classroom, which sometimes exists' (p. 122) and Brian (44, scale 4, Head of Art), as a union representative had come to feel that teachers had to be on their guard and united against heads.

I got more involved in the union when I began to see that there were various things happening in schools and in education that couldn't just be solved by going to a representative of management, usually the head, and saying 'please will you consider this as an idea', because all that happened, you got this sort of rather authoritarian figure who regarded you as completely out of order for questioning anything, and it sort of began to dawn that the one way to sort of perhaps achieve, just a simple thing like getting someone to listen to you and to actually appreciate that maybe one in ten of your ideas were workable, was simply to approach it as a body, staff, but only so far and that sometimes you need to do that as a body, teachers ... We had this head who decided that he wasn't going to accept that lunch time duties were voluntary it wasn't going to be binding on him and he was going to have everyone doing lunchtime supervision as of his right to dictate ... things like that made me aware that if you weren't careful you could end up by worsening conditions, not only for yourself but for people following you ... teachers are not above society, but they're not below society, they're entitled to the same breaks from their work as other workers ... These sound trivial issues but to people involved in the game they're big issues.

Participation: an Alternative to Bureaucracy?

According to Daunt (1975) and Hargreaves (1982), a school in which there are strong divisive cliques is unlikely to have a positive atmosphere or to be 'successful'. In such a school, teachers' commitments will probably tend to be individualized or partisan and the satisfactions of participating and working in a purposeful community will not be available. One of the main responsibilities of a Headteacher is to make sure that staff have a common challenge, a shared aim that cuts across the boundaries of any coterie. But how are they to discharge this responsibility? People's views and expectations concerning authority and the amount of control they should have over the various aspects of their own lives have changed (cf Hunter, 1980).

I think in the early days of my teaching you did as you were told ... I didn't expect to be involved in devizing courses and so on when I started. I think they expect more involvement these days. (Dave, 44, senior teacher, Head of Science)

Well, in school in the past, as I say, probably the Head was the policy maker and I suppose as a young teacher one tended to accept the Head as the senior manager, as the policy maker, and also, because most of the heads were considerably older when they were appointed than they are now, one I suppose accepted the fact that they had, if you like, more experience and wisdom — an odd word, perhaps, but it probably dates me; but one accepted that, I think, and so you went along with it and probably assumed 'Well if they think that's correct they are probably right; let's see'. And yes, by and large, I think teachers did accept them ... I don't suppose everybody agreed with everything *anyone* said or says, but I think they tended to go along with it and work to the best of their ability within it. You see now, as I say you have more consultation generally speaking, although that's not always 100 per cent true, but generally I must say we have more consultation. (Brian, 44, scale 4, Head of Art)

And all the mid-career and retired teachers were of a similar opinion. A possible explanation for this apparent consensus is suggested by Lortie (1975, pp. 55–81), who hypothesizes that the occupational socialization of teachers begins when they themselves are pupils. Pupils learn 'to "take the role" of the classroom teacher, to engage in at least enough empathy to anticipate the teacher's probable reaction to his behaviour. This requires that the student project himself into the teachers position' (p. 62). Pupils observe teachers. They observe relationships. They become aware of the extent of a teacher's power and authority vis a vis themselves, and vis a vis other teachers. To illustrate, most teachers have had experiences when pupils have said things like 'You aren't allowed to hit us, only (the Head of Year, Deputy Headteacher) can do that'. 'You can't make us do that'. 'You're only a new teacher, we don't care what you think'. The point, continually highlighted by our life history data, is that teachers are influenced by their past. They belong to, can draw upon and are influenced by a latent culture based on the experiences and observations of their pupilhood. To some extent partly perhaps because of habituation and the special sense of security the past offers, their perceptions and actions perpetuate the order and norms they experienced as pupils — usually the order and norms of traditional authoritarianism. Nevertheless, regardless of their previous experience, it seems that all teachers *believe* that for the success of the school and for their own job satisfaction, they should be more involved in the running of their school (see also Alutto and Belasco, 1972; Conway, 1980; Roy, 1983; Secondary Heads Association 1980). Bureaucratization does not necessarily preclude this, but it takes some time to organize, involves cumbersome details, elaborate protocol and complex networks of communication, as well as formalizing and thereby depersonalizing the relationships teachers say they value. At this point, we might re-emphasize the need to take a phenomenological approach because, as the following quotes show, teachers' perceptions vary regarding (a) successful management; (b) participation; (c) the role of management staff; (d) management-teacher relations; and (e) the nature of the involvement and the extent to which teachers say they would like to participate.

I mean a Head obviously can, and *should* determine basically what his or her policy is going to be and teachers I think, generally, will go along with policies, sometimes even if they disagree with them they will go along with them ... if there is an apparently good enough reason for change and if it is explained and if it is talked about and if all sides can put their three pennyworth into the pot and then out of that very often comes something that everybody can feel 'Yes, we've all thought about this', and 'Yes, let's not do that but let's do that', and there is a consensus of opinion. And I think that, to some extent, didn't happen when I first started; it was very much a Headteacher determining a policy and saying 'This is the policy', and everybody just went with it. But I think because of all the other reasons for change, people feel that they need to be consulted, they need to discuss changes, they need to be able to suggest changes; they need to feel that they can listen and be listened to, and *not* just totally ignored and have some sort of idea, change, or philosophy dropped on them without really thinking anything about it: What the hell am I doing this for?' That is when you get a problem in a school or anywhere. I don't care where ever. At Leylands, if suddenly management at Leylands want to change everything ·round and never talk about it with the work force then, you get your lay-offs. (Brian, 44, scale 4, Head of Art)

I would never go into a school which had a staffroom where every decision we made had to be by vote and we followed the vote. There's got to be somebody to make decisions ... you can end up with ridiculous situations ... There's got to be a leader, somebody's got to take the can. Everyone should have the opportunity to put their ideas forward and to have them fairly discussed. So I want key figures to manage the school ... but I want them to be perceptive enough to listen to what the people who are actually doing the job feel about the job they're doing. (Dave, 44, senior teacher, Head of Science)

For a scale 1 teacher like me there's absolutely no way anyone's going to listen to anything I say. We have staff meetings once a term, unless there's an extraordinary one called but they're about general things. (Sarah, 25, scale 1, art)

If I went to all the meetings I would have the opportunity to put my point of view and it would be acted upon if it was a worthwhile thing. It doesn't seem to matter so much where things come from. I think nobody bothers where they come from if it's a good idea. There's no sort of 'I didn't think of it so I'm not going to do it'. But I don't go to the meetings because they're getting away from what I'm interested in. It's into more like career teaching ... getting involved with the subject of teaching rather than teaching people art ... I would go to ones ... directly relevant to me but on the whole I don't want to waste my time. I don't want to have to think about some things that aren't involved either for work or what I want to be interested in. (Chris, 28, scale 1, art)

Despite these differences all the teachers we talked to said that they believed that ideally every teacher in a school should be able to feel that everyone was working towards the same aims, that there was consensus of opinion, that there were no secrets, that staff were kept informed about things which were likely to affect them and that mutual support could be counted on. Dave's (44, senior teacher, Head of Science) view is representative:

> I feel that in a school you ought to use your staff by discussing issues with them, major and minor. You might not accept what they say but the fact that they've had a chance to say it, the fact that they've had a chance to argue their case and then you argue your case and then to pick at it has got to bind you together. If you put too much down on them without discussion, then that resentment or disagreement is there and disagreement will become resentment very quickly and you actually cut your staff into factions.

Participation and involvement on the other hand can have an integrative effect, 'in that the requisite cooperation with others ... facilitate(s) the identification and linking of public and private interests' (Hunter, 1980, p. 215). This would thereby reduce management, teacher and inter-and intra–departmental tension and rivalry, for if people feel themselves to be involved in the same enterprise, there is likely to be more communication and hence greater mutual understanding. Furthermore, grumbling cliques would not perhaps be as likely to develop, since if everyone is involved 'we' are not so easily distinguishable from 'them', and there are fewer justifiable grounds for negative criticism.

As Dave (44, senior teacher, Head of Science) saw it:

> If I am not involved, then I'm a shop floor person. I'll snipe, I'll disagree, I will grumble in the staffroom and I won't be so happy about coming to work. I'll enjoy the kids, of course I will, but I won't be so keen to put in time and effort.

and herein lies the clue to why so many teachers appear to favour some form of participation. It potentially offers considerable opportunity for self actualization (cf Maslow, 1943). It also brings responsibility and perhaps the chance to try out one's ideas. These are among the aspects of promotion that teachers value most highly, and it seems that participation can help to compensate for the lack of, and even reduce teachers desire for, scale post promotion (see Sikes, 1984a and 1984b).

By comparison with bureaucratic and traditional authoritarian systems, in which the individual is told what to do and is expected to fulfil the requirements of a pre-specified role which serves the pre-specified aims of the organization, in a participative structure, theoretically at least, the individual contributes to the development of the aims of the organization and then orients what they do towards realizing them. It is this responsive element of participative management, that makes it better able to cope with change. This is because in a bureaucratic, or a traditional authoritarian system, communications are all vertical through a series of defined levels, whereas in participatory frameworks. particular problems can be simultaneously considered in all their aspects, from all perspectives and in relation to the whole situation. Therefore all those involved can state their case and work out the best all-round solution. This process often involves many meetings and much time and therefore calls for considerable commitment. But as Spooner (1979) writes 'the exploited teacher is the committed teacher'. Even so, commitment and satisfaction is less likely if:

(i)   teachers do not see active involvement in policy and decision making as part of their role. Some people sometimes do prefer to be told what to do, perhaps because (a) they might not want, or do not feel capable of taking on responsibility; or (b) they have been socialized into a traditional system', or (c) they may feel that a Head who delegates more than they think he should is not doing his job properly and, in a sense, has abdicated (cf Sikes, 1984a). These teachers may well say they favour participation but in the sense that it means that the Head and the staff are in agreement about aims and goals and are participating in working together, each in their own bureaucratic way within their own sphere of competence, to achieve them.

(ii) teachers feel that not everyone is pulling their weight, particularly with regard to classroom teaching, for example:

> I get very annoyed about it, it's no secret I would walk out into the corridor now and say to the Head, to the Deputy Heads, that I think they get away with murder because they don't do enough teaching ... if I become Deputy Head I will not accept the sort of teaching level they have here which is far too little. I don't believe their job is that difficult and if it is they ought to be doing more at home. (Dave, 44, senior teacher, Head of Science)

(iii) they feel, as Keith did, that less attractive groups are not fairly shared out:

> The people who are on the scale 3s and the scale 4s, they teach mainly the sixth-form and the academic kind of kids and they leave the dim kids for the young teachers to cut their teeth on and you either stand or fall by whether you can cope with these low ability children. (Keith, 39, scale 1, biology)

To be fair, it is perhaps less easy for heads and deputies to commit themselves to a heavy and difficult timetable when they are likely to be called away to deal with other matters (see subject Chapter 7).

(iv) demands, usually with respect to work load, are perceived as unreasonable:

> The demands that the Head puts on teachers are, I think,

completely unreasonable ... I think the trouble with a lot of education is that you know, you read job specifications in the Times Ed. and your mind blows. What do they expect? They want blood as well. And part of my disaffection at the moment is that I feel what the head is getting is, he's getting something on the cheap. You know he's getting one person doing two jobs right? I'm Head of Year and Head of Biology which is very nice for him I suppose and so on, I mean its good experience for me as well but ... (Ray, 39, scale 3, Head of Biology)

It strikes me that they (senior staff) just expect people to work and work and work and they don't consider the consequences of it. Now what they've done this year in this school is generate admin., marking, etc. all of which need to be worked by all members of staff ... and it generates even more work for people who are already pressurized. All this is being thrown down on us and they never consider what it's actually doing to us in terms of morale ... there are loads of people trying to leave. It's just an epidemic that's sweeping through our school. (Pete, 25, scale 1, biology)

(v)   recognition and appreciation are felt to be lacking:

There's no recognition, no appreciation of anything you do. They only come when they want pictures for speech days, or if the governors are coming in. You stop bothering eventually. (John, 44, scale 4, Head of Art)

(vi)   teachers feel that their experience and/or valuable situation specific knowledge are disregarded:

I can accept it if a person said to me 'look, just accept it for a moment, I've got better knowledge than you on this', then I'd be a fool not to take notice of that. But when your experience is thrown out of the window, when the knowledge you have, the knowledge you've built up, the ability you've built up is not accepted, no, I can't accept that easily. (Dave, 44, senior teacher, Head of Science)

(vii)   teachers feel that they are being manipulated and that participation is 'objectively real but subjectively false' (Conway, 1980, p. 213; see also Hunter, 1980, p. 226).

I think it is more noticeable now if we talk about here; we are involved at the moment in complete curriculum changes and OK, we probably would all feel that there should be changes in all sorts of ways, in all sorts of areas, and we all, to some degree are involved, from the most senior right down to the most junior, and so, yes, in that sense there is much more opportunity at the moment for people to say what they think and to state their own preference for any particular way, or whatever. However, I am still sometimes left with the doubt as to whether we are all running around like little goats chasing our tail and somebody is eventually going to give us the bone and say 'Well that's what you are going to have anyway', or whether we actually all *are* going to make a positive contribution. But that's perhaps a bit of cynicism: I don't know. But we seem to be involved in so many groups, sub-groups, sub-sub-groups, working parties, working parties about working parties, and meetings about working parties having meetings about working parties: it gets so involved it becomes a little ridiculous at time. (Brian, 44, scale 4, Head of Art)

It is perhaps at times when some sort of change is being proposed or affected that teachers are most likely to feel that they will not be consulted or that if they are, their contributions will not be valued.

Teachers, Management and Change

Adaptation to Change?

Change of any sort, whether at work, or in any other area of life, provokes anxiety because it threatens a person's life world, their reality, their identity, their sense of security. Even changes that a person deliberately initiates are stressful, so what effect do imposed changes have? How do teachers perceive and adapt to changes at school? To what extent do their adaptations affect the realization of change?

Independently of any 'formal' mechanisms for participation, teachers affect the success or failure of management policies through their response. Whether they 'internally adjust', 'strategically comply' or 'strategically redefine' (cf Lacey, 1977), the way in which they adapt is a consequence of their past, present and expected career experiences and perceptions. For example in the following two quotes Dave (44, senior teacher, Head of Science) and Pete (25, scale 1, biology) both describe respectively their adaptations in terms of their characters:

I conform outwardly because there's no choice. I can't do my own thing in the school ... You also make value judgments on the other people, which is a thing that affects the inner man, and therefore anything that the other person deals with, your value judgments are then changed ... I have different opinions about some people now, and what they say and do I look at in a totally different light to what I did eighteen months ago. I also did something which I thought would be foreign to my character this last year. Being perfectly honest I withdrew my services, in the sense that I didn't agree with the decision, the argument left no doubt of their opinion of my opinion so I said fair enough, you get on with it. It's a question of timetabling quite honestly. I didn't agree with it, I hadn't a chance to explain why I didn't agree.

If there's something I'm supposed to do that I don't really agree with then I'd rather not do it ... the one example that really springs to mind is assemblies. We have to go to assemblies and the kids have to sing hymns. I mean I never sing and I keep getting told off about it 'don't you think you ought to set a good example and sing?' and I say 'No.'. And when they play hell at the kids for not singing, the older kids, I'll challenge 'em and say I don't know why you go on at them because I would do exactly the same, and I do exactly the same. I think you're fighting a losing battle, you're just making them more resentful ... I do go along with some things I don't agree with, some silly little quirks of school uniform that I know I've got to check up on and I occasionally check up on 'em and say 'You shouldn't wear that any more'. But if they keep coming in it I'm not going to say anything. I've done my little bit. Like everything else in life you try and keep everyone happy. I wouldn't want one of the Deputy Heads to come down and say 'so and so's been wearing ten earrings for three months. Have you said anything to her?' I like to be able to say 'Yeh I've said something'. It's compromise all the time I s'pose.

What ostensibly appears to be strategic compliance is usually, in some respects, strategic redefinition. Pete, for example, had personally redefined to suit himself the rules about singing in assemblies and uniform — the former more obviously. His lack of belief in these rules weakened them, not least because pupils were probably well aware of his opinion. Dave, similarly, had outwardly conformed, or strategically complied, but his perception of, and relationships with his superiors had changed. He had personally redefined the situation and this was reflected in his actions.

As it stands, Lacey's model does not differentiate this type of strategy in which the individual outwardly complies with the authority figures definition of the situation but is not in agreement with it, and by their disagreement, reflected in their actions does in effect change the situation. Most teachers do this at some time over certain issues — but it is not always sufficient — and other more obvious and active strategies or combinations of strategies are necessary.

In due course teachers usually let their feelings be known. They don't do it straight away ... I think you find that first of all they accept the set up as it is for a while and they see if they can adjust it to suit themselves, work the system you see, and if they can well nothing happens (i.e. no overt complaints) but if it becomes obvious that the system is a bit rigid and they're not being considered, or their views and ideas are not being considered, then in time . . . if one thing builds up to another, eventually the pressure comes, they eventually find that somebody else feels the same, then they begin to make their feelings felt. (Jim, 65, retired, science)

The way in which management presents itself, its policies and how it justifies these is, of course, a crucial element influencing how teachers respond to them. Brian (44, scale 4, Head of Art) explained why he tended to be initially suspicious of change:

I think heads, the new breed of head, and by that I mean the type of head who appears to be the appointment made today, or in the last four or five years, they seem generally to be the sort of innovator head, people who want to come in and change, almost for change's sake . . . I suppose the older one gets the more difficult it is to come to terms with change, especially if you have been doing something in a certain way for a long time. I suppose when proposed changes are floated — as they are being done at the moment within the school — I suppose I'm suspicious. I am maybe suspicious of the reasons for changing, but that doesn't necessarily mean that I want to block change. I would like to think that I am open to suggestions, whether it is change, or anything else, if there is a good enough reason to do it. If it is just change for change's sake: 'Today is Wednesday. Tomorrow is a different day so we are going to change things', I don't really want to know, for that reason; it is not good enough. There has got to be a justifiable reason for changing and it has got to be a change for the better. Now that doesn't mean to say that I am always right in what I think is better. Often enough I am probably wrong, but it has got to seem justifiable to go along with and participate in changing some-thing; just to change it for the sake of saying you have done something new I don't think is good enough. If what one is doing at the moment works, seems appropriate, I hesitate to say 'gets the results' because that is usually implied by people as being 'Oh yes, we are only talking about examinations', but I don't mean it in an examinations' sense, but if the results that one achieves are as good as one can expect, then I don't see any reason to change something just for the sake of changing it. There has got to be a logical reason for changing things. Nothing else satisfies me. I can't quite see the point in tearing down a system within education, just for the sake of putting something else in its place so that, maybe, the person who wants to put a new system into operation can either go on an ego-trip for themselves, feed off me and live off my back or just experiment and the people caught up in any change, any experiment are the kids and if they are not going to benefit from it, or, if it doesn't look as if they will benefit: one never knows what benefit is going to accrue until you have tried it but if the risks seem to far outweigh the results, or the assumed results, it would be very difficult to persuade me to change. But I *will* change if it seems feasible.

Dave (44, senior teacher, Head of Science) similarly required convincing:

In timetabling, in staffing departments, where somebody's imposed something against my will . . . In areas like that, if I'm allowed to say my piece, if I'm allowed to point out the faults in the other person's argument, and therefore negotiate, whoever, and we've got to use the word, wins, provided I'm allowed to explore it and fight it out and show alternatives, even to my own initial thought, and therefore negotiate, and not lose absolutely, I mean that's normal and you can accept it, but I've found it very difficult to have things imposed on me, particularly now, when there's been no negotiation at all, little discussion, and the discussion has been very one sided, and the change has been against my will, against what I believe to be right.

Yet, even if negotiation is not possible, and if the balance of power does appear to be one-sided, the strategies teachers use to adjust to situations have an important influence on the atmosphere of a school, and can have an influence on the Head's own career. For example:

It's a bit of a difficult thing for a Head to decide how far he allows authority to go out of his hands. If there appears to be a vacuum there's always someone ready to step in and fill it and take over, and then he's lost control. (Jim, 65, retired, science)

The last person anyone went to for advice or help was the head. The school was in a roughish sort of area and the kids were rough. The Head didn't have any discipline, he took a gentle approach, tried to reason with them. And of course this didn't work, so the deputies had to take over. They supported teachers on matters of discipline. (Helen, 40, scale 3, Head of Art)

The way in which a traditional authoritarian head can continue because his style has pay-offs for the teachers has already been described (see also Sikes, 1984a, for a description of how teachers can have a negative influence on the career experiences of a head they perceive as having inappropriate ideas).

Change and Tradition

So far we have only considered internal changes and situations initiated or provoked by senior staff themselves. It is, perhaps, particularly difficult for Heads who have to manage an externally imposed change, such as comprehensivization, or, as is likely to become more common, school amalgamations and reorganizations changing the nature of the school, for example, from

11–18 to 11–16. Such changes can have an enormous impact upon all aspects of school life. Here, we will look at just one aspect, tradition.

Change and reorganization threaten traditions. Traditions can be a central aspect of a school's atmosphere. They can be viewed, too, as a sort of informal, though nonetheless effective, manifestation of the control system and can therefore be very useful as a management tool (Bell and Grant, 1974). Traditions are consensual rituals. Knowing about the traditions, learning what is expected is a rite de passage: being able to do what is required, almost as unconsciously as if it were natural, is proof of membership. It also, and this is of central importance to the concept, provides a sense of security. Mr Count (54, retired, science) explains:

> If there is a certain pattern to events in the school, of whatever nature they are, then, within the school environment a person is likely to feel more secure because he knows what is going to happen and can rely on this sort of thing. And I think this is possibly what appealed to me. Perhaps it was the security of it; that I knew what to look forward to and I enjoyed carrying on traditions ... traditions mean that you grow up expecting to do and expecting to take part in certain things and I think that this is why they are important to a school to give a sense of continuity and community.

Staff play a critical role in initially creating traditions (cf Berger and Luckmann, 1967). Mr Count (54, retired, science) describes how:

> We didn't sit down and say 'What traditions are we going to establish?', but the first thing we had to do was if you like, establish an academic tradition. People came here to work and therefore we had to offer them suitable courses. So I suppose we established that tradition first. The atmosphere was one of work mainly. Then the other things grew quite naturally. At the end of the first term, the Headmaster and his wife had a sherry party for the staff, this sort of thing. We had a concert; we had a carol service to which wives and families were invited and it became very much a family sort of atmosphere. I think that first term established Christmas in the school and the fact that the families were always welcome in the school, parents as well as members of staff, wives and so on. Then gradually the emphasis on the syllabus side began to emerge as being science and craft combining together to become the 'technical subjects' — and so that tradition was established very early on, the first year almost, or two. But then other things came into being like the staff cricket team; things like house activities were gradually built up. I suppose again, modelled on the public school as much as possible, or the traditional grammar school, let's say.

And it is largely the teachers who maintain them — for instance:

> Things like the Christmas decorations, it's an awful fag and very
> difficult on a split site school to organize it and the kids who take part
> in it are really getting to the cynical age about Christmas decorations,
> and yet because I've always done it I know that once I stop doing it
> I'm giving in to pressures which keep saying inside me 'Oh it's a fag,
> it's a fag'. But I keep doing it because I think it's important that, for
> myself, and for the subject and the kids. You're advertising the subject
> when few other people are prepared to. And it's a positive thing, kids
> will remember it, it'll be part of their experience of school and it may
> positively affect the attitude towards school they have when they are
> parents. (John, 44, scale 4, Head of Art)

As John suggests, tradition relies on repeated celebration and either the
support and belief of those celebrating, or a strong custodian who can enforce
celebration, though in these circumstances, the spirit may be lost. Traditions
can be about any aspect of school life. According to what teachers say,
traditions can reflect and strengthen shared values, understandings and aims.
They can give participants a sense of purpose and belonging and encourage
commitment. But they can also become out-moded and inappropriate. If
traditions ossify and are not revised they can become the foundation for a
clique divided staff and school, with factions for and against. As those for the
traditions are likely to be older and to have been at the school or in teaching
longer, a division in terms of age is also a probability. Thus, when Roman
Comprehensive School was formed by the amalgamation of grammar and
secondary modern schools, the majority of senior positions, including the
headship, went to ex-grammar school staff who brought with them and
perpetuated their traditions and values:

> The wearing of academic gowns surprises me and really gets up my
> nose. One of the features of the school calendar is speech day which
> the staff are asked to attend in academic dress and I just cannot find
> any excuse for such behaviour ... to insist that staff attend in their
> own time and how they dress on that occasion! I don't, I put my suit
> on for that one night. I'm entitled to wear academic dress but I never
> have and I never will and I think, in a comprehensive school, to parade
> around with coloured hoods and gowns is, is dreadful I think, it really
> turns me over. And this morning, the sight that you saw (people
> wearing gowns to assembly) when the comprehensive school came
> into being, that shocked me too, because I thought it was perpetuating
> a thing which we're supposed to have just abolished, the elitism, not
> of the school but of a section of the school, of the staff within the
> school, that there's an elite section, those who've chosen to train in
> one way rather than another way. (John, 44, scale 4, Head of Art)

Progress and development becomes difficult in such situations.

On the whole, it would seem that most of our teachers want what Argyle (1972) calls 'democratic leadership.' 'The democratic leader really does lead and sees that decisions are taken and carried out — but he involves the group in these decisions' (p. 148). So, the major task of management would appear to be creating a common challenge and facilitating the development of an atmosphere and of the mechanisms whereby teachers can get together to create traditions, a working consensus, and a sense of purpose appropriate to the circumstances. It does seem, from our research at least, that a participative, organic type structure is most likely to be successful in opening up more opportunities for personal fulfilment for all staff, and in eliciting the sort of commitment to a community that Dave (44, senior teacher, Head of Science) describes:

> Teachers can contribute to building up a sense of community. It's many-faced isn't it? You can go to the text books and other jargon phrases you know 'A caring nature'. What does that mean? But it's there and it has to be there. Everybody working with commitment; and not at the same level but with commitment. Not idling along. People not stopping off when they have, you know, a sore finger; that commitment to your colleagues and the kids, of coming in when you're a little bit off colour you're going to come in. When you're really off colour you stop off because it's better to. Of working together completely, of having some common standard, common approach.

Chapter 6

The Pupils' Influence

Pupils are undoubtedly an important influence upon teachers' career perceptions and experiences. After all, people can only become teachers because there
are pupils to teach in school, and, while there are many reasons for taking up a
teaching career, it seems unlikely that any intending teacher does not recognize
and look forward to contact with pupils as a major component of the job. It is
so obvious that it may be taken for granted; and this may help account for the
comparative neglect in research of the influence of pupils on the teacher career
(though see Becker, 1952; Grace, 1978; Beynon, 1984; Riseborough, 1983).
Furthermore, pupils have often been seen in educational research as passive
subjects with teachers characterized as the initiating actors (Riseborough,
1983). From this perspective teachers are a part of the school as experienced by
pupils. If the focus turns to teachers' experiences then pupils become part of
the school as experienced by teachers and we are better able to see them as
initiating actors with teachers as reactors.

To date, this perspective has perhaps best been represented in autobio-
graphical accounts (for example, Blishen, 1955), but these lack comparative
and critical analysis. What they do illustrate, however, is the potential effect
pupils can have on classroom interaction. As Arthur (69, retired, art) said:

> You've got to know what's going on in the kid's mind, you've got to
> understand the kids, plus the fact if you like kids they can sense it, if
> you are hostile to kids they can sense that too and to hell with all
> cooperation if they don't want to cooperate they won't.

Becker and Strauss (1956) noted that 'a frame of reference for studying
careers is, at the same time, a frame for studying personal identities'. This is
because new experiences and changes in status within social relationships
require the individual to 'gain, maintain and regain a sense of personal
identity'. Identity is never gained nor maintained once and for all (Becker and
Strauss, 1956; Erikson, 1950, p. 57). Through their interactions with teachers,
pupils influence teacher identities over time. As Pollard (1980) writes 'The
issue here is that of the degree of maintenance of a particular self-image or

belief compared with pragmatic adaptation to situational necessities ... This occurs a lot with teachers who recognize the discrepancy between educational ideologies and practical realities' (p 37). Pupils are very practical realities, and, in adapting to them teachers are, in effect adapting their identities — not always in a way that they would have predicted or that they find to be totally satisfactory.

So what happens to teachers? What do pupils do to them? What do they want from teaching in terms of what it means to them to work with pupils in school and to be and be seen as a teacher?

Pupils and Job Satisfaction

A Good Pupil Response

Most of our teachers looked for a great deal of their job satisfaction from relationships with pupils. One teacher spoke for many when he said:

> a good pupil response is what you talk about absolutely ad infinitum at college. And quite a lot after too!

What counts as a 'good pupil response' and what constitutes the nature of a satisfactory relationship varies, both between individual teachers, and for the same teacher at different times. It can be to do with successfully passing on and sharing subject knowledge, with getting pupils through exams, with preparing them for adult life with mutual enjoyment and fun in each other's company, and, especially for older teachers with hearing about how they have got on since they left school.

> I like kids. I used to take parties in Derbyshire hiking. I've filled my car up with kids and gone painting and sketching on Sundays and Saturdays and all that, and I used to organize school excursions, local at first and then abroad ... I remember a group of seven sixth-form girls I had for 'A' level art. I had a look at what they'd been doing, I thought God help us! This lot! There isn't one that really should be taking the exam or even the course (but I got going on them) and I dropped bow-legged, all seven of them passed. I've been as chuffed as a devil since about that, I reckon that I passed that exam, they didn't. I spoon fed them that much that they got through ... I've often said that teachers ought to pay entertainment tax because they, if they enjoy the job, the playback if you like, the compensations you can't measure in terms of LSD the job satisfaction if you like the job that's it, the job satisfaction is tremendous. I've been lucky I've always managed to get plenty of that. (Arthur, 69, retired, art)

> It is very entertaining. No, I mean, I like young people, I like the dynamism of it. I like the challenge of their young minds really. I

mean, it sounds very airy-fairy, but I get a big kick out of discussing points with pupils and seeing the intellectual process working in them, and them using me as a sounding board. I think this is very exciting. (Ray, 38, scale 3, Head of Biology)

I wanted to explain my subject to people who know nothing, or very little, about it. It's the explanatory process . . . The reward of the job is that you get people in at, say 11, and after you'd had them for five years, they'd gone through the process, they had some academic success and knowledge of your particular discipline and just getting them there, looking at a particular problem and tackling it from perhaps two or three different points of view, different ways of explaining things, was what I enjoyed. (Mr Count, 54, retired, science)

Jim (65, retired, science) actually wondered about the ethics of getting so much job satisfaction from pupils:

Teaching satisfied, it satisfied. But it's a damn selfish view, what satisfactions I get isn't it? . . . I mean, teaching's very selfish in a way . . . You use other people to find yourself in some way . . . When I say that teaching is in some way very selfish, I mean it's because you think that it is a good thing to educate other human beings. It gives you that feeling of having done something. I sometimes wonder whether we are justified using people to satisfy yourself to that degree. I think the thing to do is to think you haven't done anybody much harm and perhaps you've done some good. You've done yourself some good at any rate. But I think this applies to everything anybody ever does, doesn't it?

Teachers' Influence on Pupils

By being the sort of teacher they ideally would wish to be, many teachers hope that they will have some influence on pupils' lives. Indeed this may be a strong motivation for going into teaching in the first place — they may have a missionary type commitment (whether in a religious or social/political sense — see Nias, 1981). Or, like Sarah (25, scale 1, art), may hope for a special sort of personal effectiveness:

What's important to me about being a teacher is having an influence on kids . . . being able to think back in years to come, 'Ah, Miss General said this' so I s'pose I'll be part of their lives. That bit of it fascinates me, how much, or how little you can influence them. I s'pose that's the need for recording for posterity isn't it? The need to make your mark upon the world.

However, although some pupils may well remember Sarah, what evidence we have suggests that teachers have negligible influence on the character or the future life of the majority of pupils (Peck and Havinghurst, 1960; Adelson, 1962; Musgrove and Taylor, 1969). Because teachers themselves have often been influenced by a teacher (approximately 40 per cent of our sample said they had been) they sometimes expect others to be too, and it can be disappointing to discover that this is rarely the case (see Edelwich with Brodsky, 1980, p. 50). Nevertheless, 'having some influence' does continue to be important — perhaps especially because in teaching it is so difficult to ascertain 'results' objectively — and older and retired teachers in particular derive a great deal of pleasure from meeting and hearing about their ex-pupils:

> I can't go into a bank or a building society in town with any privacy because the old grammar school kids are the ones who went to work in banks and building societies, 'Hello, Sir? How are you?' Oh my God, here we go again! . . . I think it's a compliment directly that the kid'll come and talk to you, even if it was one of the dead-end kids who you didn't get on with. They're always very keen to come and say hello. I'd one come up to me about three weeks ago. A girl who was a proper little bitch and we'd had lots of hard words. And she came up to me in the market place area, 'Hello Sir, I bet you don't remember me do you?' And it was one of the kids I could never forget. I said 'I do, you're so and so, aren't you? You failed 'O' level. You let me down'. 'I didn't think you'd remember, I'm married now you know. Well in fact I'm getting divorced next week'. And they come and tell you all their life's story. 'I've got two youngsters but I'm getting married again. I've got another one lined up so that's alright'. My wife was with me at the time. She said 'Who was that?' I said 'that was one of the dead end kids we'd got'. But now, she'll come up to me in the street, 'Hello'. Friends for life. (Arthur, 69, retired, art)

> Occasionally you pick up little bits from people who've passed through your hands. You hear about what they're doing and you say, well, it wasn't completely lost. Yes we did do something worthwhile . . . that sort of thing keeps your flame burning a little bit. (Jim, 65, retired, biology)

However, just as pupils can provide strong intrinsic rewards, they can also promote considerable dissatisfaction.

Pupils and Teacher Dissatisfaction

Research (for example Kyriacou and Sutcliffe, 1979, Dunham, 1980 and 1982) suggests that 'teachers are more likely to attribute dissatisfaction to external, working conditions, for example staff management, resources, facilities, salary — what Herzberg *et al* (1959) term the 'hygiene factors' — rather than to intrinsic ones — but this is generally the case in any job (cf Sofer, 1970). It is perhaps easier to cope with externally-caused dissatisfactions than with those experienced when the fundamental nature of the job, in this case, pupil response, fails to provide the hoped-for results. This has been the experience of many teachers when schools are reorganized, and particularly perhaps when they have become comprehensive (see Dodd, 1974; Sikes, 1984a). Mr Count (54, retired, science) is typical:

> When we went comprehensive I wasn't happy there any longer; it wasn't the school I knew and I couldn't see any alteration taking place, any betterment ... you see under comprehension there was the addition of people further and further down the academic scale ... and I couldn't teach my subject in the way that I liked to teach. I had the sixth form, of course, but I'd go out of there into a near remedial class, and there were behavioural problems. The kids weren't particularly interested, they didn't respond in any sort of positive way, they didn't have the ability. Consequently they'd play up which meant that I was getting involved, in a forty minute period, half was spent organizing the kids and getting them settled down and this sort of thing, and I didn't like that.

Mr Count took early retirement — an option not open to everyone. Another, less drastic and apparently very common way of coping is through verbalizing and sharing experiences (see Hammersley, 1984). Consequently much staff-room conversation is anecdotal and about naughty children:

> In the staffroom, teachers mostly talk about kids, they vocalize problems that they don't really need any help for, but just need to say it. (Sarah, 25, scale 1, art)

Too much complaining can have a detrimental effect on an individual teacher's status or on staff morale (see Chapter 5; Riseborough, 1981; Sikes, 1984a). However, occasionally something extraordinary happens which has the effect of formalizing and thereby increasing the value of the problem-sharing. For example:

> A lot more recently some of the older teachers here have not been sort of ashamed to admit that they have problems with pupils. People started discussing those problems in meetings, as well as in their general staffroom talk when the authority set a date for the abolishment of corporal punishment ... People were sort of standing up and saying 'yeah well, I've got to admit this and then somebody turns round and says, well it's happening here as well' ... I found it reassuring. (Chris, 28, scale 1, art)

Pupil Behaviour and Teacher Stress: A Sign of the Times or Old Age Creeping On?

A frequent topic of staffroom conversation is the alleged deterioration in standards of pupil behavior.

> Times have changed, attitudes have changed. I think, gone are the days now, in a school where you can be absolutely authoritarian, but perhaps you could when I started to teach. You could say sort of 'do this', and children would jump and do this, and nobody questioned why or 'Do I have to?' or 'Why have we got to do this' . . . which is what you always get now. (Helen, 40, scale 3, Head of Art)

Not only is this felt to have made teaching more difficult, it is also believed to have led to an increase in teacher stress and a higher incidence of mental and physical ill health (see Pollard, 1980, p. 29; NAS/UWT, 1979). It is interesting that while teachers are often sceptical of educational research they often quote studies, such as that of Kyriacou and Sutcliffe (1979) which was extensively reported in the *Times Educational Supplement* as evidence of what pupils are doing to teachers. Not actually 'cracking' up is becoming a sort of (inverted) status symbol indicating super resilience. Keith (38, scale 1, chemistry, late entrant), for example, didn't think that he was going to be able to hold out:

> It isn't the really low ability kids, they are obedient, it's the middle band. They are awful. They're just in school to be contained. They're terrible. I'll kill one of the little buggers one day soon, that is if I'm still there. It's driving me nuts and I shall have a nervous breakdown come Christmas.

(Neither of these things in fact happened because Keith took a job outside teaching).

And yet, although teachers today say that the situation is bad compared to the past, and that it is worsening, Grace (1978, ch 2) provides evidence to show that their complaint is not new, as Arthur's (69, retired, art) story about the early 1930s illustrates:

> It nearly broke your heart in college on school practice. If you got one of the schools in the nice residential areas you thought you were doing nicely but I got Fortby. One wall of Fortby school playground was the boundary wall of Handley jail and you sometimes wondered what side of the wall you were on. First time I went in front of a class of forty-two kids, the teacher was glad to get rid of them. I never saw him again. He just said, 'here, they're all yours', and he went . . . I hadn't a clue what was going to happen. It was murder. It was one big fight between you and the kids and the rest of the permanent teachers didn't want to know. This was their time off. Let the college students take over . . . But I managed to get by one way and another.

During his second school practice, Arthur was in one of the 'posh schools' and a friend of his in Fortby. This friend caught the train for Fortby on Monday morning, and was not seen again until Friday morning:

> ... Somebody going down early found this bloke at the bottom of the drive wandering about, and he'd lost his memory. This school at Handley had preyed on his mind so much it was such a tough area, that actually his mind had gone. And he remembers being on Blackpool promenade and that was the only thing that registered, and then the next thing he remembers he was in Lefield somewhere, which wasn't very far away from where he lived and then he'd lost his memory again in Lefield and somehow he'd got back to Shefley — and he's wandering about the bottom of the college drive there, shoes are worn right through. He must have walked miles and miles. (Arthur, 69, retired, art)

Clearly, there has always been difficulty with pupils for some teachers in some schools. But it is also the case that mores change with each generation, and as teachers get older and generationally further away from pupils they are more likely to complain about indiscipline (see Peterson, 1964, p. 276). The fewer the shared understandings and the more distant the cultures — whether social or generational — to which pupils and teachers belong, the greater the likelihood of conflict.

Teachers come into teaching with certain expectations concerning pupil teacher relations, expectations which tend to be based on their own, usually positive experience of education (see Lortie, 1975 pp. 61–7.) Such expectations are part of an idealized view of the sort of teacher one wants to be and be seen as being by pupils and colleagues, the sorts of things one wants to do as a teacher, and of the sorts of outcomes one would hope to achieve. These idealized views, which presuppose idealized, compliant, cooperative pupils (cf Hammersley, 1977, p. 13) reflect the teachers' world view, their philosophy of life and humanity, their politics and, more specifically, the nature of their commitment to teaching (cf Nias, 1981; Sikes, 1984b).

However, pupils are real, and they have their own expectations of schools, teachers and education, which are frequently different from the teachers' (see Berger and Luckmann, 1971; Edelwich with Brodsky, 1980; Grace, 1978; Hammersley and Turner, 1980; Musgrove and Taylor, 1969). And pupils are not the only threat to ideals, for in the staffroom the new teacher is likely to be told that 'experience will knock out all those airy fairy ideas'. Pete and Sarah were not so sure, and John, an experienced teacher, had retained much of his idealism by avoiding the cynics.

> Oh, you get all this 'wait till you've had a bit more experience, you won't be so optimistic and enthusiastic then'. It gets on your nerves. (Sarah, 25, scale 1, art)

In the staffroom I've always tended to sit with the younger teachers. It seems to me that the longer some people are in teaching the more cynical and bored they get. It doesn't have to be like that, I can do without hearing their views. (John, 44, scale 4, Head of Art)

However, no doubt many new teachers inevitably do have some unrealistic ideas and expectations which is why the experience of early encounters between a teacher and a group of pupils, whether on teaching practice in the probationary period, at a new or different type of school, or with a new class, has been described as one of culture or reality shock (Peterson, 1964, p. 268) during which the teacher experiences role conflict (cf Musgrove and Taylor, 1969, p. 57) and goes through a critical period, variously characterized as a 'baptism of fire' (Cole, 1984), or an 'initiation by ordeal' (Grace, 1978). They may be tested, or 'sussed out' by the pupils (cf Hargreaves, Hestor and Mellor, 1975; Ball, 1980; Beynon, 1984; Measor and Woods 1984a). On the other hand, even if the teacher feels that they are being tried out, it may be that the pupils are acting out their culture and behaving in their normal manner. Either way, teachers become aware of how pupils can behave. This is an important part of their professional socialization.

During their initial encounters pupils and teachers form impressions of each other. These become the foundation of reputations which influence future relations. Jan (25, scale 1, art) provides a good illustration of the process (another one of those 'critical incidents').

> In my first year I literally had to push one child out of the classroom who steadfastly refused to go ... She's since been expelled, which shows what she's like. She swore at me I think, she certainly gave me a mouthful back. So I said 'I'm not having that, go out' and she turned round 'I'm not' and planted herself firmly, and all the others were going 'she's not going out' and I frog-marched her out, pushed her out and closed the door, and I was leaning on the door for the next ten minutes to stop her coming back in ... Oh I laugh about it now but I really felt inadequate in front of those kids because what I'd said hadn't gone ... the next time I had that class they were horrible — they still are.

For both teacher and pupils initial encounters are trials to establish a basis for negotiations (Werthman, 1963; Woods, 1980). This was Arthur's (69, retired, art) experience:

> In the beginning they were a hostile tribe and you were at your wits' end to know how to get hold of their interest and how to maintain law and order, that was your first priority, without that you were flogging a dead horse. And you found out little tricks of the trade that you know you could crack a joke but you've got to know how far to go with that. If you went too far then you got mayhem and they've got to laugh with you not at you, do you know what I mean? And kids have got a good sense of humour and that was one way of getting a bit of rapport.

Pupils' Effect on Teacher Careers

Teacher Reputations

Teacher status is largely founded on classroom control (Denscombe, 1980b; Hargreaves, 1980) and one's promotion chances can depend on it. Teachers quickly acquire reputations based on their approach to discipline, and pupils play a large part in establishing these reputations. As Mr Shaw (45, scale 3, Head of Department, rural science) explained:

> You build a reputation in a school. It's basically a question of catching the first instance of misbehaviour because if you don't catch the first one you don't get the second one and the third one and so on. And it's a question of knowing who to watch and who to catch.

Having established whether a teacher is strict, short–tempered, fair, good fun, easy to play up and so on, pupils disseminate the information via their grapevine. Some reputations are really rather exotic, though none the less useful. Ray's (38, scale 3, Head of Biology) fell into this category:

> When I first started I had this group, this was in a grammar school mind the B–betas, when I ended up as a year tutor this was where all the fun was really. They really were quite prepared to take a new member of staff apart. I should say a crisis point occurred half-way through the Easter term, the second term, and I ended up carrying this fifth year lad out and I had him up against the wall nearly by his neck, and it was just very fortunate that the Deputy Head walked along and quietly removed me from the situation; took this lad off, and after that there wasn't that sort of trial ... it's reputation entirely. It's myths that generate ... I mean I get first years in this school asking me if I was a boxer ... Now I don't know what has generated this myth that's around me. At my previous school and when I was at college I did do a bit of boxing and I did quite enjoy it, but I very soon lost interest in it. I don't know what it is, perhaps I've got a flat nose ... But you know the number of pupils that ask me that question. So I say, no I'm not boxing professionally and leave it at that!

Reputations are not confined to the pupils community. By various means, teachers get to know about the pupils' opinions of their colleagues and sometimes this influences their own views:

> You have to go and cover somebody else's lesson and you ask the kids what they're supposed to be doing and they say 'oh it's old so and so, we never do anything what we're told, it's so boring', and I think, yes, he must have a few problems. (Chris, 28, scale 1, art)

> Sometimes they come out with it before you can stop them, but I . . . always make an excuse for a teacher or say I'm not sure about that or something non-committal if I can stop them I say I'm not interested and I don't want to hear. (Ann, 43, scale 1, art)

> I was talking to two of the fifth formers last week and they were saying 'What do you think of Mr T?' I said 'I think he's a great bloke'. 'Oh he's horrible, he's so strict, he never lets anything go. He's absolutely 100 per cent school rules and anything, anything that you do that's against school rules he'll have a go at you about it'. I said 'Well, he's obviously very good at his job . . . but . . . that doesn't stop him being a great bloke'. 'I know but he's always on at us about silly things'. (Pete, 25, scale 1, biology)

Some reputations and rumours can be quite damaging:

> Oh you get to know from the kids who's got a reputation as a dirty old man. You know, teachers who're supposed to be a bit too friendly with the girls, who make innuendoes, are always touching them and so on. Half of the time it's in the kids' imagination and that's why you've got to be careful. (Pete, 25, scale 1, biology)

Squeezing Teachers Out

Teachers sometimes are unable to cope with the way in which pupils behave towards them. But pupils are not always solely responsible. Sometimes, other teachers, including senior staff, appear to 'collude' with pupils in 'cooling out', or getting rid of 'unsatisfactory' teachers (Riseborough, 1983, p. 72).

> This chap had been redeployed from being head of department in a teacher training college. He was still on that salary but he'd only got a scale 1 sort of job, and he couldn't cope with the kids. They really messed him about, threw his briefcase in the pond, things like that. In the staffroom, he never went in there, he was always preparing lessons and things, the teachers' opinion was, this is a specialist. He's supposed to know how it's done and he can't even cope. Anyway, one day he didn't come into school and the Head 'phoned his wife, as far as she knew he'd gone in. They found him some weeks later. He'd killed himself. He left a letter and in it he said that he felt a failure, inadequate, because he couldn't control or get through to the kids. (Keith, 38, scale 1, chemistry)

The teacher Keith talks about may have coped more successfully with academically-oriented pupils, but they were the minority at the school and his contact with them was minimal. This is why timetabling can be such an important issue. Classroom teachers often judge heads of department on the basis of 'the fairness' of their timetabling:

With promotion comes the more academic kind of kid that I would wish to teach ... I mean the people who are on the scale 3 and the scale 4s, the heads of department, they teach mainly the sixth-form and the academic kind of kids and they leave the dim kids for the young teachers to cut their teeth on and you stand or fall I suppose, on whether you can cope with these children, I don't think it's very fair at all. (Keith, 38, scale 1, chemistry)

I've got a really super head of department. He's really good. When I started out he gave me mostly the better classes, now I get a range because I feel confident to cope. (Jan, 25, scale 1, art)

Heads of department often stressed that they made a point of sharing out the classes fairly:

When we went comprehensive, I said, as Head of Science, we will all teach all the pupils. It's important to be fair I think. And I took the second bottom stream. The bottom stream were almost ESN, they didn't do chemistry. (Mr Count, 54, retired, science)

When we went comprehensive my view was that the first people who should teach these comprehensive children were the heads of department because how can you do anything when you've no idea yourself? So I volunteered to teach this intake when it came. Not all the heads of department did though. They kept the sixth-form and the exam groups and gave the others to the junior teachers (Kath, 59, retired, science)

Margery (45, scale 3, Head of Chemistry) (Keith's Head of Department) however felt quite justified in teaching the most able groups herself:

When we first went comprehensive most of the heads of department really did bend over backwards to prove that they could teach all the ability ranges and many put themselves on almost remedial classes just to you know, get on with it ... I've obviously had to take a share of all ability work and even general science and things like that, but I suppose I've always kept more academic work than most people because the numbers of trained chemists are not tremendous, and the two men who are in the Department are not superbly qualified.

Pupils as Staff Selectors

Margery's school has something of a good local reputation for academic work, examination success and reasonably behaved pupils, which dates back to its grammar school origins. It attracts staff who favour a traditional grammar school type approach, and who prefer teaching academically-oriented pupils. This is but one example of how pupils play a vital part in the selection of staff for a specific school. Although the choice between grammar and secondary modern is now rarely available, new hierarchies of schools, catchment area (i.e. the social class of pupils) and reputations identify schools just as effectively. (cf Becker, 1976).

> When I first came to this school the authority had this system of grammar schools, junior high and high schools which meant that some secondary moderns, the junior highs were declared better than others ... So rather than just having your grammar school and your secondary modern school you had your elite and your nearly elite and your remainder, which was a destructive process. We were a high school — the remainder. The school had a lot of problems. For a start we are one of the worst areas, socially speaking, in the city. Then the Head was ill, he left. The old deputy retired. There was a terrific staff turnover and I think to some extent we are still suffering because you know, once you get a reputation it takes a long time to shake a reputation, it's more than a generation really that it would take and I think we have suffered a long time, I'm talking about years. It was so bad at one point they even changed the name of the school, it's taking a long hard slog to pull the place back. (Brian, 44, scale 4, Head of Art)

Even though teachers often comment on the inaccuracy of their own school's reputation, they seem not to apply the same scepticism to what they hear about elsewhere. Pete, (25, scale 1, biology) for example, worked in a school that was regarded as rather tough, yet he still says:

> When I left college I made a pool application. I had two interviews, one at Otterdip which I failed, much to my eternal delight because it's a dreadful school. It would have destroyed me if I'd tried to teach there.

Sarah (25, scale 1, art) whose, mainly middle class intake secondary modern was being reorganized into a larger comprehensive was prepared to sell her new house and if possible take a job elsewhere:

> *Sarah:* I don't think I'll be all that happy in the new school. I've got my doubts ... I know what some of the kids are like ... they are thieves and vandals, and people who burn people's hair, I mean they're vile, they really are vile.
> *R:* Have you had any work with them?
> *Sarah:* No, thank God. But the primary schools they come from are all special priority area schools. They are awful, and I think they'll get worse. I mean some of ours from the council estate are by no means little angels, they're sly little swines. I'm not really looking forward to it.

Yet, nine months later, having decided to 'give it a go' Sarah felt these pupils were

> all right when you get to know them. It's just that they scream and shout on the buses and they look a bit scruffy. Some of them are awful of course, but not the majority.

For Sarah, as for other teachers at her new school, there was some status attached to working with 'difficult' pupils, but even so the school and pupils were not her 'ideals'. In these days of contraction her situation is common because it is not always possible for teachers to get a job in schools where all the pupils meet all their requirements. So, if they do not actually leave teaching, they have to adapt to pupils.

As we have already noted, these adaptations can have implications far beyond the work situation. Keith (38, scale 1, chemistry), for example, believed that since he had become a teacher, his view of humanity and his attitude towards his family at home had both changed:

> Originally I thought that people were, as I s'pose they are really, basically honest, that they were willing and wishing to learn, that they had desires to kind of create a better world. A kind of optimistic view I suppose of society but I'm gradually changing to think that perhaps people do as little as they can get away with and people are not really at all bothered about creating a sort of better society, by and large. This is my view. But I s'pose it's very dangerous to draw conclusions about people in general when you're only looking at a very young slice of the population ... But this is what I'm doing ...., I see all mankind differently now, because I'm a teacher because I kind of think to myself, all these people around me are only grown up children, and look how they are as children ... I think I have changed. I tend to be more short-tempered and nasty at home because I have more bad days and yet in some respects I think I have become more tolerant because I've met a much greater cross-section of the community, in a sense ... I mean I've come into contact with people of low academic ability and I'd never really mixed with people like that before ... And in a sense I regret it, because if I'd never become a teacher I'd never have known that all these rotten, badly behaved, ill-mannered, not very intelligent kids existed and I'd have been a lot happier in my ignorance I think ... Yet I think I'm more intolerant of my own children perhaps ... because I don't want them to be like the kids at school and I think I chastize them more than I would have done previously.

Pupils, Curriculum, and Teacher Role

Lesson Content

Pupils influence teachers' ideals about what they teach. Sarah and Brian illustrate how reflective and adaptable teachers need to be especially. But not only in the early days of their careers:

> I think my ideas have changed slightly. I mean I had all these wonderful ideas about giving children art so that they could do it in their leisure time, in all this leisure time that they're going to get when they get unemployed and all this sort of malarky, but, . . . the children we've got, I'm sure I have no influence whatsoever on what they'll do at all . . . it was quite difficult for me to have to modify my plans . . . the work I anticipated doing when I first took the fifth years over was sort of more formal 'O' level type work . . . and they couldn't do it . . . and they hadn't got the need, or the want to do it . . . I think it took me about eighteen months to realize I'd got to revize my ideas . . . by the time I'd settled in and I'd done the work that I'd expected to be able to do, and found that it was failing and they weren't getting the results. I had to, I mean, even now with the third years, I'm having to change everything that I've done with the other two groups of third years that I've taken because they're so totally different. (Sarah, 25, scale 1, art)

> I don't think I gave a lot of thought to what I was going to do when I initially started out, I don't think a lot of people do. You assume that you are going to do this particular job and you are going to change the world. You are God's gift to teaching: I think ninety-nine people out of 100 people think that, whatever job you go into, you are going to be the answer; you are going to sock it to 'em. It is only when you find that you have run up against a brick wall and you sit on the floor sort of thinking 'God, that hurt!' that you actually then begin to wonder what you are about. But I think probably, after about the first two or three years, I would think I had 'come down to earth' and was more realistic about what could be achieved and, perhaps more to the point, what it was worthwhile attempting to achieve. For many years when we were asked 'Have you up-dated your scheme of work?' my answer is 'I'm up-dating it every-day', which is true. I am continually re-writing, chucking things out. (Brian, 44, scale 4, Head of Art)

Even though many teachers continually update their work in order to meet the needs and abilities of particular groups of pupils, first impressions (which are frequently coloured by specific reputations and more general expectations) of teaching a class may affect later interpretations. As Ball (1980, p. 149) points out, such expectations 'have their own impact on classroom relationships by self-fulfilment in the strategies that teachers employ in anticipation'. For example, in Chapter 7 we discuss teachers' feelings about doing practical work with pupils who could not confidently be expected to behave appropriately. If teachers decided that the risks were too great, they were likely to feel that they were being prevented from doing the sorts of things they wanted to do, and thereby from being the sort of teacher they wanted to be and to be seen as being.

Sometimes teachers will negotiate quietness and cooperation in return for favoured activities or other pupil valuables. For instance:

> I'm not very happy for them to copy from magazines and by and large I've banned it. I'll let them do it as a special treat. If they behave through the half term I'll let them do whatever they want in the last lesson. I remind them of this if they ever got a bit high. (Sarah, 25, scale 1, art)

In his elementary school days, Arthur (69, retired, art) had been able to exploit this strategy because as a class teacher he had wider bargaining power than the specialist teacher has:

> If you had a kid who was particularly naughty in the class, if they made themselves a nuisance, the teacher used to get mad and the whole class had to suffer. And of course in art or games or that sort of thing . . . it was a doddle, you could use that as a lever if you wanted to. You could blackmail the whole class because of that one individual, if he made a wrong step, 'You've all had it'. And they used to put their fists up 'you'll get it if', you know, but they kept law and order, not me.

Another way of attracting pupils' attention is for the teacher to set the work they want to do within the context of a topic that pupils are interested in.

> All some of the boys want to do is motorbikes, so I'll try and use motorbikes to illustrate various points of technique and so on. And they quite like that because it means they draw better motorbikes! (Sarah, 25, scale 1, art)

> Working with teenage girls — and boys these days, I often do things about fashion and things that they are interested in — cars perhaps. I manage to get them interested and then I can slip in a few things that I feel are worthwhile and they might not have seen. (Ann, 43, scale 1, art)

> I try and link what I'm doing with things the kids are interested in. For instance I might notice that some of them are wearing tie-dyed clothes so I'll bring that in. (Dave, 44, senior teacher, Head of Science)

Either way, the pupils have influenced lesson content (cf Ebbutt, 1981). They are also quite effective influences on teachers' pedagogical style, mainly as a result of their expectations and perceptions of the 'ideal teacher'.

Pupils' Expectations of Teachers

Pupils' expectations concerning what constitutes a good and proper teacher (cf Musgrove and Taylor, 1969, p. 17) make them one of the most potent forces for conservatism in education. Pupils expect teachers to teach, they expect them to know, to be experts. These expectations are rarely modified, higher up the school (Rudduck and Hopkins, 1984), and even sixth-form pupils expect teachers to transmit knowledge. Some teachers find this a problem:

> I think pupils have a great deal of influence on the sort of teacher you are. I think when youngsters quite obviously expect you to know, you're in a bit of a cleft stick sometimes because whether you can say I just don't know and we'd better find out together, with some, if you allow that to happen it's possible that they'll lose everything, they'll say well, nothing is reliable at all and you have to be a bit careful about it all. It's not so much a problem at the top end of the school, and it doesn't really matter to them if you don't know ... Yet, I wasn't after, sort of rote knowledge, I wanted something different to that ... but the trouble is that there are so many basic facts and rules in science, laws and so on, and you trot 'em out as a teacher, just like this, and they say 'Good God, he's like an encyclopaedia'. And this isn't a good thing for them to think ... But they would expect you to produce an answer, they wanted an answer and they would expect you to be able to produce something on any topic they wanted to bring up. (Jim, 65, retired, science)

The examination system is often held to be responsible for these attitudes. Pupils and their parents largely want exam passes and they want the formula, that is the notes, that will enable them to collect these. For some teachers, providing the notes and attaining examination passes is what teaching is all about. Others, while recognizing the dilemma, would prefer a different emphasis and greater pupil involvement in the learning process:

> When I first came into teaching my idea was that I was there to educate kids in chemistry and quite frankly I wasn't too bothered about what the syllabus said. And I certainly wasn't too bothered about whether they were going to pass their exams or not, and in fact, I remember saying to one kid one day, look, I'm here to teach you chemistry, I'm not here to teach you 'O' level. You see there's a difference between teaching a kid 'O' level and teaching a kid chemistry, there's no such thing as CSE chemistry or 'O' level chemistry, there is chemistry ... now, having taught for six years I come to realize that it is important, the exams are important, artifically, so I think, from the parents' of the pupils point of view, because they want, like me, I mean I wanted my child to get X number of 'O' levels and X number of grade As and whatever, the

parents of the pupils by and large, the ones who care, want their children to get so many certificates. They come up at Open Evenings, 'how's he going to do in his 'O' level'? 'Is he going to get a grade A?' I feel like saying I couldn't care a damn providing he gets educated. (Keith, 38, scale 1, chemistry)

As Jim's earlier quote suggested, some pupils may find this approach difficult to cope with, especially perhaps if their other teachers favour a transmission method. They may reject it outright, and make 'official' complaints that the teacher is failing to do his job. Whether out of sympathy for bewildered pupils, or because of 'consumer pressure', it is difficult for the teacher to persevere:

So, what do you do? I mean they get so panicky. They've no confidence in themselves, they look to you to tell them, to give them notes. They say the other teachers do, and because they do it's a bit difficult to get the kids to understand why you personally don't. God knows how they cope when they get to university. (Bill, 39, senior teacher, physics)★

Similarly teachers feel that many pupils expect 'proper teachers' to be strict disciplinarians. And if they assume that guise, it of course influences the pupils' response. Jim said:

I think anything that tends to fit you into a mould, it's difficult to avoid it, but it produces a barrier between you and a particular youngster because my idea is that ultimately it's on a one to one basis that you really teach and if there's anything in the whole situation that sets you up as a particular sort of a figure and you've got a nice hard shell around you, you don't, you can't break through the barrier and it's difficult to avoid in some cases, but you've got to be conscious of it and the fact that it's likely to happen because it harms relationships. (Jim, 65, retired, science)

Expectations put people into moulds which categorize and depersonalize. As we have already remarked, teachers who have their own children seem to be more understanding and report fewer problems or dissatisfactions with pupils' behaviour than do those who are childless. It seems that if pupils recognize the teacher as a real person with a life outside school, their expectations of the teacher and the nature of their relationship may well alter. It does seem that pupils do tend to regard teachers as 'sub-human' (Blackie, 1977). Yet, contradicting Waller's (1932) assertion that to their pupils the effective teacher must be 'relatively meaningless as a person', teachers often say that if pupils can see that they are human, it can help in establishing positive, friendly, more cooperative relationships. Furthermore, as Denscombe (1980c) suggests, friendliness can be a very effective control strategy

★ A teacher in a related piece of research

(pp. 60–5). Friendly relationships are satisfying and often approximate to the teacher's ideal conception of what the job should be like.

> I think you've got to let them see that you're human on occasions because they tend to think you're just a teacher, that you don't have a life outside. If you can do that then it's much better, you can talk to each other, do many more things, they listen to you. It's fun. (Jan, 25, scale 1, art)

> We fall out occasionally of course and I rant and rave and keep them in but usually we quite quickly come to an arrangement between us where I don't have to shout and rant and rave and I enjoy the relationship I have with them. Because I'm not really a formal person, it's more of a friendly relationship that I have ... and because I get a good relationship with them, eventually they don't like to upset me. (Ann, 43, scale 1, art)

As Ann suggests, with this sort of relationship it is perhaps more difficult for the pupil to practise role distancing successfully (Goffman, 1961). Berger and Luckmann (1967) write 'The roles of secondary socialization carry a high degree of anonymity; that is, they are readily detached from their individual performers', and that therefore 'teachers need not be significant others in any sense of the word' (p. 161). Knowing that teachers are people basically like themselves, perhaps gives them more significance to pupils.

But it isn't only pupils who see teachers as distant. Some teachers see pupils as sub-human, or as undifferentiated cohorts (Lortie, 1975) and respond to them as pupils rather than as individuals. And this may be the reason why 'parent-teachers', who associate pupils with their own children and thereby recognize them as individuals, find it somewhat easier to have better relationships with them.

However, the teachers' professional socialization tends to militate against them, treating pupils as individual people, which, in turn, reinforces pupils' stereotypical perceptions of teachers. This is because, as we noted earlier, many teachers are advised to use a 'social distance' approach to pupils (Waller, 1932). For example:

> They told you at college don't be nice, don't talk to them, tell them, that sort of thing. (Ann, 43, scale 1, art)

> At college they were very strong on the 'Don't smile until Christmas' sort of approach. (Chris, 28, scale 1, art)

In effect, such training has the character of preparation for a conflict in which the teacher has to try to maintain the upper hand, to establish 'tactical superiority' (Doyle, 1979). Any softening can afford a breach to the enemy hordes. Such an approach, based on the presumption of 'trouble' seems likely to serve to buttress the widespread 'Us versus Them' mentality of both teacher and pupil (Hammersley, 1977, p. 14; Hammersley and Turner, 1980), Denscombe's (1980) findings suggest that this is the case. Arthur (69, retired, art) tended to agree:

> You should aim to get a voluntary discipline if you can. But if it starts a battle between you and the kids you might as well give up . . . if you can get some sort of friendship with the kids and they get a feeling that you're not their enemy, you are on their side and it pays dividends.

In any case many teachers are not at ease using a social distance approach because it is contrary to their nature and/or the nature of their commitment. For instance:

> I'd rather be too friendly than the other extreme so I'll go to that way. It seems to be more pleasant . . . and it's the easiest for me to do, so I won't go against what I'm personally like. (Chris, 28, scale 1, art)

> I used to try and be more of a friend really, an adviser, where I could, rather than tell them 'you will do this' or 'you will do that' because I found that you just got nothing from them, and those who were reasonably good, they just didn't want to know them and I'm not an authoritarian person, I wasn't there to be authoritarian but I am human so if, after I'd tried to be a friend, they took advantage, I might occasionally, in frustration, give them a thump, but it wasn't a formal thump, it was a human one. You can't do that now of course. (Mr Bridge, 58, retired, art)

Yet, even if teachers would rather not, they may find themselves being 'teacherly', especially perhaps at the start of their career, simply because it can give the appearance of success, and because pupils — and colleagues — expect and respond to it. What this means is that pupils play a significant part in the process whereby the prospective libertarian, idealistic, critically aware teacher can become the authoritarian, disciplinarian, 'proper' teacher. Keith certainly felt this to be true for him:

> I think my approach to kids has changed since I started right at the beginning. I was, I won't say I was more relaxed, because I'm not a relaxed sort of person. I don't know whether lackadaisical is perhaps the right word, I had a less formal approach to them perhaps, whereas now I suppose I tend to be much, I deliberately try, if necessary to frighten them. I think this is what teachers do and this is probably why I've never really liked teachers to be honest . . . in that I think they go out of their way to frighten children. But I can see the reason for that now . . . I've been told by quite experienced teachers that when you go into the room . . . when you meet a class for the first time, if nobody's doing anything wrong, you've got to find something wrong, to pick on them, that sounds awful doesn't it, but I can see the rationale, you've got to somehow imprint the fact that you are,

if you like, a sort of nasty person. And really in some ways I think that's why I don't feel I have been or perhaps ever can be a proper teacher because I am not basically, I don't feel that I'm a nasty person ... and I think to be a proper teacher you've got to really have some sort of nasty streak in you. Anyway, that's the impression I get. And I'm getting nastier because I'm getting fed up with it, I'm absolutely sick of kids treating me as if I was dirt, so therefore I tend to treat them back as if they were dirt. (Keith, 38, scale 1, chemistry)

Teachers and the School

One of the reasons why some teachers engage in extra-curricular activities may be because they allow them to relate more closely to pupils, free from the constraints of the formal curriculum. For instance, Arthur, Sarah and John had all taken pupils on hiking and sketching expeditions; Keith, Dave and Mr Count had coached and played games; Pete went birdwatching, and Mike and Ray ran science clubs.

Chris illustrates the stark change in relationships that can occur:

There's a very strange difference when you're outside school and when you're in and I've never quite worked it out because some of the kids live round our way and they won't speak to me until I get off the bus, just up the road here, they won't start talking to me. When I get off the bus it's a little bit better, some of them don't speak to me at all until they come into the classroom, they open the door and say hello! I can't get used to it, it's really strange. Some of them probably think I'd be embarrassed to talk them outside school, I suddenly turn into a member of the public out there, in here they treat me differently. They can come in here and swear at me as they like. I don't know it's strange, I'm sure they must see me in a different way. (Chris, 28, scale 1, art)

If teachers have to enforce rules which they feel are petty, or administer punishments that they think are unfair, they may see these tasks which they have to do because they are teachers in that specific school, as coming between them and the pupils.

I think to teach in a school you're concerned with petty things ... you're supposed to look to see what colour socks somebody's got on and that sort of pettiness ... I couldn't be bothered ... there are things that I think are silly about the school but I have to do them. (Ann, 43, scale 1, art)

But they are in a paradoxical situation. If they do not do these things, they may (i) lose the respect of their colleagues; (ii) jeopardize their career prospects; and (iii) be seen as 'soft' by the pupils. Some teachers have found a way round this:

I tell them the day before that they'd better come in proper uniform because I'll be doing a check. I give them plenty of warning. (Pete, 25, scale 1, biology)

If somebody's not wearing the right coloured socks I warn them . . . I also try and explain, I'll say 'You know I do think you ought to be able to wear leg warmers. It's cold and I think you ought to but the rule is that you're not allowed to and in life, wherever you go, there are certain rules. I mean when you go to work there will be rules and you've got to learn to accept them and obey them even if you think they're silly. . . . but the petty rules I suppose you've got to try and change those if you do come up against them, and I do in my own little way. I argue at staff meetings but it doesn't often do much good. (Ann, 43, scale 1, art)

I was a housemaster and if teachers had a problem with a kid they used to send it to me, I was one of the few on the staff authorized to give the cane . . . and the kid used to come to me, 'Mrs So and So sent me for the stick'; 'Well, what have you been doing?'. 'Nowt, I only did so and so', and knowing Mrs so and so herself and knowing the kid himself you could soon weigh up who was the guilty one. Very often it was the teacher at fault, not the kid . . . so, you went through the motions. You got the kid to bend down and you waved the magic wand around his backside and he hardly felt it and got up and he looked at you and you looked at him and he knew what was meant. 'Alright, you tell her you had the stick'. It was alright from the professional, stick-by-your-colleagues point of view, it probably wasn't right, on the other hand it was not right to have a kid sent to you in cold blood to be thrashed for something which you weren't quite sure who was guilty or how guilty, or how serious the offence. (Arthur, 69, retired, art)

In the above accounts, teachers are describing how they sometimes collude with pupils. We were told of many instances of teachers supporting pupils who they believed were being unjustly treated by officials. And pupils can also help teachers. They can, for instance, be especially kind if a teacher is unwell (Measor and Woods, 1984a), and Riseborough (1983) quotes a teacher whose class of troublemakers 'were as good as gold' when an HMI observed a lesson. Less extraordinary, but perhaps more important, is the way in which pupils by their everyday behaviour allow teachers to be the sort of teacher they want to be, and to experience teaching as satisfying, rather than stressful work.

Teacher Presentation of Self

So far the emphasis has been on how pupils can influence teachers' career experiences and intrinsic aspects of their identity. They can also have an effect on teachers' outward appearance and the sense of self they derive from it. How a teacher looks can be a significant factor influencing how pupils perceive and adapt to them. For example, when working as a supply teacher with a group of fourth-year boys, one of the researchers was asked:

> Are you in the CND? You look like one of those peace women. Yeh, a lot of young teachers look like that, like social workers. Do you dirve a car? I bet she drives a Fiat Panda?

She did!

Not surprisingly perhaps, given this acute degree of analysis, some teachers take care how they present themselves to pupils. This may involve cultivating slight eccentricity on the part of the art teacher, or even taking elocution lessons to get rid of the 'wrong' accent:

> I had a class laughing at me when I said 'Lizen' not 'Listen' because that was the way I spoke, and the class openly laughed ... what was the other thing I used to say? I can't remember; oh yes, I used to say 'fud' instead of 'food', and they couldn't stand that either you see. It would be as soon as you said it, laugh, which hurt. I spent quite some time training myself to speak more like them, or more BBC standard, than like the Geordie which I am. Most people can't tell now. (Dave, 44, senior teacher, Head of Science)

However many cosmetic changes teachers may make in the hopes that relationships with pupils will thereby be slightly easier, they cannot disguise their age. Age makes teachers different — as Ann (43, scale 1, art) describes:

> I've noticed how strange children are in the way they regard their teachers. When I was, first started teaching, in the secondary school and obviously I looked much younger and I was only 21 and I had a student in, for her teaching practice and she looked older than me really, because I've always looked younger than I've been. I used to hate it when I was 16 and I looked about 12 and I heard them say, how old do you think that student is, you see, and oh she's bound to be a lot younger than Mrs Bakewell because I, well I was Miss then, because Miss is a teacher, so I think that children sort of think that Miss is a teacher and something entirely different from a normal person.

Age is an extremely important influence on many aspects of pupil-teacher relationships. For instance, age differences carry implications concerning power and authority, personal identity and sense of self, shared experiences and common understanding, interests and concerns, ease of communication, and so on. The way in which throughout a career a teacher's age changes with respect to pupils' age and how this change is reflected in relationships with pupils, would seem to be central to the experience of being a teacher.

The characteristics often said to distinguish teachers — bossiness, preoccupation with trivialities, meanness, ignorance of the real world, the inability to talk about anything except school and pupils — all perhaps have their origin as classroom survival strategies. As Riseborough (1983) writes, teachers 'become what they are culturally by negotiation on the chalk face' (p. 50). This may make them more of a 'proper teacher' and less of the sort of teacher, and person, that they would like to be.

The problem seems to lie in the role teachers are often expected to play. But, as is clear from the teachers in this study, by rejecting parts of the role and being 'oneself', teachers can survive and indeed have satisfying, unstressful relationships. Undoubtedly, because of tradition and cultural expectations on both sides, this is difficult to accomplish, but teachers who do attempt it, even if they are not always successful, are unequivocal about the rewards they reap.

Chapter 7

Subject Identities

The Head at my second school said to me, 'You teach children, you use your subject as a vehicle with which to teach children'. And I've always felt that's right, as far as I'm concerned, I'm much more interested in children than I am in the subject. (Mr Shoe, 63, retired, science)

I think one of the troubles you see, of the last, what, thirty odd years, ever since the war, has been this business of specialization. I don't know whether it's a good thing in the long run ... You don't teach the subject, you teach kids, and you should be prepared to teach kids, within reason, any sort of thing. Quite obviously there is a limit to what you can do. It's no good expecting me to have taught music on any sort of really effective scale at all but I could cope with the odd music lesson and if it was necessary to encourage a group of kids to sing songs, sort of have a reasonable time and enjoy it and so on, I could make a go of that ... Do you think somebody who is going to be a teacher, in the sense of teachers in the general mainstream of education, should be people who are only prepared to say 'My narrow little thing and nothing else'? ... Of course teachers have changed, the demands on teachers have changed. (Jim, 65, retired, science)

Subject Perspectives

The Specialist Teacher

For the largest part of their career, most secondary school teachers are subject 'specialists' who work in relatively discrete subject departments. This is because the majority of comprehensives tend towards what Bernstein (1975) describes as a 'collection code' type organizational structure. Reasons for this include:

(i) The tendency for bureaucratic structures to break down a large group into smaller units which are easier to administer. However, by definition 'specialization fragments the occupational culture' (Bucher and Strauss, 1961) and generally leads to the development of status hierarchies (cf Hargreaves, 1980, p. 133) and partisanship. In many comprehensives, as Musgrove and Taylor (1969) noted, 'academic subjects have become highly organized social systems with heavily defended boundaries' (p. 70). The grammar/secondary modern dichotomy thus still survives, although in a more subtle and complicated form, with academics (teachers) on one side and artisans (trainers or instructors) and pastoral caretakers on the other (cf also Richardson, 1973, pp. 107–48).

(ii) The fact that specialization was central to the grammar school tradition, and it tended to be ex-grammar school, rather than ex-secondary modern school, teachers who were appointed to senior posts in comprehensives. There, they have established a specialist tradition which is generally resistant to change. This is largely because, as pupils and students, most teachers experienced a subject-based education and are likely to have developed subject loyalties and identities which they are concerned to protect. They often do this by reproducing the structures which they experienced (cf Lortie, 1975).

Apart from Jim and Arthur, who had started their careers as general class teachers in elementary schools, the subject had been the major factor influencing all of our teachers' decisions to teach (see also Lacey, 1977; Lyons, 1981), and all of them were teaching for the majority of their time the subject they had specialized in at college or university. This may have something to do with their being artists and scientists, because, while at the present time many other teachers are having to teach subjects in which they hold no formal qualifications there is still a relatively good match in science and art (HMI, 1979).

I love my subject and I wanted to stay in it ... I really enjoy it, and when I was thinking about jobs I immediately thought of what else can I do in my subject. (Pete, 25, scale 1, biology)

I wanted to do something with art and it was while I was in the sixth-form that I decided on teaching. (Jan, 25, scale 1, art)

As you observe schools and find the subjects that you enjoy don't seem to sink into other people and you feel a bit like converting them or getting them to see the simplicity or the pleasure of knowing something which you see yourself, it's a sort of question of sharing one's pleasures. (Mike, 46, scale 3, physics)

Becoming a teacher was suggested to me by my mum and I never thought twice about it because I knew or I thought my career would have to have something to do with art because it was the subject I enjoyed most and at the time could excel at when compared to other people that I knew of my own age, and I couldn't really see any other way at the time of making it support me other than through teaching. (John, 44, scale 4, Head of Art)

I think I was attracted to science because I liked things, albeit living things, I'm a biologist, rather than human beings! (Mr Ray, 38, scale 4, Head of Department, science)

A Collective Philosophy?

Going through our transcripts it became apparent that, in some way or other, most of what teachers say about their careers relates to their subject. This reflects the findings of research on other subject areas (e.g. Ball, 1982; Ball and Lacey, 1980 (on English teachers); Hendry, 1975; Jenkins, 1974; MacDonald, 1979 and 1981; McNair and MacDonald, 1980 (on P.E. teachers); Goodson, 1981 (on geography and rural science teachers)).

However, the extent and nature of influence varies, perhaps as a consequence of there being a number of different routes into teaching. For example, the experiences of those with a subject degree and Postgraduate Certificate of Education are likely to be different from those of people trained in a college of education, or of those who have had no formal training to teach at all (Bennet, 1983; Burns, 1983; Grace, 1978). Thus art, science and English teachers may have more in common and identify more strongly with teachers of the same subjects in other schools than they do with colleagues teaching other subjects in their own schools. Certainly, it does seem that teachers' experiences as subject specialists lead, as Brian (48, scale 4, Head of Art) suggests is the case with artists, to a sort of 'collective philosophy', a subject perspective, although by no means necessarily a collective view of content and pedagogy (see Ball, 1982) which is distinct from the common 'mode of consciousness' (Cole, 1984) they share with other teachers (cf Hammersley, 1977).

Art is viewed as a slightly dubious subject area . . . art has always had this image from the 1880s hasn't it? I mean you go back to Lautrec and the French Impressionists . . . but I mean you know people sort of see that and automatically, they, everybody is painted with the same brush. Added to which maybe we are slightly strange, in that I think we do tend to, I'm not trying to sound pretentious, but I think we do tend to see things perhaps differently to a lot of other people, we interpret things differently. Perhaps we have, although it may not be a collective philosophy, we may have different philosophies to other people. And I think historically as well, you know, the artist in a way has had to fight for a position and to some extent if you are going to fight then you are going to have a lot of aggro coming your way. You have got to be single minded to stick it out, and I think that sort of image has rubbed off, but I think some of that determination has rubbed off as well, and I think, especially today, in education. I mean art's got to fight like mad, there's no chance of anything else.

As Brian notes, collective philosophies have historical origins and yet, to some extent and in certain respects they seem to transcend contemporary paradigms of content and pedagogy. Thus they are reflected in characteristic pedagogical styles; views of the teacher's role; relationships with pupils; views of the purpose of school-based education and the part that subject plays in this; classroom ambience, and even the physical appearance of the teacher. We shall consider these in the rest of the chapter.

Images of the Specialist

Subject-associated characteristics form the basis of expectations which can influence both teachers' and pupils' approach to lessons — as these art teachers who had taught other subjects explain:

Last year I took some English. I couldn't teach it. I was nervous and besides not being able to do it as well, you need a different approach to what you take in art. You couldn't treat the kids as individuals like you do in art. You had to be a teacher in front of a class and tell everybody what to do. You had to be specific about what they had to do whereas in art you can rely on them interpreting. In art there's more than one 'answer' to any problem you set them. In English if they couldn't spell and they couldn't write then they got it wrong. There were more rules ... and the kids saw me as an art teacher in English ... I could tell ... it was just the way they said, 'Right, draw us a picture', you know. I would hate to think that I looked like an art teacher when I was teaching English, but perhaps I did, the way I kept drawing diagrams on the board. Yes I did. I was thinking all of it in images a lot more than I was in words. (Chris, 28, scale 1, art)

Well I've got two styles of teaching. I've got the one that I deal with in the art room and the other that's formal because I teach part of my timetable in humanities ... in art I can relax and go round and talk to them individually ... with the humanities it's a case of come in in silence and sit down ... definitely teaching from the board. (Jan, 25, scale 1, art)

It can be quite difficult for the individual to override stereotyped expectations, especially if the stereotype is as strong as that of the art teacher. As we noted in Chapter 4, appearance is central to conceptualizations of the proper teacher. Similarly, there is a general view of what a proper art teacher looks like, although it seems that schools vary in the extent to which their art teachers are expected to fit the stereotype.

Sarah and John, for example, both expressed the opinion that in some schools the candidate whose appearance came closest to the stereotype was the one most likely to be appointed, whereas in others it was irrelevant, or even a disadvantage.

Art teachers vary in the extent to which they conform to the stereotype. We did notice a geographical variation with southern art teachers tending to be more avant garde, but in any case fashions are usually more advanced and extravagant in the south, the north taking a while to catch up and being generally more conservative. Nevertheless, art teachers in both areas can usually be distinguished by a certain style about their dress, and perhaps as Chris (28, scale 1, art) suggests, this isn't really surprising:

> *Chris:* I wonder if art teachers do consider their image a bit more than others. It would be strange if an art teacher was totally unaware of the way he appeared because that would be against what he's supposed to be all about. He's supposed to be visually aware. If you're not aware of how you're looking then there's something strange. You must be in control of your appearance.
>
> *R:* I've found with lady art teachers they often wear a piece of jewellery or something.
>
> *Chris:* Yeah, that's right, obviously something artistic.

There are practical considerations of course:

> I dress to feel comfortable in the sort of work that I'm doing ... I've got clay on my trousers, I've got plaster, I wear a smock, not because it's an image smock but because it keeps me clean, so it's purely practical. I mean I dress like this most of the time anyway, so I don't try to create an artist's image and I don't really know many art teachers who do. (Brian, 44, scale 4, Head of Art)

There are also practical considerations for scientists:

> You have to wear a lab coat, it can be messy doing experiments, there's always a chance you might spill something and you don't want to get acid or whatever on your own clothes. (Dave, 44, senior teacher, science)

It is perhaps significant in terms of status hierarchies that, in most cases scientists wear white 'lab coats', whereas 'practical teachers' usually wear the same type of coat but in brown, green, grey or navy. This mirrors the white coat, blue coat divide in industry.

However, on the whole, although they can often be identified by their clothes, as can drama and PE teachers and teachers of practical subjects, dress would seem to be relatively peripheral to the stereotype of the scientist which focuses almost exclusively on cognitive style and general ambience. For example, the absent-minded but scientifically brilliant professor, the Professor Branestawm, the cold, logical scientist, or the flat-chested, flat-heeled, masculine lady science teacher (see Ebbutt, 1981). Physicists, in particular, are often singled out, even by other science teachers:

> I think you often find that physicists are rather peculiar. They keep themselves to themselves but they are rather odd. (Margery, 45, scale 3, Head of Chemistry)

While scientists are perceived as logical, practical problem solvers, artists tend to be seen as impractical and unrealistic:

> You get many of them (artists) who are airy fairy people. (Jim, 65, retired, science).

And sometimes as anarchistic and subversive. The following quote suggests why this might be:

> Art is an individual expression. I think it's a development of a person's individuality. I find school a bit difficult in a way because the basis of school is getting people to conform. You know, they put them in school uniform, when bells ring we all move, all the time we're trying to get them to conform whereas I'd rather they were themselves. (Ann, 43, scale 1, art)

Ann works in a school where hierarchical statuses and subject boundaries are clearly delineated and vigorously maintained. In these circumstances her integrative, questioning, interpretative, pupil-centred approach, which is representative of the 'collective philosophy' of art teachers, is highlighted. At many points it is clearly at odds with the ethos maintained by the formal structure which is supported by the Headmaster and majority of staff. Art, therefore, as represented by Ann and the others in the department, appears rather subversive within the context of that specific school, though it would not necessarily be so in another school.

Subject Aims

So, what did these teachers see their role as subject specialists to be? On the whole the differences between art and science teachers stem from their views of their subject, and in particular; (i) the ways in which they perceive the nature of their subject to differ from other subjects; (ii) their perception of their subject's relationship to other subjects; (iii) their perception of their role as mediator between subject and pupil; and (iv) their own personal relationship with their subject.

While each individual has his own idiosyncratic view, and perhaps a view which reflects a paradigm which he associates himself with (cf Ball, 1982), scientists tended to share a view of science as a body of knowledge to be learnt about, and artists saw art as a fundamental, integral part of life, 'as something the child already possesses (which) must be drawn out and developed' (Ball and Lacey, 1980, p. 156). What does this mean for the teacher?

Overall the aims of scientists and artists presently working in school had many similarities. They are perhaps, above all else, comprehensive school teacher aims, because they take into account what is realistically possible given the school, the pupils — and also given the historical development of the role of the school and of the teacher in England and Wales. English teachers cannot, perhaps, be specialists in the same way as French agrégés.

None of the art teachers said that they realistically expected their pupils to become artists.

> Not every child is a born artist and I don't think you can make them into artists . . . and I wouldn't want to, I mean I'd be out of a job eventually wouldn't I? They'd all be artists! (Sarah, 25, scale 1, art).

> I know they've chosen to do art, but they're not going to be artists are they, many of them? (Ann, 43, scale 1, art)

> If I were just trying to aim to produce fine artists, you'd better forget it. I've produced, well it sounds big-headed to say I've produced, I've had a hand in the production of two in, what, twenty-three years? (Brian, 44, scale 4, Head of Art)

Scientists did not expect to produce many scientists either:

> Where do you get your satisfactions from in teaching? Occasionally, occasionally, you do get one, I had two or three who went on to become scientists, who did PhDs. One youngster I taught now works in a high level job with a Swiss pharmaceutical firm. But you don't pin your hopes on those . . . and that's not what you're there for either. (Jim, 65, retired, science)

> My central drive isn't to produce scientists. You don't get scientists in school very often. (Dave, 44, senior teacher, Head of Science)

Some of the retired ex-grammar school, science teachers however had been strongly committed to turning out specialists. They had worked towards excellent exam results, university places, Oxbridge in particular, and so had their pupils who, more relevantly, stood a reasonable chance of success. That these grammar school teachers were quite likely to achieve their aims is very important, for unrealistic aims often lead to dissatisfaction. A 'pragmatic' approach to the job may well represent an adaptation for, as Brian suggests, teachers of all subjects probably start out with dreams, and most probably do retain some vestiges of them.

> I think everybody, when they start, no matter what they say, I think everybody imagines that they are really going to make their mark and do something for their subject, I don't think I ever said what it was I

was going to do, but I don't think that there's anybody who doesn't feel somewhere or other, or why are they going to do it? 'Because I believe in'. I've no doubt there's that there, but I don't think that really works ... you have to adapt your view to what's possible. (Brian, 44, scale 4, Head of Art)

Realistically, artists hoped to give *all* pupils the opportunity to experience being involved in creating something, and to gain the satisfaction of successful achievement.

I think everybody can find something in art that they like to do and I think you can get a great deal of satisfaction out of doing something, making something, and I think it's my job to help them find that something. (Ann, 43, scale 1, art)

I say to some children, art's given me a life, I don't expect it to give you the same, but if it gives you some pleasure and enjoyment then it's been worthwhile, and it's going to be worthwhile cultivating your skills in it, even if you do no more than drawing or painting while you're on holiday, it's going to give you some satisfaction and pleasure and an interest, and something to look forward to. (John, 44, scale 4, Head of Art)

I've got very conscious of teaching them something that will be useful to them later on, so I do things like colour, and design, things that they can apply to their clothes, to their homes when they have them, and so on. (Sally, 44, scale 3, art)

And scientists wanted their pupils to experience some sense of satisfaction through understanding.

I see the importance of chemistry, and of all kids knowing something about it as a feature of their life ... not that they should know that if they've got stomach ache they should take bicarbonate of soda so much as try to make them aware of the changing thing and that the fact that when they eat a plateful of peas, they're not eating just peas, they've got dyes and flavouring in and God knows what, and that's part of the chemistry of life. I don't see it as a panacea to solve the world's problems ... I just want to make them aware of what's going on. (Dave, 44, senior teacher, Head of Year)

I think chemistry is a very good background to the material world in the sense that all the modern things that we have around us in the modern world have been through some sort of chemical process. I mean there's very few natural things ... so from a purely materialistic point I think that children should know, should have some idea of chemistry ... so that when they go into their factory or whatever it is at whatever level, they will take with them the ideas of chemistry, the transformation of material ... the chemistry gives them a logical method of thinking so that you don't naturally jump to so-called illogical conclusions about things. (Keith, 38, scale 1, chemistry)

Views and syllabuses vary and by no means all chemistry and other science teachers were of the same opinion as Dave and Keith. There were those who thought that chemistry, as they saw it (as a fully developed school subject — see Layton, 1972), was not particularly relevant or useful to, or a valuable experience for the majority of pupils. Margery and Kath both said they were happy teaching chemistry at 'A' level to pupils with special needs and interests, but not at 'O' level to a wider section of the pupil population. Their reasons for this are rather different.

Chemistry is becoming a much more rarified subject, more on the lines of Latin and things like that. Obviously it is essential for certain careers ... medicine, dentistry, agriculture so you can never be without it. Lower level chemistry is much more difficult to justify really, because I think physics and biology are much more applicable to most children, more understandable, and more tangible to them ... It's easy to say that in the outer world there's a lot of chemistry, well there is, but I'm not quite sure that children of low ability need to be made all that much aware of it ... I think ordinary children can see a little bit more relevance in physics than chemistry. (Mrs Morris, 45, scale 3, Head of Chemistry)

When I first started teaching you didn't bother, you didn't have all this about examining objectives and how you're going to achieve something, this just wasn't on. Now when I started examining my objectives and how I was going to achieve them, I thought there was nothing more a waste of time than 'O' level chemistry, because I didn't feel you were achieving anything other than giving some children a basis for 'A' level, but educationally I didn't think you were doing anything ... I felt it didn't really matter to youngsters if they knew that *that* gas existed and they had *that* properties, I didn't see anything educational in that. (Kath, retired, science)

Pete, a biologist, also had views about the value of chemistry:

I think, with a few exceptions that don't really impinge on exam syllabuses, chemistry is so remote from a lot of what goes on. I mean physics, fair enough, there's a hell of a lot of physics that can be useful and applied and also it's very much a thinking subject, I think more so than chemistry. Biology, well, there's so much about the human body that kids just love to find out about, but chemistry! It would really get me down trying to teach chemistry, trying to explain that when copper sulphate mixes with sodium hydroxide we get such and such a colour or whatever. So what? (Pete, 25, scale 1, biology)

In arguing for chemistry as a generally relevant and applicable subject, Keith (38, scale 1, chemistry) raises an interesting point concerning the nature and implications of views like those expressed by Margery, Kath and Pete. He also perhaps displays an attitude of 'missionary enthusiasm' (Goodson, 1981, p. 167) for the subject, which contrasts with Kath's and Margery's opinions and which is consonant with his view of chemistry and his desire to share it:

> I can't see how you can't justify teaching chemistry . . . that's rubbish. I think chemistry is a very important background subject for everybody . . . what we've got to do is adapt it and simplify it down to a level at which all kids can understand it. Teachers who say they can't justify chemistry for everyone are the ones who need educating. If they can't see the relevance and practicality of the subject they have a very narrow view of chemistry.

In general, teachers of science and art both hoped to equip pupils with the means of becoming aware of understanding and interpreting the world. However, there were some differences of opinion of what this meant, and these appeared to be subject related.

Artists tended to stress personal understanding and communication of that understanding, sometimes in a sense that could be regarded as therapeutic. They did teach techniques and skills but these were regarded as incidental necessaries to the central aim of self expression. The following quotes are typical:

> For me, art is a sort of chance to express and develop ideas, to be able to have a sort of style, not only to yourself (clothes) and to where you live (decor) . . . it's sort of a whole thing. To be able to go out into the country and see beautiful things, to be able to appreciate things, which is what I try and instil in, no, give the kiddiwinks, to me it's all around . . . I'm happy if they are happy with their work . . . I say to them 'What you're trying to do is get that little feeling inside you, that tells you when you've done something that you're pleased with', and if they get that, even if I don't know about it, sooner or later one of them's going to get that little tingly feeling, which you do get when you know you've done something good, and you've worked at it and you've sort of slogged and you've got 99 per cent perspiration and 1 per cent inspiration and all that, that's what I think I'm aiming for. To develop, to make them have that feeling and then want it even more, sort of like a drug. (Sarah, 25, scale 1, art)

Although not many put it in similar terms, some scientists felt the same way. Dave (44, senior teacher, Head of Science), for example said:

> Obviously I think chemistry is important, obviously I can see that a lot of kids need to have chemistry for their career, the rest of the kids I want to have an awareness of science, chemistry is just a feature of

that, you know ... There are particular aspects of chemistry that might just influence their decision making later, but basically I want them to come along, to use their hands, use their minds and enjoy what's going on and contribute, to communicate ...

Scientists and artists both aimed to teach skills, provide experiences, and pass on information which has some application in every day life:

I see my role as being to show the relevance of basic principles, I suppose, and their application in life, their practical application. I mean there's no point in teaching some kids high falutin' theories that they can see no use in, but why a fuse works and what sort of a fuse you want to put in a plug, then fair enough, that's got some real meaning to them. (Christine, 33, scale 3, Head of Physics)

Being a teacher is partly about showing them how they can use art to better their environment, to make something pleasant, to be aware of which colours go with which colours. (Sarah, 25, scale 1, art)

I think biology is a very useful subject for kids to do especially when we do the human body and health and so on, the bits I enjoy most are those, because they want to know. They want to know about teeth and how to look after teeth, they want to know about alcohol, they want to know about smoking and lungs and kidney diseases and diet ... they enjoy it and I feel it's useful information for them. You're explaining things to them that they've just heard, they might have seen something on *Tomorrow's World* and never really understood it, and you can see them 'Oh! That's why such and such and so on and so on'. (Pete, 25, scale 1, biology)

I'm teaching art as a chance for individual expression. I think it's a development of a person's individuality ... I'm sort of working towards them being themselves ... I'm sure that children should learn that, and do learn that what they do in their way is as good as what another person does in their way, and it reflects their personality. That's why I try to give such a wide variety of things to do so they can find their way ... Techniques of course you need to touch, but they don't take a lot of time. They need to be practised and a person's imagination needs to be stimulated to make a person a whole person. (Ann, 43, scale 1, art)

I would hope that they would be appreciative of the environment in which they find themselves — I don't just mean the local environment, but the world, if you like — and that by appreciating that environment they can perhaps, through some means or other, be that through painting, ceramics or whatever, communicate their response and their appreciation to others.

(R) So it is a communication thing essentially?

Yes, communication in art ... If we are talking about art, if you can get people to appreciate what they themselves can do and if they can appreciate and respect what other people can do. I mean this is one of the most abysmal things I find, that kids don't respect what they do themselves, a lot of them; they have no self respect, so therefore, they have no respect for other people's things, and I find that very distressing, so if we can get them to realise their potential and to respect another person and, perhaps try and communicate what they themselves feel, if they feel anything at all, with others. This is what I'm about. *'I think, I feel',* then we are beginning to be successful. I am not out to make artists out of them. They can still go home and they can still drink out of plastic cups and have a Trechicov green China woman on the wall, which is a god-awful picture, but they can have it on. They can have the plaster ducks flying over the mantelpiece or go around every morning sweeping the mantel-shelf and all that. They can have that. That's their taste, perhaps. I am not putting them down. I am not putting the kids down and saying 'You are rubbish'. If that is their taste, I might try to widen their experience and say 'Well look, there are other things. Let's look at other things'. But if that is their taste and if that is the level of artistic life that they are exposed to at home, though it is my job to expose them to something wider than that, but if after all they go back to that then I have got to accept that. It is not for *me*, though you can't help sometimes doing it I suppose, it is not for me to say 'They are wrong and their parents are wrong', it is not that. If they go back to that, and that is what they want, if they can make a value judgment and say: 'That is what I want because ...' then fair enough; I have succeeded. It is when they don't think and they accept anything that is put in front of them and these are the things in a way I would like to try and overcome. I don't want to make them into potters or painters. I want to make them aware. (Brian, 44, scale 4, Head of Art)

As earlier quotes show, the scientists tended to be much more objective. They strongly emphasized the practical applicability of the knowledge they were passing on to pupils. None of the science teachers left much room for the pupils to personally interpret the phenomena and relationships they were studying. Hypotheses, doubt and relativity were rarely mentioned. This is, perhaps, to do partly with the requirements of exam syllabuses, partly with the teachers' own educational experience and partly with a general feeling that:

There's no point in introducing pupils to relativity, it would only confuse them. (Jim, 65, retired, science).

Physics is uncertain in the sort of boundaries, the frontiers as it were ... As far as what you're doing in school is concerned, I think the very elementary stuff that you do there, even up to sixth-form is still elementary physics really and most of that has been tied up and explained and so on. There are very few things there where you've got to say to them, 'Well we think so and so, we're not sure'. So it is tidy within the school concept. (Mr Count, 54, retired, science)

I don't think it's necessary to complicate the matter by talking about relativity and doubt. It wouldn't mean much to most of the pupils anyway. We are teaching very low level science most of the time. (Margery, 45, scale 3, Head of Chemistry)

In other words, for the majority of the time science teachers were teaching facts, and herein lies what is probably the fundamental difference between our artists and scientists as *subject* teachers. Being in possession of the facts puts the teacher in a superior position vis a vis pupils. This, together with the need, promoted by exam syllabuses, to pass on these facts relatively quickly and in a particular, developmental order, has implications for pupil teacher relationships and for the working pattern in the classroom. It is likely to be a great deal easier for the teacher to fulfil the requirements of teaching science in schools if they take a formal authoritarian oriented approach. Art teachers also have to follow syllabuses. They usually chose to teach techniques, but in the last resort they were aiming to enable the pupils to express themselves. They are therefore in a co-worker, less formal and less authoritarian type of relationship.

Despite a shared perspective of science as a body of knowledge, among themselves our science teachers expressed a range of different opinions as to how they should approach teaching it. Mr Count and Mike, who were both, perhaps significantly, physicists, stressed the importance of teaching facts:

You have to teach facts, and they have to learn them. If they don't grasp the basic principles then they won't be able to go any further in the subject. (Mr Count, 54, retired, science)

There are some people who think that teaching should be concerned with teaching skills and not the content of information. Well I don't feel this, and it may be because perhaps it's physics, but I mean so much of what I do, is the sort of underlying pivot of so many things that they're going to do, that I mean they've got to get a lot of information, and a lot of understanding. (Mike, 46, scale 3, Head of Physics)

As Mike suggests, some people are critical of a fact oriented approach and advocate a skills-based approach to science teaching.

I love the notion of teaching science based on skills and I try to weave that into biology whenever I can. I think there's too much science which is just factually based. (Pete, 25, scale 1, biology)

The way I try to teach is not to be in transmission mode all the time. But rather to force them into assimilating the information rather than sheets of notes and 'go away and learn' — this type of thing. Get some sort of activity into what you are doing. (Ray, 38, scale 3, Head of Biology)

If our exams are nothing more than teaching ability to learn, really, is that education? I know you can't get by without some learning but there's got to be more even right at the start of taking science, for it to be worthwhile. (Kath, retired, science)

Subject Commitment

Teachers differ in their commitment to subject, teaching and school. Our art teachers were heavily committed to their subject above all else and used a sort of role-distancing strategy in order to redefine their position in school. They tended to see teaching as something they could do for the time being before going onto other things. Usually they said they were waiting until their families were no longer financially dependent on them. Brian (44, scale 4, Head of Art) is typical:

I am going to stick it out because there is nothing else I can do. I don't mean there is nothing else I am capable of doing, because there is, but I can't do what I would like to do ... What I would like to do is be an independent potter, but that means throwing my family's future very much into the melting-pot and rightly or wrongly I'm not prepared to gamble their futures at this stage ... I'm 44, my little boy is 7, therefore I've got a bit of a wait. I am looking forward to early retirement when I hopefully will be in a position to do something about the potting.

This attitude is not exclusive to art teachers. Research (for example Dale, 1976; Kyriacou and Sutcliffe, 1979; Lacey, 1977; Lortie, 1975) shows that many young teachers do not see themselves as committed to a life-long career in teaching. However, while teachers of other subjects, as they get older, seem more likely to come to accept that they will stay in teaching until they retire, art teachers continue to look forward to getting out. The dream of several of our art teachers was either to obtain a 'part'-time lecturing post in an art college and spend the rest of the time on their own work, or to be in a financial position to be able to live entirely on their work (see Bennet, 1983). This was even true of Sally who had taken on a scale 3, Head of Year, when it was offered to her. But this does not mean that these teachers are not committed to doing a good job, as Ann and John said:

If I got my ideal part-time job in an art college I wouldn't miss school or teaching one bit. I'm fully committed when I'm in it. When I'm in the classroom I'm thoroughly committed to what I'm actually doing. If I'm tired and I've had a late night or something and then next day I think 'I'll take it easy today', I can't. Once I'm there, once I'm in and somebody says 'Miss, will you?' and then I do and I can't stop, but when I leave it I usually forget it. (Ann, 43, scale 1, art)

When I'm in a classroom with a class I can lose myself in what's going on and enjoy it. I can still do that and I can ... get excited thinking, oh, it's so and so today, I'm looking forward to that class coming in. (John, 44, scale 4, Head of Art)

It is just that if it were possible, they would be quite happy to leave tomorrow. This is largely because these artist teachers' first commitment was to art. Their own work played a central role in their lives.

I do art for myself. I mean if I wasn't an artist I don't know what I'd do. If I didn't have art as something, as part of me, I don't know what I'd do ... I need something, to sort of manipulate my own living space and to express myself. (Sarah, scale 1, art)

I don't just like art, it's sort of my life ... it's very important to me ... I can't imagine life without it. Without it I'd be bored and when I'm not doing some work I feel sort of depressed, fed up. (Ann, 43, scale 1, art)

A lot of what I do out of school is wrapped up around art, because in that sense that's part of my life. (Brian, 44, scale 4, Head of Art)

Art is incredibly important to me, in my understanding of the world and everything because I've been doing it so long, all the time when I was at school. It must be the way I have for learning, and other things and understanding what's about them ... I get ideas from images rather than in mechanically writing it down ... to go and *see* something and respond to it, it's much easier for me. (Chris, 28, scale 1, art)

Science teachers did not talk about science in similar terms. Keith (38, scale 1, chemistry) was the exception and, in fact, has since left teaching and gone into a job in which he has closer and more exclusive contact with science.

For me, really, chemistry is not so much a technology ... my motivating drive to study science, at least on the conscious level, is to find out what the universe is made of and why it's here and how far it goes and so on, and chemistry is a means of doing that, because in studying chemistry you're studying the nature of how the universe is made. Now, for me, that's philosophy.

Teachers whose 'core commitment' is to their subject frequently have more in common with other artists and scientists than with other teachers in their own school. Some of the art teachers are in fact practising professional artists and, in many respects this tends to exacerbate their marginal status in school. Artist teachers may complain about marginal status, especially when it affects resources, but this may be what the artists who happen to be teaching really want. Their preferred identity is very much as artist rather than as teacher, as Chris suggests when he explains his perception of a 'career' teacher and why he is not one:

> A career teacher is somebody who spends all their time sort of learning how to do something without anything to do. You know, how to be a teacher without having something to teach, without the information and ideas. It's like some of them learn how to be good at art but they've got nothing to say, so its really stupid, not stupid, I shouldn't say, but there's nothing there. (Chris, 28, scale 1, art)

Indeed Bennet (1983) suggests that it is the deviant art teacher who wants to get on and make a career in school. This seems to be particularly true of those who had had an art school training and whose early professional socialization was oriented towards being an artist. By comparison those who trained at a teachers' training college do perhaps have more invested in identity as a teacher. There are exceptions of course, and Ann was one of them. In her case inaccurate careers' guidance had led her to a college of education instead of to an art college which she would have preferred. In general though, John's (44, scale 4, art) personal interpretation, given below, would appear to hold true:

> I had an opportunity to go for year tutor and I couldn't see my way of making an impact upon the school and the children through doing it, I thought I could do it better through my subject. I've always thought of myself as an artist first and a teacher second and that's always been my criticism of training colleges, they think of themselves as a teacher first and their subject is second. Now that's my own personal interpretation of it but I've seen other people doing art who were teacher trained from a college and they say 'Oh I think we ought to do some printing this week with them, or this term. What can we print?' 'Whereas I work the other way round, 'What are we going to do this term?' and then find a way of expressing it. But it's the subject that's important to me. If you go into things like the year tutor, it's the administration that becomes important then, over-riding really, how you organize things rather than what you're organizing.

For teachers of all subjects, a strong subject commitment has implications for career development in terms of progress up through the scale post hierarchy. Insofar as promotion tends to involve more administrative, managerial or pastoral type work and has less subject teaching, teachers have to weigh up their needs for greater remuneration — which may be an important consideration as their familial and domestic commitments increase. They also have to weigh the attractions of enhanced prestige against their needs for contact with their subject:

> I don't want to take on any more responsibility at school, and I'm not interested in admin or naughty children or anything like that. I came here to teach art and that's it really, and if I was to have more responsibility at school, I'd have no energy at all left for doing my own work. (Ann, 43, scale 1, art)

> One of the reasons why I stayed in teaching was because it kept me in contact with my subject, whereas if you become Deputy Head then your teaching goes down and you're running round after caretakers and silly things like that. (Christine, 33, scale 3, Head of Physics)

Art teachers' promotion prospects are comparatively poor (cf, Hilsum and Start, 1974). This does not necessarily cause them a great deal of dissatisfaction or mean that their morale is low, for there are other aspects of being a teacher which they value. For example, 'art' can encompass many different techniques, processes and skills and therefore offers the opportunity to focus on and develop areas of special personal interest. Most art teachers confessed to a pottery phase, during which they did little else; photography, screen printing and sculpture 'obsessions' were also mentioned. Marginal status can mean especial freedoms, because if art is regarded as relatively unimportant, people in authority are less concerned about what pupils do, although, as Brian said, they can have definite ideas about what this should be, and this can prove obstructive. This chance to diversify is something not available, at least to anything like the same extent, to scientists who are more constrained by syllabuses, and by what they can hope to teach pupils in the time they have. These factors, together with the satisfaction they get from working in their subject, may explain why, despite general peer pressure to climb the promotion ladder, art teachers are able to maintain their marginality.

Mr Bridge was perhaps the ultimate marginal art teacher. His wife got him a teaching job when he came out of the army at the end of the war. This was intended to be a short-term contingency while he looked round for a job, preferably as a technical illustrator. In the event, it seemed that his time in the services had put him behind — younger artists had 'stolen a march' on him. He taught for approximately thirty-three years but during that time he never saw himself as a teacher. He continued to do commissions, kept trying to get out of school, and never got to know anything about the career structure. He knew that he was on scale 2, but claimed not to know how many scales there were. Mr Bridge is exceptional, but it does seem that few art teachers would perceive themselves to be 'proper teachers, and as Bennet (1983, p. 10) argues, many art teachers 'regard senior posts as a threat to, and incompatible with, their selves'.

Scientists, according to Hilsum and Start (1974) have relatively good promotion prospects — although, as with all subjects, men's prospects are believed to be better than women's.

> I s'pose a woman Head of Physics is quite unusual, but it's not as rare as it used to be I don't think. I occasionally meet other lady Heads of Physics when I go on courses. There's one in Leffield. (Christine, 33, scale 3, Head of Physics)

> In this school there are women teaching biology but apart from me there's no woman in chemistry and physics. In general I think there are more now than there used to be ... I think you find it difficult to find women science teachers in positions of responsibility because single sex schools have gone. (Margery, 45, scale 3, Head of Chemistry)

Nor would it seem are prospects the same across the sciences. Biology is often said to hold out the least and chemistry the greatest, opportunities for promotion. Hilsum and Start (1974) noted a higher percentage of physics teachers in headships, though the position may have changed since they gathered their data in 1971–72. However, within schools, and even LEAs, traditions may develop, as Christine (33, scale 3, Head of Physics) describes:

> My next step would be to go to Head of Science, but it's difficult to go to Head of Science in this area cos Head of Science in this area is generally a chemist ... the posts usually advertised for a chemist so you can't really go for it. I was excluded from applying for the Head of Science here because of that.

Nevertheless, science teachers do, in general, tend to have higher promotional aspirations than art teachers. Apart from the fact that these aspirations are more likely to be realized, one motivation may be the difference between the earnings of scientists in schools and scientists in industry or medicine. This is something that university trained, specialist science teachers are perhaps most likely to be aware of, because they may have friends from college working in other occupations. Indeed all those in this category, together with most of those who went to colleges of education did mention their low salary compared to scientists working in industry. At first, science teachers may earn more than their non-teaching peers, but they quickly get overtaken (cf *Times Educational Supplement*, 27 January 1984, p. 17). As Ray (38, scale 3, Head of Biology) said:

> You get a bit fed up you know when you look at your particular salary level and compare it to other people of your age and this sort of thing, doing perhaps less stressful jobs anyway.

Perhaps feelings of relative deprivation make promotion seem more attractive. Artists, by comparison, are well aware of their financial security and well-being compared with the position of some of their peers, who are attempting to live on what they can sell of their own work. They may know of people in, for example, advertising, who are reputedly earning substantial sums, but on the whole the art teacher appears fairly content, and comparatively unambitious, from the money point of view.

Another possible reason why scientists seem more keen to be promoted is that scientific knowledge, particularly the more specialized areas, develops quickly. While art teachers can continue to improve their skills through doing their own work, it is hard for scientists to keep up to date with developments in their field.

> I suppose we all left university with high ideals, I can remember trying hard to keep up for just a short time but ... because the available journals just weren't appropriate it became obvious very quickly that you couldn't keep up ... I keep some files of cuttings ... things that I've been doing with sixth formers and in general studies. I don't really keep up to date. I mean the stuff that I was doing at university it never even got into the popular journals. I certainly don't take Abstracts of the Chemical Society or what have you because the sum of money involved there is absolutely enormous ... I don't think I really have access to the sort of thing I did at university at all. It's almost always the case that your knowledge goes out of date very quickly ... I think everyone knows it will be, as soon as you've left its gone. You can't really keep up to date by reading ... techniques are the thing that scientists could never pick up except by working with the equipment. This is the big cut off point between arts and science because you can't do science in abstract, you have to have loads of equipment, technique, money, even assistance to feed you information that you can't get, like X-Ray photography, that sort of thing. I certainly don't think you can go back, you probably could with great dedication if you didn't leave it too long, but twenty years or more is hopeless. (Margery, 45, scale 3, Head of Chemistry)

> I found it impossible to keep up with the way things were going because there was too much to read and not enough time. (Mr Count, 54, retired, science)

This has two important effects on their careers. Firstly, it becomes increasingly unlikely that they could leave teaching and go into industry or research, especially if, as is often the case particularly with men, their qualifications are not strong and they are in teaching because they couldn't get in anywhere else. This was Dave's (44, senior teacher, Head of Science) experience:

> There's school chemistry and chemistry. Chemistry's the outside world which is moving so fast, its industrial chemistry, and I learnt that when I tried to get a job outside, they just don't want you, not at 30-odd, you've got to train up ... chemistry has passed me by now.

Secondly, it is less easy to maintain an identity as a scientist. The teacher identity becomes more realistic, as Margery (45, scale 3, Head of Chemistry) explains:

> I suppose other things take over really, you become very busy in your present job and there's things to look out for there too ... chemistry was important to me as a student, I was good at it and keen on it. I suppose I've got a bit more away from the mainstream chemistry and it's become more of a methodology thing as you might say, the teaching method rather than the subject. Having been away from sort of mainstream research for so long, that has inevitably, you know, ceased to be so fascinating, because I don't know much about it now. So it's really concerned with the teaching of it to school children.

As was the case with artists, college-trained scientists may be at something of an advantage. Because they have more invested in an identity as 'teacher', it is easier for them to make a shift from subject commitment. Perhaps because it tends to be a less significant aspect of their whole life experience their subject becomes less important to some science teachers. Science teachers therefore more easily become administrators while art teachers remain artists.

Integration

How do recent trends toward integration affect subject commitment and identities? At a fundamental level, the issue of integrating science is political and ideological (cf Bernstein, 1975), and some teachers supported integration on these grounds:

> I did my TP in 1968, 1969, and I had this political orientation toward comprehensives, and integration was the name of the game. (Mr Ray, 38, scale 4, Head of Science)

Others who did not mention the political implications favoured an integrated approach saying that it is a more relevant and meaningful way for children to learn science.

For example Mr Count's (54, retired, science) feelings were that:

> I think it is important for a physicist to look at the implications, or the applications of his discipline on, say, biology and chemistry, and if this can be done by someone trained so that you don't just get a single biased view of things, such as I might have, then I think this is excellent ... I think it makes a much more complete scientist of you if you can interweave the three sciences and look at things from various points of view.

With special regard to their involvement in the Schools Council integrated Science Project, Jim and Kath made the following comments:

> You've got to watch science. If you're not careful it can become cigarette card science, in other words, little snippets of nice firm information, but no underlying theory or built-in system about it, no organized scheme of knowledge, and that is what SCISP in fact did ... You have to have an organized idea, now of the whole aspects of science; one is integrated to another. You may be talking about a biological subject and it will turn out in fact, the lesson will be physics ... you might say to yourself, well this is going to chemistry and lo and behold! it turns out to be biology — if you deal with the old groupings. And you can certainly expect to incorporate a certain amount of geology. And in some ways that is the challenge for most science teachers. (Jim, 65, retired, science)

> I have been influenced by SCISP, although some of my traditionalist colleagues damned it, because it teaches children to think but especially because ... it horrified me when, in a chemistry lesson I introduced a concept and someone would tell me 'That's physics', and so on and I would go on 'but this is not physics, this is science'. And I thought, how ridiculous that this is all compartmentalized and they can't see it's the same concept, same principle, same laws. (Kath, retired, science)

Kath also argued that when separate sciences are taught, time is wasted because pupils often cover the same topic more than once, but there are those like Pete (25, scale 1, biology) who think such repetition is not necessarily a bad thing.

> I teach the eye and I daresay physics teach the eye. I've no idea what they teach. It doesn't worry me at all really because the things that I did at school, that I understood best, were the things that I'd heard three times from three different people ... that worked for me ...

Despite what many of them say about school science being relatively basic, teachers opposed to integrated science frequently explain that they do not feel competent to teach the sciences they have not specialized in. For instance:

> If you're a languages teacher, if you teach maybe French and Spanish shall we say, they don't expect you also to teach Russian do they? and German? I mean they assume, they say 'Right, obviously you can't teach everything'. But because you're a science teacher they kind of expect you, they think you're going to be able to teach anything to do with science, you know, you're the sort of expert on it and therefore you get lumbered with everything. (Keith, 38, scale 1, chemistry)

> I don't feel much of an affinity with the integration lark. It's because of mixed ability, because of class size, because I believe my skills are best in the chemistry and weaker in physics and biology ... If you're going to teach mixed ability and you only teach a single subject the

person teaching has got to have a very good knowledge of that subject to range over the full range and to cope with the various capabilities of the kids. That needs various explanations and the possible deep question that the kid might ask you ... in any case staff don't like to teach outside their discipline, they really don't. It's no good saying, as the management people will, as some science advisers say, that you're not a good scientist if you can't teach at least third year any science. You find me a scientist who wants to teach all three disciplines and can do it to the satisfaction of the Head of Biology, Head of Chemistry, Head of Physics, and I'll find you fifty who can't or don't want to and that's the ratio you're in. All right, they'll teach chemistry and physics and loathe biology, so what's going to happen in the biology element in that er, first year, second year, third year syllabus. They'll teach biology and chemistry perhaps and loathe physics. (Dave, 44, senior teacher, Head of Science)

Ray, the Head of Biology in Dave's science department, did not agree and believed that integrated science would be a much more practical proposition, both from a manpower point of view and because he himself was a 'synthesist'. On the other hand, Pete, a junior member of the biology department, supported Dave:

I'm much happier teaching biology because I do feel much more knowledgeable about it and I feel much more interested in it and I'm sure that would convey itself to the pupils ... I don't think I could teach physics as well as a physicist and I don't think a physicist could teach biology as well as I could. It's not actually the syllabus, its answering the questions that the kids throw up. (Pete, 25, scale 1, biology)

Mr Count, (54, retired, science) who incidentally never taught 'integrated' or general science had conflicting feelings, similar to many teachers who only had experience of teaching their own specialist science.

I don't think there's anyone born yet who could tackle something satisfactorily, who has the experience, the background, the academic qualifications that are really needed to provide the depth of subject knowledge ... you may well be able to deal with the subject matter of any subject, but you're drawing on your own background knowledge and experience an awful lot to highlight what you're saying. I don't know that many people could do this from the point of view of physics, chemistry and biology. People say you're teaching well below degree level but you're drawing on degree material to illustrate what you're saying. So I have mixed feelings, yes (the integration is very important but the detail has got to be done by specialists).

Some teachers objected to integrated science on the grounds that it is less intellectually demanding and is detrimental to the chances of pupils who might go on to study a science at university. Margery's (45, scale 3, Head of Chemistry) view was that:

> Integrated science is interesting but I think it takes away from the academic strand. You've got to separate them out again somewhere in order to get the university requirements. I would enjoy it as an interesting experience but I don't personally believe in it very much.

For Margery, integrated science is not a recognized intellectual discipline because it is not taught at university. This is perhaps a major reason why integrated and general science have such low status, as indeed do integrated courses in general (Burns, 1983, p. 3). Being required to teach it can be perceived as threatening to one's professional identity as a subject specialist (cf Musgrove and Taylor, 1969, pp. 70–1).

The following quote from a teacher who did not regard himself as a specialist, tends to support this argument:

> I think, for me, education was more important than the science. I never minded integration. The trouble was I never saw myself as a particularly competent science teacher, since I dropped out of 'A' level physics at school and I didn't bother with chemistry at university. I didn't take maths above 'O' level. So I didn't really feel in touch with other areas of science. (Mr Ray, 38, scale 4, Head of Science)

Similarly, as Head of Science in a recently reorganized comprehensive, Jim (65, retired, science) had introduced integrated science without facing any opposition because the teachers concerned did not have specialist subject alliances or identities:

> We did SCISP ... in a way it was lucky to be able to do it, it was a lucky situation because having been a secondary modern school it had never had built into it this sort of three separate sciences ... it had never had that system in it. It had always had general science for everybody and it was lucky from my point of view that we hadn't got three separate sciences because, for one thing there was no-one in the school who said, could say 'I'm a physicist, I can't possibly teach any chemistry, I'm a chemist, it's no good expecting me to deal with physics'.

The art teachers I talked to did not express quite the same concerns. In fact many of them were quite critical of the way in which the organizational structure of the school required that they teach art as a separate body of knowledge. All of them had been, or were presently involved in integrated design courses and they said that they welcomed links with other subjects. They claimed that it was other teachers, particularly of metal and woodwork, who were resistant. For instance:

I did a course in design, craft and technology — you know 'boy's crafts' ... I wanted to use wood and metal and plastics in an art kind of way ... But I haven't got any wood, and I haven't got any plastics. You know I have asked for odd bits of things from time to time. I'd like to do, oh, what do you call it, enamelling, which is an artistic type of thing but it's all somewhere else, and when I mentioned it, I'm not really, you know, in their department. (Ann, 43, scale 1, art)

It is perhaps significant that art, being a subject that can in itself be studied to degree level, carries more prestige than most craft/technical subjects. Possibly teachers, particularly older ones, of these craft subjects are concerned to preserve what status they have and are not prepared to risk losing it to art teachers. This may be especially so at a time when the position of craft/ technical teachers in schools is potentially increasing in importance because of the introduction of City and Guilds, TVEI and other MSC sponsored courses. What art teachers did object to was the way in which teachers of 'academic' subjects would use art to fill up time.

If you try and take the whole job-lot, art is something which I regard as very valuable, even in terms of actual visualization of situations around you, the art of advertising and things like this, not necessarily the straight fine art sense; but art is very often seen by people as purely a therapy. It is an area where when kids have had enough of thinking — that means when they are full to the gills with maths, English and science and whatever else — let's pack them off to art, they can have a play around down there and that is providing they don't play too loud of course: 'He is not doing a very good job that man', but it is a place where they can dump; and when you have an option system as we have seen developed in all sorts of schools, 'the able shall do this, that and the other. The unable ...', and as one head of department said to me two or three times: 'Well you can always give them a piece of paper and a pencil and they can draw. In *my* subject: AND IT GETS UP MY BLOODY NOSE. Yes, I can give them a piece of paper and a pencil, but they won't do anything. That same person can give them a piece of paper and a pencil and they will get the same result, so, why put art as a dumping ground, a dust-bin, a second-rate subject, a time filler? (Brian, 44, scale 4, Head of Art)

There are subjects when the kids are sort of casually asked 'right, do a drawing'. I'd like to know how it's asked and how it's used, art and graphic skills in other subjects, and how the teacher perhaps views it. Often, it's just sort of used for something you can fall back on, suddenly when you run out of ideas. I don't really think that's good enough. (Chris, 28, scale 1, art)

When art is treated in this way, when it is regarded as a time-filler, as a dumping ground, as therapy, the art teacher is, in effect, deskilled. This illustrates how a teacher's identity is affected by subject status, which we consider next.

Subject Status

Influence of the Head

As was illustrated in Chapter 5, the character and atmosphere of a school tend to reflect its Headteacher's orientations. Thus the status accorded and the resources allocated to a subject owe a great deal to how the Head regards it.

> At the old Roman Girls' Grammar School, the set up was absolutely perfect, you got a big room with lots of light and the PTA were very cooperative and very often they'd raise money for our extra apparatus. The Headmistress used to come 'Is there anything you'd like for the art room?'. 'Well, we could do with an electric wheel because youngsters find it difficult to use the kick wheel, they are very cumbersome things'; 'And how much do they cost?' 'Oh, a hundred pounds'. 'Right, order one then' ... on the other hand, when I was at the Lincolnshire school, the Head there was inclined towards history and the geography and those sorts of things, you know. Art to him was something that kids, it was a bit of a fiddle and so it didn't merit very much money, and you found yourself, you were the poor relation in the staffroom and when it came to requisition and your stock was very meagre. (Arthur, 69, retired, art)

> In this school art is way down at the bottom, very much so. Languages, anything classical, comes top in this school, which is understandable considering that the Head is main language, most of the hierarchy are as well. But you can understand it in the fact that it's a very academic type of school, it's run on the lines of a grammar school rather than a normal comprehensive school. (Jan, 25, scale 1, art)

> Perhaps I've been lucky in this school, when I listen to other art teachers and how they seem to be fighting tooth and nail, or that's the impression you get, for their own subject and for the status of their own subject in school. Whereas we've got a head who is very keen and interested in art. This may come from the fact that he's an English specialist, he's very keen on drama ... and he sees ... the creative side as an important balance. So I've spent the time I've been here with the subject where I've not had to battle for what I've wanted ... we get a fair crack of the whip. (Helen, 40, scale 3, Head of Art)

Now Parklands High School was not unique, but exceptional insofar as the Head of this girls' school was a chemist. It had a lot of girls doing science in the sixth-form. I mean obviously we had a lot of arts, and many more of them, but nevertheless we always had some good large science groups going through, and it was exceptional in that. The fact that we had a Head who was a science person, she realized you can't do science without it costing money, and it was a well equipped school too, and I got my hands on quite a lot of money. (Kath, 59, retired, science)

I've now got a department of three whereas I had a department of six. If I compare it to the secondary modern school days when there were three full-time art teachers and two part-time teachers in this building, I now operate in a school twice the size, on two sites, and there are only three of us, and I feel that it's an attitude towards the subject on the part of the head. (John, 44, scale 4, Head of Art)

It was a very good school in Coventry and the Headmaster was a man who was passionately keen on art and music and drama and things like that and of course, anybody like me was made you see, so the Head was a great asset in that way ... I didn't enjoy it in Exeter though because he was a sort of a Headmaster who was trying to run a secondary modern school on a very tight academic basis like a grammar school ... I moved from there because of the Head's attitude to art and his penny pinching over materials. (Mr Bridge, 58, retired, art)

In our school, I would say, science has top status ... we lead the way. (Pete, 25, scale 1, biology)

There are always the Cinderella subjects. Science doesn't usually do too bad. (Christine, 33, physics)

As Christine suggests, science is usually a high status subject, not surprisingly in view of its academic pedigree (Ball, 1982; Goodson, 1981) and marketability (Ball, 1981). In addition very few art teachers become Heads (Hilsum and Start, 1974) which is probably both a reason for, and a consequence of, the marginal position that art and art teachers have in many schools.

An interesting and illuminating insight into how teachers experience subject status hierarchies can be obtained by comparing the accounts of two teachers, Mr King and Mr Ladyhill, who taught art and science respectively, in the same school, Valley Boys, at the same time:

When I first went to the school the status of art was appalling, absolutely unforgiveably bad. The art master set them work on little fiddly bids of paper. Art was a suppressed subject. I had to break that at Valley. It was a science school, art was nothing. I broke it. Mind you, with a lot of very great aggression. I'm afraid that was the only way. Well that's the only way I succeeded. And I was prepared to. A lot of staff left because they disagreed with what the Head did. I decided it had reached the point where he was going to change and not me. To some extent I was a bad lad, but I had to stick up for the kids. My attack was 'You appointed me, and you appointed me presumably because I have the guts to do what I'm doing, and if you don't like it, bad luck. It was a science school, as Ladyhill would be pleased about. But I robbed him, you see, it would take me years to get something in the region of £300–£500 a year, and he could spend that on a microscope or a balance. I pulled the socks right up in the art department too, anything up to fifteen going to art school a year. (Mr King, 65, retired, art)

Mr Ladyhill: Science had very high status in the school, and it has been my intention to keep it that way. I believe very much in a balanced curriculum up to 'O' level. When I first went to the school my then Head of Department was a chemist, a very fine teacher, and a very good Head of Department, and during the time I served with him, there was a building-up period, the science was already quite high, but I like to think I helped him in building. Science did enjoy a very strong, justifiably strong reputation in the school, if one looks at the number of successes we had at 'O' and 'A' level, the number of open scholarships, the number of people who've gone for higher education in the sciences then I think it becomes obvious to anyone. The teaching, the reputation of science in the school, was already quite high when I came, and I like to think it has gone on increasing in reputation.

R: So did science have good resources in the school?

Mr Ladyhill: Facilities — in respect of laboratories, yes, in respect of equipment at that time, I suppose adequate, but not excessive, and it has been our policy among the science staff, and particularly the Head of Department, to fight and fight and fight again for more money, and this is what we've done very successfully I think. You see Valley had grown from a municipal secondary school, it didn't get grammar school status with the 1944 Act, and a new Headmaster. As far as the laboratories are concerned it was fairly well off, one of the physics labs was better equipped than the other, the chemistry labs about even, but I think we all felt that the amount of money that was available for science was inadequate, for the things we wanted to do, in fact one always feels this, and this has been a perpetual theme I think, during my teaching. (67, retired, science)

Gender Differences

Differential subject status is also sometimes associated with gender, and the Head's view of what are appropriate subjects for girls and boys to study. In the light of this it is interesting to consider what Mrs Castle and Miss Coal, who taught art and science at Valley Girls, Valley Boys' sister school have to say.

> *Mrs Castle* (64, retired, art):   The Headmistress was interested in art, and she was a water colour painter in her spare time. She was a very jolly lady and art had very good status, as had music. Music had top status and art about the next in the school ... The timetable was quite well organized, when I first went there, except that the lower age group classes were very large, and it wasn't until we got a new Headmistress that she cut down drastically at all levels ... The Headmistress encouraged me, in order to keep up with her. I took myself off to London on Saturday mornings to have some private pottery lessons, to be in a position to develop the pottery, in a way she pushed me.
>
> *R:*   As you talk, I keep thinking of Mr King's experience at Valley Boys' School, fighting to get art some credibility. It was science all the way in the boys' school. It seems like an absolute reversal.
>
> *Mrs Castle:*   Nice girls were expected to be able to draw and paint and do nice things. There was never much of a problem and quite a lot of girls wanted to do it.

When I came to Valley Girls, there was no sixth-form in my subject. There was sixth-form chemistry and sixth-form biology ... oh and maths, but there was no sixth-form physics. They didn't even take physics to 'O' level or School Certificate as it was then. Oh yes it was wonderful. I was there one year with Miss Wells (the Headmistress) who appointed me. And the following year, when Miss Knight came — well we were all introduced to her you see — and she said to me, when I was introduced 'Oh yes, you're the physicist' or 'You teach physics' and I had the common sense to keep quiet, and not let on — because physics didn't exist in the school. So I was introduced to her like that, I didn't say anything and then, when the timetable was made, in September, I had a timetable in which I was teaching sixth-form physics. Nobody had told me. I was there, confronted with teaching sixth-form physics. Anyway there I was, but it didn't matter, I wasn't that long out of college, and I kept about two lessons ahead of them ... But it was frustrating there, you see we did this awful exam, which I think now doesn't exist, called 'physics with chemistry' and I mean I was perpetually at every Headmistress that I could get at, to say that this was a ridiculous exam. You see, they wanted to do physics with chemistry, because they were only prepared to give you four periods a week. Well, you couldn't do physics and chemistry as separate subjects on two periods a week each — it was impossible. This is where I say the girls were at a disadvantage, because you would *never* get that at a boys' school, *never*. You see they weren't prepared to give you the time for physics and chemistry, so they stuck the two together. We did physics with chemistry until the end — until I retired. I mean it is quite nonsensical. I fought that right the way through and I got frustrated more and more. (Miss Coal, 68, retired, physics)

There were some girls' schools such as those attended by Margery and Christine who went on to become chemistry and physics teachers, where girls were strongly encouraged to become scientists. But it was unusual, and if girls did a science, it was more likely to be biology.

A number of teachers felt this was sometimes regarded as the least prestigious science, and it is taken by a disproportionate number of girls (cf HMI, 1979, pp. 164–205). Dave (44, senior teacher, Head of Science) recalled that in the grammar school where he worked in the mid 1960s, the option scheme worked so that it was:

Physics for boys, boys and physics in a mining area and engineering and so on. Girls have to take biology haven't they, you know, end of story. That was the regime in that school, and it was by no means unusual.

This 'biology for girls' notion may be a reason why, in girls' grammar schools, biology often tended to be more generously resourced than did the other sciences.

Resources

Art is usually one of the areas that suffers most at a time of contraction (cf Goodson, 1983).

There were changes occurring all the time throughout my career (a) the environment; (b) the facilities as the economic climate changed, the money available for art in particular which was a cinderella subject at my particular last school anyway. The amount of money varied quite a lot depending on what was left over very often ... it was national economics and this much was granted for education, each authority is given that much out of the rates sort of thing from that each school is allocated in order of different priorities depending on what the Director thinks and his minions. This much for that school and then you come back to the head, then his favourite themes, they get the money and if he's an art sympathizer you are alright, if he's not you are all wrong. (Arthur, 69, retired, art)

What is done in the classroom depends to a large extent on the resources that are available. Art teachers often complain that they are unable to do the sorts of things that they would like to do because they lack the equipment and staff. This is a major source of job dissatisfaction among them especially as they feel they often even have to cope with an inadequate supply of basic materials such as paper, paints and brushes.

> If you have less money you narrow the field down and you cut out the luxury activities. More money, alright they can dabble in this, that and the other, and some kids like experimenting with new materials, you give them a bucket full of plaster of paris and stuff like that and some sponges, a fantastic atmosphere, but on the other hand when you are limited you've perhaps only got drawing paper and pencils and you tie them down to portrait studies and pencil studies and all that. Even the best of art teachers, you are going to have problems pinning some kids down because they can only take so much of that. (Arthur, 69, retired, art)

> I've just submitted some figures to the Head to show how the money that I can spend on the pupils has been eroded since we became a comprehensive school, and the allowance for the department has gone down from £2500 to £600 per annum, and that's in spite of inflation. So we don't do things now that we used to do. We used to do a lot of screen printing, now it's a sort of special event for examination candidates ... I think it's a philosophy in the school that there's less money for art. (John, 44, scale 4, Head of Art)

Scientists also complain about the effects of contraction upon what they are able to do in the classroom (cf *Times Educational Supplement*, 17 February 1984). But, by comparison with art, at least in the schools where our teachers were working, science still attracts a large share of capitation, although it may no longer enjoy the generous provision of the late 1960s and early 1970s. In those days a lot of money and expensive equipment was available for science as Kath (59, retired, science), who was perhaps particularly fortunate, remembers:

> In those days ... of course money was different from what it is now. The LEA gave the schools an awful lot of money to buy equipment, they called it Nuffield money, but the science adviser, he used to ring up, most unfair system, he used to ring up the folks he knew, I did very well out of him, and say 'Would you like XY and Z?' and of course I said 'Yes' to everything. Equipment used to pour in, and one time, just before we became comprehensive, 'Would you like, I've got a lovely analytical balance here, would you like it?', 'Yes'. It came. We didn't really need it because we'd got plenty. So I rang him back and said 'Well, you know, a lovely balance this, how about me getting it back to you, and I have the money for something else?', and I sold it back to him and got the money for something else. Those were the days when money was easy.

Artists didn't always do too badly from expansion and comprehensivization either:

> For five or six years you were in clover, you could have anything you wanted to ... they were just going into comprehensives. You see Squirreldray School, the old secondary modern school, ceased to exist and the new Squirreldray Comprehensive began at phase one which was the same school, the same numbers and the same staff in a new building. Well you carted all of your old stuff from the old school up to the new building, you had that year's requisition money plus an initial settling in allowance, so you'd really three lots of money to go at. And then when phase two began you got another art room, you got another initial allowance and the ordinary year's allowance, and they were quite good allowances anyway. Money was no object. (Arthur, 69, retired, art)

But it hadn't always been like that, and in many, secondary schools, it never was. An interesting geographical variation emerged here. Retired teachers in the south continually stressed that the resources and facilities available for science teaching had been inadequate. This was said to be particularly so in girls' grammar schools where, by comparison, art was abundantly provided for. It may be that the northern teachers did better because they had access to more industrial companies who were prepared to 'sponsor' the school by providing it with equipment and setting up regular visits for pupils.

Yet even in the north it seems that all schools were not equally favoured. For instance, in the early 1960s Jim (65, retired, science) had had to make his own apparatus — and he was not the only one:

> I spent an awful lot of time concocting simple scientific apparatus, make your own! Oh yes! Actually I used some of it right up to the very end. I can remember making a simple electric motor, made of cut up bits of tin and folds of tin and carefully wrapped coils and so on. Everything could be seen and you could easily understand the process, but it was worthwhile doing it because it was a useful teaching aid. But there wasn't much choice, there was nothing bought for you. If you wanted to cope with these ideas, of what happens to conductors and so on, well you've got to produce the stuff yourself, you've got to make it. So you made it ... on scientific apparatus there just wasn't any. I think it must be a shock for many people in the profession now to come up against some of those sorts of attitudes. In the very early days I met the business of, well, 'if you want a set of pencils for this class where are the stubs of the old pencils before you can have the new ones?'

Going further back Arthur (69, retired, art) recalled the depression of the 1930s:

> If you saw a job that you had the faintest chance of getting you went to it, wherever it was jobs were very scarce, it was a worse depression period than the one we're going through now. Teachers actually gave up 10 per cent of their salary, well, they didn't have much option really, it were taken from them. I mean I'd only been teaching about eighteen months and they took 10 per cent off my salary, which wasn't all that big anyway at the time ... it was very tight and requisition money was always tight ... It was grim, your art lesson was on a piece of paper eleven by seven and you used both sides of the paper, use the other side next week.

It was partly because he remembered those days and suspected that they might return that he took every opportunity to take advantage of a sympathetic head:

> I could see it coming just before I retired and for a number of years I was hoarding these odd little gifts the Head came around with. 'Can you spend £20 now?' Even if I couldn't have, I would never have said no I can't. I always said 'Yes I'll have it', and I'd find something to buy that I could stick in a cupboard until next year, and when I retired I handed over reams and reams of drawing paper and parcel paper and all that which was very scarce, the last couple or three years ... I retired nearly five years ago now ... It was all beginning to tighten up, the requisition allowance.

However, Arthur was perhaps something of an opportunist, for in other circumstances, under a less generous Head, he found other ways to supplement his allocation:

> I taught night school classes ... The actual payment when you took income tax out of it was nothing, but on the other hand you met people. And through the night school set up you were able to order pottery, clay, and glaze and that, ostensibly for the night school class which in reality was used for the day school classes as well. I was able to get by like that — by fiddling.

Timetabling

A number of studies (Hargreaves, 1967 and 1980; Keddie, 1971; Lacey, 1970; Riseborough, 1981) have shown that in schools where pupils are streamed on the basis of their ability as judged by a selection exam or primary school reports, teachers are also streamed on the basis of their ability as judged by qualifications, experience and the value accorded to their subject. Generally speaking, pupils and teachers at similar 'levels' on their respective ladders work with each other — and have a similar school experience.

People in practical subjects aren't allowed anywhere near the A or B forms for registration, we're only allowed the C or Ds ... that's the philosophy of the school. (Jan, 25, scale 1, art)

Where practical subjects in general, and art in particular, are regarded as low status, art teachers often feel that the subject receives less than fair treatment on the timetable. Also, it is often scheduled predominantly for lower ability pupils. This is understandably a source of dissatisfaction and was emphatically mentioned by *all* art teachers.

I think that because the school is controlled by ex-grammar school people their way of thinking puts more store on traditional academic subjects. You see, if they feel it expedient they will allow so many kids to take Latin and those will be taken out of other lessons to do Latin. But if I wanted so many kids to do art, they wouldn't take them out of other lessons to do art. All the kids have to do three sciences, it seems ridiculous ... I could equally well say all the kids should have to do three crafts ... you could make a case out for it if you wanted to, particularly in a comprehensive school, when at least a proportion of the kids are non-academic ... I've tried to argue for timetable space ... I don't even see the third year kids. We get them in the third year once a week. (John, 44, scale 4, Head of Art)

Able pupils may actively be discouraged by it being made very difficult for them to take art. But teachers do persevere:

I think the number of very bright kids that I get, there's an awful lot of pressure put on them to take other subjects and two of my best pupils in the sixth-form for example, come to lessons when I've got other classes in the room and they don't come when the main group comes in the sixth-form, because they've been pressurized into taking other subjects which conflict with the timetable. Now they don't go to French when the French teacher has a third year, but they come to art when the art teacher has a third year. (John, 44, scale 4, Head of Art)

The Head doesn't like it (art). He doesn't like the bright children to do it really. I think he restricts them because there aren't a lot of jobs in art and you need to be bright to do it. I mean, to do a degree in it you need to be bright in it but he doesn't let them have many lessons a week. (Ann, 43, scale 1, art)

We do take pupils down to the art school and we've had people up here to give talks. But there's a certain amount of reluctance on the side of the school, in fact the Head this year has said no to having somebody from the art school come to talk to the fifth years ... because he thinks it might encourage them to leave and go to the art school instead of staying on into the sixth form, and I do think there is a reluctance to encourage them to go in for an arts' subject. (Sally, 44, scale 3, art, head of year)

In an attempt to improve the standard of art in an academically oriented school, one group of teachers — Sally, John and Ann — had proposed introducing a history of art 'A' level. In the event they were unsuccessful, but had they succeeded, it is somewhat ironical that within their school art would have been differentiated, with one aspect of it being available only to the privileged few; while practical work, the mainstream art, would perhaps have been further downgraded.

If teachers are so acutely conscious of the status of their subject within the school, pupils can be expected to be similarly aware. As Ball and Lacey (1980) write, 'the subject department is a crucial mediating context in the translation of curriculum knowledge from the level of "subject communities" into the pupils' experience of "subjects" in the process of classroom interaction' (p. 150). Frequently, the nature of the translation means that pupils pick up and internalize 'the traditional belief that there is a body of content for each separate subject' (Schools Council, 1967, p. 3). Consequently, in many cases pupils' major, and perhaps only, experience of a 'subject' is their experience of it in school. This experience is quite likely to colour their perception of it and their approach to it (Ball, 1982). Chris (28, scale 1, art) is a committed and enthusiastic art teacher in a school where art is relatively well regarded and resourced, yet has been led by his experiences to say:

> It's very hard to justify art for the academically capable. I could have done before I was a teacher but I think I'm beginning to believe to some extent that if the 'able', I don't know how I'm going to judge ability, the really able pupils are wanting to get to university, they're not gonna get there by doing 'A' level art. They're gonna have to do other subjects that are regarded at university as more academic.

It is not really all that surprising that art teachers therefore often complain that

> Some kids come to art because they think it's a doss and they would fall out, people wasting their time, and I feel I work quite hard usually, and I don't like it if I feel people are not working. (Ann, 43, scale 1, art)

(cf Measor, 1984, on pupils' views of art).

Art teachers who see art to be a valuable subject having equal status with others on the timetable often have to combat the view that it is not seen as being particularly important, and therefore does not demand the same sort of hard working, committed approach of science, maths, English and humanities.

Strategies for Protecting Status

Within their specific schools, science and art teachers were equally protective towards their subject. Although no doubt teachers of all subjects share this attitude, it may be stronger amongst art and science teachers who may develop a more potent and cohesive sub-culture through spending less time in the staffroom, and more in their own specialist rooms. The chief indication of this protective attitude was the frequency with which comments like these were made:

> If the Head made any sort of general policy decision to do with teaching, curriculum and so on, even if I disagreed with it and argued with him about it, in the end I would have to go along with it. But if he said something like 'You will teach the moon is made of green cheese' and I know for a fact, because it was within the area of my subject, that it wasn't, I would definitely not do it. (Mr Count, 54, retired, science)

> I'll comply and do all the administration we have to do, though I don't agree with it, but when it comes to things that affect my subject I won't, because I feel that I'm right. (John, 44, scale 4, Head of Art)

In some schools, scientists convincingly argue that it is impossible for them to teach mixed ability groups and are therefore allowed to set (Ball, 1981), and Margery had been able to get smaller classes for separate sciences to be taught.

Dave, on the other hand, was prepared to accept large classes because to have them smaller would have meant teaching integrated science, which was what the head and deputies wanted, but which Dave (44, senior teacher, Head of Science), as Head of Department, was resisting.

> The labs are designed for twenty-four and they put thirty-six in ... but I've accepted it because I'm at the moment insisting upon single sciences. If I want smaller classes I'm told 'Right, you can't teach single sciences unless you do it on a rota basis, two terms this, two terms that, you would have to come down to four periods in first year and second year as opposed to six, unless you teach integrated science, or something like that and then they could cut the class size down'.

Christine felt that she was able to get her own way by blinding her historian head and his classicist deputies with science. But strategies such as these are not always successful, and teachers, and perhaps art teachers in particular, because their subject seems more frequently to be threatened, may feel that they have to resort to private, underground strategies.

Brian (44, scale 4, Head of Art), for example, describes the defensive perspective he has developed:

It's perhaps a survival instinct. I don't know, it is just a feeling, at times, that in order to survive and in order to protect and I am not thinking of being purely conservative, with a little c, but in order to protect perhaps what I value — but in terms of things like my subject, within a committee room, in order to protect that and let it retain some kind of status you have got to be open and you have got to lay your cards on the table but I think at times you have got to be bloody minded, you have got to dig your heels in and say 'enough is enough', or 'no' or 'yes', or whatever. You have got to be, and I think it is very closely related, if you want to use a word like I do 'devious', you have got to be. That sounds very scheming and underhand and I don't mean it in that way. You have got to be willing to look at the problem and try and work out what the opposition is going to be. It is just like playing chess, though I can't play chess. You have got to try and work out your opponent's next move ... because if not, some rather astute guy is suddenly going to wipe you clean off the board and you are going to think later, 'God if only I had done so and so, that situation wouldn't have arisen' ... I think this approach is something that's grown, something I've developed over the years as a response to circumstances you might say.

It is perhaps significant that a number of art teachers described themselves as 'devious' in their dealings with management and in their attempts to get a fair deal for their subject (cf Woods, 1984).

A common cause of dissatisfaction amongst art teachers, and one which often provokes them into taking some action, is the way in which, although little interest is shown in their work for the majority of the time, they are asked to put on displays when the school is on show.

Somebody will say 'We've got a parent's night tonight Mr Baden, if you've got a spare minute we'd like some work in the entrance hall, tonight please'. They don't say 'We've got one next week if you can be thinking about it'. It makes you cynical. (John, 44, scale 4, Head of Art)

Brian (44, scale 4, Head of Art) had also become cynical:

You get, 'we have got governors coming in next Tuesday, smarten the walls up please'. ... In other words: 'Can we have the cow in the corner of the field chewing the cud on the wall because the governor is coming and he will think "Aren't these kids great". In actual fact, child art is usually lousy: it is terrible, because of that very philosophy that some people approach it with. Go back to your junior schools: Christmas, nativity, right, the hall. So out comes the tinsel and the coloured and crêped paper and we make a whacking great manger scene on the back of the stage wall. Now, I am not saying there is anything wrong in doing it, but sometimes it is done for the wrong reasons. It is not always what is done, it is why it is done. 'We have got a school play; we need the scenery doing. Oh, the art department! Mind you, of course, we can't offer to let you have any time to do it, or any extra money to do it with'. In other words, it's a means, and very often it's a mean means and I think it is through things like that that I have grown cynical, I have grown more stubborn and I have grown resistant to pleas for help and things like that not 'We won't help' but it sometimes falls on deaf ears now because I won't be used.

Art teachers see these requests, which are in effect demands, as indicative of a slighting trivializing, yet at the same time, instrumental and mercenary attitude towards their work. They have their counter strategies, which may not produce any immediate dramatic changes, but which give them some personal satisfaction and which may have an effect in the long run.

You tend to withdraw and say, well I'll work with the kids in the four walls of the classroom. Occasionally I will have a burst of blood and come out and put an exhibition up somewhere and that gives my ego a boost ... I will go and put art work in geography rooms and in the corridors and the libraries and the foyers, entrance halls, as well as the three art rooms, just to show what work is going on and it's about time somebody else noticed ... Christmas decorations, although I can't afford to do as much as I used to, I still try because I've always done it and I feel that if I give up doing that then that's a symbol of giving up to the system. (John, 44, scale 4, Head of Art)

The Head now complains when work isn't displayed around. I think he's coming round to see art as a viable subject. I think with the more we put on the walls, the more he can see what we're doing and that's why we do insist on these displays. (Jan, 25, scale 1, art)

At other times teachers may appear to comply, but this is only because they have successfully redefined the situation to make it acceptable — they resolve their cognitive dissonance. This is what Ann (43, scale 1, art) did when the Head required her to set homework:

I don't like giving homework but we have to do, we're supposed to give homework, the Head likes everybody to have homework and they have these homework notebooks and I start at the beginning of the year and give them homework. They have sketch books and they're to do this drawing. And they draw a jar of jam, a toothbrush and a view from the window and I try to think of things and about now at this point in the term, in June, I run out of ideas. ... You're supposed to go through with the fourth and fifth years giving them homework and marking it ... well, I don't really think you can mark art but I've got a lot of marks in the book I must admit and its useful to look through I suppose and the drawings are not a waste of time of course. Drawing isn't ever a waste of time and you can use it for the 16+ as well. They need to practice it and so on but when I get to the fourth year, to about now, I expect them to do things at home without telling them to do things at home because I'll let them take things home, paint and anything they ask and so my fourth year red band now, I don't set them any homework ... I just expect by now it's become important to them.

What, then, actually happens in the classroom?

The Classroom and Teaching

Organization and Pedagogical Style

Art and science teachers both have to organize and manage practical lessons involving messy, expensive and potentially dangerous equipment and substances. In this respect the two subjects do have a great deal in common.

There's lots of things in the art room that you can be naughty with, you know. You can throw paint up and you can paint each other and you can tip water over. (Ann, 43, scale 1; art)

The amount of bumf we get out from the authority which warns us that we are accountable for anything that happens in the lab impresses the dangers on us. (Dave, 44, senior teacher, Head of Science)

The way in which a teacher approaches and organizes a practical lesson determines the atmosphere in the classroom (of which more later) and can influence pupils' receptivity and response. In art, for example, Sally (44, scale 3, art, Head of Year) felt that:

In a way, if your discipline is too good, then the art lesson will fail. You've got to have children confident enough to do their own thing or it's a waste of time, if it's too regimented and organized I don't think it's art at all.

She saw the difficulty to lie in achieving an acceptable balance:

because some children will go too far and be noisy and take advantage of it, it is an awkward system and simply because they should be able to sit and talk really, while they're working, as an ideal situation, but you do get some classes who are incapable of sitting and talking ... not constant chatter, but they shouldn't have to sit in silence for the whole of the time I don't think.

By trial and error, teachers learn and develop strategies aimed at encouraging the sort of working environment they prefer. Ann and Jan had a similar approach to the earlier encounters between a teacher and a class when the class may be trying to 'suss out' (Beynon, 1984) the teachers' approach to discipline.

> Once they've thrown clay up to the ceiling and you've sent them out or give them a detention they don't generally do it again, it's not worth it, plus you get them interested of course which, you know, that interest survives throughout the course, hopefully. (Ann, 43, scale 1, art)

> They usually have a lesson when I first start teaching them where they try and paint each other ... it's all annoying little things, ripping up a sheet of paper ... (but) ... if you just come on tough at the beginning. (Jan, 25, scale 1, art)

Artists and scientists both saw teaching pupils how to use materials properly as an important part of their job. On the whole, artists tended to have a more relaxed approach:

> They all think it will be easy to use a potter's wheel and they all want to do it. It takes a long time to learn and some of them do get impatient and want to give up ... You have to show them how to clean brushes, you have to nag at them sometimes, sometimes they aren't very thorough but I'm quite strict with them. (Ann, 43, scale 1, art)

Scientists tended towards a more formal instructional mode:

> I think, in a science subject, you have to impose a very strict code of discipline ... I started teaching in a school where the lab I was going into was devoid of apparatus because the people who had been teaching there beforehand, in that lab, were not capable of looking after it, so you realize you are going to teach kids who have had a slack regime and who are going to damage apparatus deliberately, so you set off, if you're gonna survive you're gonna be firm, if you want apparatus in the lab you've gotta convince your Head of Department they can have it and so on, so you set off in that sort of hard line that you're not gonna stand for any nonsense. (Dave, 44, senior teacher, Head of Science)

Jim (65, retired, science) was perhaps less authoritative and disciplinarian:

> One of the problems is that some of the items of scientific equipment are damned expensive to start with and it's so easy to damage them. Some of the electrical stuff, some of the meters of one kind or another, certainly a meter for 'A' level, they can be gone with just the slightest little bit of carelessness, and if you're to let youngsters use them well then you've got to go and speak to them — 'Well, there's something. It cost 25 quid'. Click. And it's gone, and in fact draft as it seems it costs more to repair it than to buy a new one. This is a horrible

state of affairs, and yes, it's a bit cruel isn't it. But it becomes a problem.

Whatever their approach, all teachers felt that learning to work with equipment had a value beyond the immediate need insofar as it was a way of encouraging self discipline:

> We are evolving a discipline as well as teaching chemistry, a controlled disciplined approach to behaviour, yes, to looking at science, yes, it's to get the discipline going as well. (Dave, 44, senior teacher, Head of Science)

It is traditional to teach science theoretically and abstractly, or with the teacher demonstrating experiments. Science teachers can therefore use practical work as a control strategy, a bribe for good behaviour (Woods, 1980). They will probably feel the temptation to do this especially with less academically motivated pupils who are perhaps more likely to misuse equipment, and who, ironically are also less likely to be able to cope with theoretical work. As Keith (38, scale 1, chemistry) points out, this is, on the whole, an unsatisfactory strategy because it leads to a vicious circle with negative effects for both teacher and pupils:

> The difficulty lies in the fact that the lower down the ability range you go, the less able, the less well coordinated they are perhaps, or the less they understand the instructions you have given them or the less they are willing and able to follow the instructions. So instead of the experiments becoming a meaningful exercise in learning, which it is to the more academic kids, it becomes just a play around to the less able kids, and this is why, I believe, a lot of teachers who take less able kids, will just give them a text book and say 'right, you will copy the pictures and the drawings', because it's such hard work to give them practical work to do. Or they're dangerous when they do the practical work, or they damage the benches or they break the apparatus, and so this is the problem. It would seem reasonable, wouldn't it, to give the low ability kids more, sort of manual tasks? And, yet, because they are low ability they're less able to do the manual tasks properly. So therefore you're caught in a sort of paradox I feel . . . you see. Other people have said to me 'Don't always let them do practical because they'll always want to do it. Don't give them too much of a good thing, kind of thing . . . So I suppose what people do, and what I do to some extent, is to use the practical as a sort of prize, you know, 'if you're good today, you will do a practical', not, 'a practical is an integral part of the lesson' but more a 'if you do not behave, you will not get any more practicals this term. You will do writing from the books'. Not very good is it? . . . and I don't know whether they tend to misbehave with apparatus because they are not familiar with apparatus, it's so much of a novelty that it becomes a game.

Dave (44, senior teacher, Head of Science) had also come to use practical work as a control strategy, but in the opposite way to Keith — and this highlights the way in which teachers are exposed to, and influenced by different school and subject cultures:

I'm very much a practically-based teacher. We spoil them in this school with practical work, do too much but that's the way I believe it ought to be done. Now that's evolved with having been in a traditional grammar school with not much apparatus and then being a blackboard teacher, in a new comprehensive I began to realize blackboard work didn't go down ... you see many times I would've talked to a class for an hour and written on the blackboard and been quite happy about it, I couldn't do that at (the new comprehensive) you had to teach them or give them something to do or show them something in order to survive, and when you think about it, it's good science. So the two come together. Nuffield was emerging then which helped in the 1960s, and (the new comprehensive) was well organized and had technicians which I'd never had, so you could get things prepared for you. You were encouraged to do experiments and anything you wanted to do, you'd have the chance of doing it. Since then I think practical has become the focal point, because I found myself at (the new comprehensive) doing what I call good chemistry, with remedial kids. I thought I'd have to do inferior chemistry with remedial kids, C band kids, but I became aware that inferior science, they got bored with ... it's far better to do your grammar school practical type science, the stuff that I was doing with the A banded kids there, I could do with the C banded kids there ... and very often their science skills handling apparatus is just as good as the A band.

Despite the potential problems, practical work was generally felt to be crucial for understanding:

I know someone who does the absolute minimum of practical work ... it depends on how much you value understanding, as opposed to learning. (Kath, 59, retired, science)

Children do like to do things, obviously, rather than just be told a lot of theory and obviously that must be an integral part of learning, since we learn not just with our minds, but with our hands and our eyes and our ears and our noses and so on. (Keith, 38, scale 1, chemistry)

However, views were divided on how practical work should be approached, and especially on the use of the practically-based Nuffield science project.

Nuffield science is about 80 per cent practical and 20 per cent theory. Now I'm very hooked on that. I wasn't at first I didn't like it because I came from a traditional grammar school and the emphasis was very much on theory with practical work to back up the theory. You know, 'This is a practical to prove Boyle's Law', rather than 'Here is a practical, what have you discovered? You've discovered something which we call Boyle's Law'. People tell me that Nuffield is very much for the top ability kids, I don't know, I think a kind of Nuffield approach for all kids. (Keith, 38, scale 1, chemistry)

We use traditional methods here, for the simple reason that we have groups that are so mixed in their ability that the Nuffield type schemes aren't any good for the less bright kids. Nuffield schemes are very good for very able children who are able to make their own deductions. But you get a kid, or a group of kids in a group who don't have the mental ability to do that, then they get very little out of the course, they just get lost. (Christine, 33, scale 3, Heard of Physics)

Art teachers also use favourite activities, such as pottery, sculpture, copying and printing as 'carrots'. In extreme cases, if the teacher does not feel confident of controlling a practical lesson they may resort to writing. In other words, they give up teaching art. This is what Mrs Castle (64, retired, art) did towards the end of her career.

There were one or two difficult classes I had from time to time, although I never got trampled on. But I did have one particular class, just before I left, that I never came to terms with. I could keep them quiet only if I took them out of the art room. It was long after we had gone comprehensive, that was OK, it was the first intake of boys. They were just wrecking the art room, so I stopped giving them art. But I had to sit with them, and I devized all sorts of moronic exercises for them. Some of it was number work, some I suppose were basically English exercises. I just duplicated papers, and gave them to them to do, and when they were all sitting in straight rows facing front, and I was sitting up front, I could just about cope with that, but I could not cope with them in the art room. I think they were the only class I really did fail with, but they just finished up not having any art lessons ... You really felt you were losing your grip. I took early retirement soon after that.

Arthur (69, retired, art) had come across young art teachers who had done this because they had not been given adequate inductional guidance:

You have got to have some system in an art room. If you want to do things it'll only work if you do them in a proper fashion but there were cases when newcomers to the profession were sort of bunged into a room with the door shut and that was it and nobody cared, and you could see them with stacks of exercise books, the only way they could keep the kids quiet was to give them writing.

Art teachers who set 'writing' are in some ways emasculated, more so, perhaps, than other teachers who have recourse to 'survival strategies' (Woods, 1979). They are at risk of losing their identity as *art teacher*.

Classroom Atmosphere and Approach to Pupils

When pupils are working individually or in groups, the atmosphere in the classroom tends to be relatively informal. There is conversation and move-ment, which can be rather worrying for the new teacher who is anxious to be seen to be competent (Denscombe, 1980b). Sarah's (25, scale 1, art) fears are typical:

> It worries me, it still worries me . . . when you go into English classes or whatever, they're all sitting down, quietly working, but they don't in art, they're all over the place, and I don't like people coming in and thinking they're not working, because they are.

However, teachers can take advantage of this relaxed atmosphere, and go round and build relationships with pupils, which are not only satisfying in themselves but also help in maintaining an acceptable level of discipline and a positive working climate.

> When I think about relationships with kids I think especially about the fifth years, who I've now been teaching for two years, and it's just, it's almost like university tutorials, it's great. I really enjoy it — it makes teaching a real joy. (Pete, 25, scale 1, biology)

> I would like to think that kids enjoy the lessons with me, not everybody will, but I would like to think that they enjoy the art room. Even if they're not good at the subject, if they can come in and say well, 'it's alright in Mr Baden's art room', providing they're not taking me for a ride. Certainly some of the kids who are ready to leave and who are in the bottom stream of the school, they're coming into my room now and not working. Now I don't mind if they behave themselves, if they want to sit and talk to me, or talk to each other or they do a bit of a drawing and throw it away at the end of the lesson it doesn't worry me particularly, if they want to come back again next lesson, it's rather nice I think, it's what I enjoy about teaching art. (John, 44, scale 4, Head of Art)

> When I go round in the lesson they sort of chum up along me, and they tell me incredible things like that they're moving house, or that their granny's ill . . . I really like that aspect of teaching. I don't mind a little bit of talk that's not about the subject, as long as it isn't too much. (Margery, 45, scale 3, head of chemistry)

Art teachers frequently said that they thought it was particularly easy for them to relate easily with pupils, partly because they liked the subject, and partly because the atmosphere of the art lesson tended to be less authoritarian and less pressurized. Other subjects also share some of these advantages.

> Getting good relationships with kids depends on the personality of the individual . . . I also think various subjects have different possibilities. I think the people who are operating in the, shall we say, P.E. field, have an easier run getting into contact with youngsters than perhaps somebody in something very academic does. (Jim, 65, retired, science)

Some teachers complained that specialization and the development and growth of the pastoral care system had made part of their role redundant, limiting the scope of their potential influence (Sikes, 1984b), and officially confining them to teaching the subject. Even so, art and science teachers' concern for their pupils extended far beyond this. For they do not see themselves only as specialists who happen to be teachers, but rather as specialist teachers.

> I like there to be a nice atmosphere in the room with everybody being friendly with each other. I think it's something to do with some sort of social training in a way that you work, you train yourself in self discipline, you know cos I don't like to stand there and . . . what I like is everybody working. And we talk about all sorts of things, politics and all sorts of things . . . I do think school is about growing up and being able to manage in the world really. The main thing about school, isn't it, if you're bright you get ten O' levels and three 'A' levels and that's the way you manage in the world, with them to earn a living and to be fulfilled. If you're not very bright there are lots of other things you've got to do in life to manage, and it's discussion of everyday things with them, which I can do in the subject that I teach, trying to perhaps change their attitude if I think it's wrong . . . If you teach children for two years you get to know them very well, especially having a small group and I think it's vital that you talk to them and help them in their everyday life. I mean I want them to get a good grade in their art exam because that'll help them if they've got sort of seven 'O' levels instead of six or a few CSEs to get a job. But I do think the main thing about teaching is developing personality, helping a person to cope in their life. (Ann, 43, scale 1, art)

> I think kids should be aware of, for want of a better phrase, middle class values, I would be horrified if I went into some of the homes that our children live in; but unless they know that there's something else in the world that they can aim for, not particularly the values that I hold or the Head holds or things like that, but I think they should be aware that there's something else apart from their pitiful life styles, and all the infighting in the streets and dad boozing down the street, they should be aware there's something else, there's a different way to

conduct themselves, there's a different way of life, that's experience. I think they should be given different experiences. I think I can help to make them aware ... and I think it's important to have an atmosphere where kids can talk because half of them don't get a chance to talk, anyway. They're either yelling and screaming at each other in the playground, they don't get a chance to talk perhaps at home so it helps them in that way. It may not help their art but it helps them and sometimes I'll introduce something, I mean I've had discussions with the second year on nuclear disarmament, this sort of thing, women's rights, you know, just bring a lot of things in which I suppose art is about anyway. (Sarah, 25, scale 1, art)

I would like to think that in some way I was perhaps, and again it may be a cliche, sorry, that in some way I was helping a young person to develop and to come to terms with themselves because, I think you have got to come to terms with yourself, with your own capabilities and with your own restrictions, your own limitations, before you can ever really begin to make any attempt at living ... If I can help the kid to come to terms with himself, him or herself, so that they can then begin to perhaps realize their own potential, realize it mentally. If they can then begin to realize it in actual terms, or come some way towards realizing their potential in actual terms, then I suppose, to some extent I could say I had been successful. (Brian, 44, scale 4, Head of Art)

I develop their skills, their powers of observation, try and make them realize that there are things in life that are important, and just being a person is important in many ways. I try to make them recognize themselves, to build up responsibility for themselves. I try to make them take a pride in themselves in that I often notice, and say that I notice, when they dress nicely, or don't dress nicely, boys and girls. (Dave, 44, senior teacher, Head of Science)

Mixed Ability Grouping

Secondary school reorganization had some profound effects on some teachers' relationships with pupils, though the experience of teaching the less able seems to stand the art teacher in good stead when mixed ability classes are introduced, or when schools became comprehensives.

When Roman School went comprehensive I'd had the experience of teaching ordinary school kids as you might say and I had no problems, and I could easily switch over. My techniques didn't matter all that much, especially in art any way, and the high flyers and the backward kids got the appropriate treatment. Art is an individual thing. You went round and talked to each kid and encouraged them at their own ability and speed. (Arthur, 69, retired, art)

Scientists, by comparison, are less likely to have had such experience and may find it difficult to cope:

> I think the kind of science teaching that we were taught was the kind of science teaching that one would do at a selective grammar school probably because the teacher trainers were ex-grammar school teachers and their expectations were based on the sort of school they'd taught in . . . It's very difficult, for me at any rate, and I still haven't learnt how to control classes and create a learning situation with the less able kids. I don't really quite know how to do it. (Keith, 38, scale 1, chemistry)

Arthur (retired, art) didn't think Margery would be able to do it either:

> People who have never had the experience of teaching in the old elementary schools, or who had only taught in the grammar schools they found they got problems. I think it is easier for an artist. People like Margery — who you talked to — would think, probably Margery had got big problems teaching the backward kids and juvenile detergents . . . I mean I like Margery, nothing personal about this, I'm just saying I can quite see where she could have problems because she'd never taught that kind of kid.

Not only may teachers find it difficult to cope with mixed ability classrooms. Some may lose the satisfaction of teaching their subject at a relatively high level to able, motivated pupils. Mr Count (54, retired, science), for example, became extremely dissatisfied when his grammar school went comprehensive and he had to teach a wider ability range (see also Sikes, 1984a). He had very strong views on mixed ability, views which Ball would identify as representing an 'academic perspective' (Ball, 1981, p. 161):

> I've no time for mixed ability at all . . . I think its true that the ones of lower ability are the ones you get the behavioural problems with. If you've got a class of thirty bright kids and you put one kid with a behavioural problem, of lower ability, in there, he can make an absolute mess of them, so why subject them to it? When you've got mixed ability the people at the top are bound to suffer, and I don't see why they should at the expense of these other goons . . . so I'm all for streaming and segregation. Perhaps I'm an out and out traditionalist . . . but most people I've talked to in the teaching profession have been against mixed ability . . . I think that the people who are for it are living in a false world.

As with integrated and general science, some scientists perceive mixed ability as a threat to their identity as subject specialists. This threat is probably behind Mr Count's opposition for he emphasized that his job was to teach physics but that he was unable to do this with low ability pupils. Margery and Keith also made similar comments.

Others, however, enjoy the challenge. Dave, for example, (44, senior teacher, Head of Science) who works in a school where there is no streaming or setting, is firmly committed to mixed ability because of its effects on teachers as well as pupils. He represents Ball's idealist perspective, (*ibid*, p. 160).

> One of the problems in schools where they stream as I see it is that you get your C band kids, B band kids, there's not much cross over, there is one but not much. You get your remedial class who are floated back into C band and there's always problems, when there are the kids who come to you and say they are C band kids they are thick, and they are determined to be thick and this is a restriction on what you can do with them, what they will achieve. Worse still you get staff who become C band staff and staff who become sixth-form or upper school staff and a number of staff are looked down on as being inferior ... I'm 100 per cent behind mixed ability and little things happen that emphasize it you know, the second year I was here we had a second chemist came in and we had two fourth year groups. Now this lad was straight out of college and we were trying to establish ourselves as good as everybody else, and still trying to get kids who were going to comprehensive, modelled on the grammar schools, back, so to take 'O' level was going to be a big thing, but to get kids through 'O' level was the drive, we had to make some mark somewhere and so I had two classes of fourth year chemists and decided that I would stream them and therefore I had to take the top stream because I had to make sure we had some 'O' level kids out of it, and if we didn't I was going to carry the can and the second stream taken by this lad wrote themselves off straight away. They knew the cleverer ones were in the other group, they therefore said within a fortnight 'We're duffers, now make us work'. Needless to say the next year I didn't, I was the first department to un-stream with the fourth year so we had mixed ability in the fourth year from then on out. It puts a tremendous strain on teaching that way but it has to do.

At the same school we were also shown biology worksheets which Ray (Head of Biology) told us could be answered at a number of different levels. Fete (25, scale 1, biology), a junior member of the department, was, however sceptical:

> What we have at this school are mixed ability classes, we don't have mixed ability teaching ... when I got the job the boss said 'Well, I know it's mixed ability but it's really no different from teaching normally'. And that's the boss, And that's how it is throughout the school. One or two departments are trying to do what mixed ability is really all about, individualized learning etc. ... but for a hell of a lot of the lessons in this school a teacher stands at the front and explains it to thirty-odd kids and there are some kids who can hardly write and

there are some potential grade 1 'A' levels and they all receive the same and they all write about it, and some write three lines and some write three pages. But they are all taught the same and they all go through the same work, it's just that some do more than others. And the teacher is aiming for exam passes. So the lower kids get bored stiff and become discipline problems.

Chapter 8

Conclusion: Teacher Careers and Identities

In this chapter we discuss some of the theoretical and policy implications of the research, selecting what appear to us to be the prominent themes running through the study. These are: the structure of teacher careers; the contexts in which they are located; how they are 'managed' by teachers; and the relationship between careers and identities.

The Structure of Teacher Careers

In one sense, there are several teacher career structures. Many teachers no doubt relate strongly to the Burnham scales, and have internalized appropriate 'timetables', 'maps' and 'benchmarks' (Lyons, 1981). On the other hand, some do not think of 'a career' at all.

> By the end of my PGCE year I wasn't sure I wanted to be a teacher all the time. I still wanted to be prepared to move onto something else. And I feel the same now. I want to still go on teaching but I don't want a career in teaching if you see what I mean. I want to be able to carry on with things, personal individual things at the same time. (Chris, 28, scale 1, art)

In between are a variety of adaptations. However, viewed from another perspective, it is possible to discern a life-cycle common to most teachers, with distinctive phases and tasks attaching to them. There is a fairly well-defined early period involving explorations and experimentations, establishing the platform enabling one to practise teaching — basic skills of pedagogy and control, and knowledge of one's subject; and being socialized into the culture. In relation to the rest of one's life, this period is also distinctive in that school-related activities can become a central focus, constituting one's social, as well as working, life. With no family commitments at this stage, and close generational ties with pupils, some young teachers can derive many satisfactions from the early years to set against the problems of induction.

We have seen, too, in Chapter 1, how these tasks and their resolution are mediated by such factors as generation (for example, the late 1960s being much more idealistic and ambitious compared to the pragmatic 1980s) and institution (for example, rural and community schools providing a more complete and rounded introduction than urban schools). Doubtless there are other factors, such as educational policy and social mix of school and area that deserve consideration. One question raised was whether the fact that there are fewer young teachers today in schools means that they will lack the traditional support of what has previously been a strong generational peer group, and become more rapidly absorbed into a school culture completely dominated by older teachers' tasks and concerns.

We detected an 'age 30' transition. Settling down after initial socialization, male teachers showed a, for men, new-found urgency, an interest in promotion, more planning, and growing interest in career timetables. Several of the women became more conscious of a dual career, and aware of facing a choice between family and job. For some, growing family commitments made money and promotion more important, and with this, other potential careers within teaching become more attractive — curriculum development, pedagogy (accelerated by increasing distance from the knowledge base of one's subject), counselling. With their awakened interest in promotion comes an identification with 'cliques' or 'cabals', depending on one's interests.

With this phase, therefore, we see a pronounced gender effect, and family life beginning to exert an influence in its own right on motivation for and direction of careers. We gain a sense, too, of a new initiation, into 'strategies for promotion', as they become aware of the possibilities and their supportive groups. Lyons (1981, p. 11) uses the analogy of a tree: 'The trunk represents the large number of those who enter teaching as the start of a career in education; with each career stage, as they progress along the main branches, greater and greater specialization is displayed ...' The age 30 transition may see a significant branching of this nature.

The 'settling down' phase (30–40) sees male teachers established and at their peak. Many women, on the other hand, by this stage have made teaching secondary to their family careers, regarding it as a reasonable way of supplementing the family income, and maintaining a sense of an alternative identity. Some men, and a few women, will be aspiring to senior positions in the school, and subordinating other areas of life to that end. Some develop an interest in management. They now have a definable group of teachers younger than them, which aids their identity as seasoned professionals still advancing in their careers. Pupils, too, now constitute a new generation and, there is no longer any generational rapport, but rather, where there is some affinity, of parental or avuncular style. Others may increasingly come to be regarded as 'proper teachers' as the role elements become those most called into play in interaction.

Some teachers may have become disillusioned by this stage for one reason or another, and may have to come to terms with the position they have reached. Family responsibilities may be considerable, restricting opportunities for a move elsewhere. Some teachers undergo distinctive changes in commitment now, and may develop alternative careers in the family, the home, a hobby or a business.

Whether it is advancement within the teacher career, or some alternative line, this is a 'settling down' phase, with the likelihood of fewer 'critical incidents' than formerly, all other things, such as government policy or world events, being equal.

Between 40 and 50/55, the aspirers are in senior or middle management. This is a stage too when married women whose families are now grown up begin to look towards these positions. The main task for all during this period is coming to terms with the plateau of one's career and with 'one's own mortality'. Around the age of 40, there may be an agonizing 'mid-life crisis', when there is a radical self-appraisal, an estimate of what achieved and what not, and a reckoning of how one might achieve self-fulfilment in an increasingly finite future.

Beyond this crisis lie calmer waters — a settling for what is; an increasingly parental role towards pupils, and now indeed toward younger teachers; a general recognition of their own knowledge and experience, qualifying them to be considered among the 'ancients' of the school, staunch upholders of standards and tradition; and a relaxation, now they have reached this plateau, and are respected and proficient. Not all, however, follow this line. Those whose ambitions have not been met make any one of a number of adaptations, for example, 'coasting'. There may well be more of these during periods of recession and resultant fewer opportunities.

At 50/55+, the major task now is increasingly preparing for retirement. As we have noted, a large number of teachers have taken early retirement in the present economic crisis, with an average age of 56. As the trend continues, it will become more of a pronounced part of the accepted life-cycle. During this period a teacher typically finds energies and enthusiasms for the job declining, especially in contrast with younger teachers and increasing distance from pupils. They may be more relaxed and free in their teaching and discipline, but this again may be taken as evidence by those younger that they are 'too old' and 'past it'. They may be critical of falling standards among the young, more evidence of the widening generation gap and the influence of general trends in society (for example, towards less authoritarianism). There are satisfactions during these years however, notably through informal contacts with ex-pupils, whose evaluation of their teaching makes it all seem worthwhile.

This life-cycle is not a rigid framework through which all teachers inevitably pass. It takes no account, for example, of teachers who enter the profession late, having embarked on a different career, or those who leave early for other careers (though they may still go through the phases of this life-cycle in their other careers). Not all teachers go through all these processes (for example, not all experience a mid-life crisis, or anticipate retirement at

55). There are overlaps between phases, and strong linkages betweeen them (for example, teachers in the second phase maintaining strong social ties with pupils). There are early ('high fliers') and late developers.

However, it is presented as a generalized outline which aids our understanding of teacher careers, attitudes and behaviours. It has the advantage of being (i) developmental — and in a number of ways, not being restricted to structured promotional routes; (ii) holistic , in that it takes a view not only of the whole career, but also of other areas of life, such as the family, so that each phase of career can be seen in context; and (iii) capable of illustrating historical, generational, economic and political influences.

The question is raised that, if the teacher career consists of phases and stages, how does one move from one phase to another? Is it a matter of smooth, almost imperceptible progression, or sudden leaps and transitions? No doubt there is a certain amount of gradual development. But there are also highly charged moments and episodes that have enormous consequences for personal change and development.

The teacher career is thus punctuated by critical incidents occurring typically within critical periods (Chapter 2). One such period, unsurprisingly, is the initiation into teaching. Here, new recruits are met with stark demands of the role in sudden, and unsuspected confrontations, which challenge their existing claims to being a teacher. Critical incidents act as cataclysmic events which undeniably and emphatically confirm some claims and reject others; but which also present one with hitherto unsuspected aspects of the self. Clearly they are of particular importance in the early stages of the teacher's career, for they help set the style of one's teaching and discipline.

Critical incidents might be compared to what we have described as 'counter-incidents', which act as a kind of contrastive shadow. Whereas critical incidents are totally unanticipated, unrehearsed, and uncontrolled, counter incidents are deliberately stage-managed. Having learned from the former, the teacher can now control the action. There may be all the properties of an incident (noise, spectacle, atmosphere), but the teacher has arranged the scene, selected the props and written the script. There may even be applause from the audience in the form of heightened respect for and firmer relationships with a teacher who has dealt with a challenge capably.

The folklore of teaching advocates an attitude of aggressive aloofness towards. pupils, at least to begin with, summed up in the advice to novitiate teachers 'not to smile before Christmas'. But our material shows that teachers are not necessarily constrained to act in ways that they feel are contrary to their own natures. Typically, teachers negotiate with the role, taking on some aspects to some degree or other (and this can vary in strength and between situations) and rejecting others in a complicated process of dovetailing self and role. The critical incident is invaluable in this process, for it highlights and defines the crucial elements of demands and resource in unmistakable and pronounced terms, and in a way that demands uncompromising solution. It thus cuts through the idealism, the woolliness, the doubt, the generalizing, the lack of knowledge that attends teachers (and doubtless many other workers) at the launch of their careers.

As a career develops, we would expect such incidents to diminish in frequency as one meets fewer totally new situations, acquires knowledge, discovers the nature, extent and limits of one's resources, and develops strategies to cope. There would be lengthier periods of comparatively quiet consolidation, marked by a number of counter incidents, during which time the teacher is practising and refining the new persona. But there are other critical periods, some anticipated in their form if not in their effects, others less so. Among the former we might include certain promotions or moves which take the teacher into new sub-cultures, or new parts of the system with new roles. For example, a teacher who becomes a deputy head, or head, is immediately confronted with completely new demands. For many, though not necessarily all, a critical period follows in which they wrestle to disentangle the possible from the impossible and to come to terms with their own strengths and weaknesses in this new situation. This is not entirely a discovery voyage de nouveau. At this stage, there are a large number of knowns which help defuse these later periods and provide firmer guidelines for action. In this sense, one stores up the gains of previous incidents and periods as one accumulates experience. But inasmuch as a new phase or period carries unknowns, or serves new challenges on new claims, it warrants being considered 'critical'. And as with all others, it can make or break.

Among the unexpected events in teaching inducing critical periods are demotion or redeployment, the mid-career crisis, and periods following major changes in educational policy, such as secondary reorganization, which confront teachers with new situations.

Critical periods or incidents occurring in other areas of life can have a profound effect on teacher careers. Marriage, parenthood, divorce, becoming a householder, bereavement, grandparenthood, all involve reconstructions of reality which can place the teacher career within a new context (Berger and Kellner, 1964; Hart, 1976; Musgrove and Middleton, 1981; Townsend 1981).

Ann (43, scale 1, art) had undergone one such critical period in her personal life, which had had profound consequences for her teaching:

> I do believe in brainwashing, I think I've brainwashed my children. I would talk to my children about everything when they were very tiny, and we would talk about anything . . . we would discuss . . . and I suppose I treat the children I teach in the same way . . . I use my lessons, not just for art, but to get them to think . . . I don't think I ever thought or questioned things when I was young, I just did what seemed to be expected . . . For example, I would always advise them not to get married until they were rather old because I made a mistake when I got married, consequently I got divorced and nobody told me, I mean nobody asked me to think about it properly, you know, the fact that you're going to get married and have children and you're

going to be the one that looks after the children in this society ... I don't think that most boys and girls think about these things ... but its something I talk about with them, like I talk about it with my own daughter. In fact I've probably put my own daughter off marriage for life!

Currently, in the mid 1980s, the whole profession is going through a critical period. This inevitably means a higher rate of critical incidents for teachers than, for example, during the 1960s. In this way we can see how teachers' careers are influenced by wider political and economic developments. Teachers are being called upon to dredge up even more ingenuity than usual, not least to resolve the various contradictory demands being made of them that we discussed in the introduction.

Contexts for Teachers Careers

Teacher careers are made and experienced within schools. The organization of the school, the personality, views and values of the head, and how the teacher relates to them, are profoundly important factors in a teacher's life. Head-teachers are gatekeepers par excellence to preferred ends. We have seen how they control advancement through promotions within the school, and the allocation of a significant element of job content through timetabling and resources. We have argued that, in periods of contraction when there are fewer opportunities and resources, the head's power is increased as the currency, though less, considerably appreciates. The gatekeeping, quixotic at the best of times in the view of some teachers, may become even more so.

This is particularly the case in tradition-authoritative and bureaucratic organizations with their top-down systems of control. There is a historical element here, accompanied by a generational one among our sample. Our older teachers had largely experienced traditional-authoritative (and occasionally, but rarely, charismatic) organizations in their earlier years, and although initially critical, came to recognize their virtues, largely consisting of a pronounced certainty and system which aided their teaching in the early stages. Middle-aged teachers have known largely bureaucracies, which inevitably followed the vast increases in institutional size following the 1960s secondary reorganization. These bureaucratic developments within schools were paralleled by the new pay structure of the 1960s, which further helped establish hierarchies within institutions.

Our research suggests that the drive for participatory frameworks is coming largely from this generation of teachers — those who began teaching in the 1960s — especially from those who were university trained. It is perhaps significant that several of them come from working-class backgrounds with a tradition of trade union activity.

Interestingly, this new trend has been accompanied by a call to change the pay structure, which would have a similar effect, that is, it would represent a move from a bureaucratic to a more professional structure (NAS/UWT, 1979). Such proposals have involved, for example, a single main professional grade, to which all teachers would progress after a far more closely supervised three-year entry period for beginners. There would be promotion prospects to posts of greater responsibility, but the net effect of such proposals would be to make school organization more collegial and less hierarchical. The lengthier and more closely supervised probationary period conducted by senior staff on nationally agreed guidelines would ensure the appropriate degree of professionalism among new entrants. Of course any new deal might equally involve a change in teachers' conditions of service which involved them in administrative duties hitherto voluntary.

It is important to note that this drive for less bureaucracy in schools is not simply to the benefit of teachers' professional development. The dissolution of some of the boundaries can enable pupils to develop wider and deeper relationships, and perhaps gain more control of their own education (Buswell, 1984). It ministers in general to the kind of community education envisaged by Hargreaves (1982).

However, bureaucracy cannot be dispensed with altogether, nor, perhaps, is it desirable that it should be (Giddens, 1982). Some organizations appear to be entering a post-bureaucratic period, as Weber suspected they might, wherein they retain certain elements, but dispense with others. Organizations will still need rules, there will still be areas of clearly-defined competence, and posts of special responsibility. Berger *et al* (1973, pp. 186–7) argue that under-institutionalized spheres are anxiety producing because they allow individuals too much latitude which they do not know how to use: 'The most fundamental function of institutions is probably to protect the individual from having to make too many choices'. This may be the main reason why some teachers prefer traditional and bureaucratic structures. They provide for guidance, security, certainty.

Paradoxically, perhaps, this may also be why some teachers increasingly object to them. For the problems which have contributed toward the crisis in teacher careers have undermined for them whatever securities and certainties previously existed. Further, our teachers resisted the role, yet prided themselves on their professionalism. They may prefer the kind of organization of the future outlined by Bennis (1968, p. 73–74): 'The group will . . . evolve in response to a problem rather than to programmed role expectations. The executive thus becomes coordinator or 'linking pin' between various task forces . . . People will be evaluated not according to rank but according to skill and professional training. Organizational charts will consist of project groups rather than stratified functional groups'. Such an arrangement offers flexibility in the face of required changes, openings for initiative, and new directions for careers that could help strengthen morale.

Moreover, though contraction is making school size less than it was (for example, the roll of an average-sized 11–18 school of 900–1000 pupils in

1979/80, is predicted to fall to 600–700 by the late 1980s, see Fiske, 1979), as Husen (1979, p. 174) has noted. 'The tendency of centralized bigness can hardly be reversed'. He goes on, 'The problem then becomes how to build in the advantages of smallness within the larger framework. In the final analysis this is a psychological problem: how to increase the sense of individual identity and participation'. It is met through sociological means — the reorganization of the basis of relationships within the school, but without giving up the benefits of bureaucracy. Though there might be some contradictions in the way some institutions have developed both bureaucratic and professional elements, there are also some complementary ones. As Dreeben (1970, p. 23) argues, 'it would be erroneous to claim that bureaucracy ... is inherently inimical to professional practice ... despite their real differences ... They resemble each other in that both are organized within specific spheres of technical competence and universalistic, disinterested conduct toward those served ... Despite the often-heard indictment, from both the political right and the political left, that professionals cannot flourish under bureaucratic conditions, the fact is that they do'.

Thus the bureaucratic/professional contradiction discussed in the introduction can be resolved by such measures as modifying the pay scales, continuing to work for the increased professionalism of teachers, and making the management structures of schools more organic, less mechanistic. Blanket recipes of this kind can only work, of course, if the principles behind them are adopted as policy by all concerned. Currently, salary levels are depressed, adding to despondency and the sense of crisis. This, of course, need not prohibit a change in salary structure along the lines indicated. Again, in some schools, there appears to be a mockery of participation (Hunter, 1980; Hargreaves, 1984). Headteachers have been observed persuading their staffs to accept their ideas by a variety of subtle tactics, or consulting them, and then following their own course of action. Such lip-service to democratic forms is, arguably, worse than the authoritarian forms they purport to replace. Further, it takes the best of teacher initiative, ingenuity and creativity out of teaching and education, and forces it into administration and strategical struggles. We would stress that it is not headteachers personally that are under criticism here. The role of head is a difficult one, a product of the system, with total responsibility for the school, a requirement to lead, and directly accountable to several different parties (Cohen, 1969). The constraints are enormous, impervious to everything except perhaps charisma, which our system of schooling does everything to discourage. Heads are constrained to act the way they do (Coulson, 1976). It takes a bold initiative to do otherwise. The current situation, however, demands no less.

If participation is chimerical in some instances, there are some who argue that 'professionalism' is nothing more than an ideology, a resource to be used by teachers in the conflictual struggle for improved status in a period that has seen them increasingly proletarianized (Lawn and Ozga, 1981). It is tempting to suggest that such a process has been furthered by traditional/authoritarian and bureaucratic structures, as well as government and educational policy. However that may be, there is mixed evidence from our sample of teachers in relation to the proletarianization thesis. We have seen, for example, several teachers feeling their subject, which for them was one of the mainsprings of their teacher identity, under attack in new integrational schemes and in 'mixed-ability' classes; and art teachers feeling their subject devalued by becoming a receptacle for the non-qualified. On the other hand, there was a strong sense of the subject surviving these onslaughts, and of teachers actually fashioning themselves new roles. There are few signs of loss of view of the 'whole enterprise', of routinization, of separation of content, pedagogy and assessment. It may be, of course, that our sample are particularly strong on resistance, which may be atypical of the body of teachers as a whole. Yet there is no doubt that, despite the increasing difficulties that have produced a sense of crisis, there have also been developments in recent years which have increased teachers' claims to professional status. These include extended training periods, a move to an all-graduate and fully-trained profession, an educational knowledge increasingly backed by theory and research (Hoyle, 1983).

However, whether one wishes to argue for increased professionalization or growing proletarianization, or a combination of both, our evidence shows that from the individual teacher's perspective, there is scope for managing one's interests. If this is somewhat under seige at the moment in some respects, there are some more favourable ongoing auspices, and they could be further encouraged by such developments as more democratic management structures, a less hierarchical pay structure and greater opportunities to further one's professional knowledge.

Managing Teacher Careers

The theme of managing or 'coping' runs strongly through our teacher accounts. The predominant theme in the literature in several disciplines on this matter is that this is done chiefly through matching one's motives and interests to the demands of the situation, rather than the converse. Festinger's (1957) dissonance theory suggests that where it is difficult to bring the real world into line with one's motives, the discrepancy tends to be reduced by changes in the perception of reality. Janis and King (1954) also argue that playing a role tends to bring opinions into line with behaviour required in the line. This is the 'internalized adjustment' of the Lacey (1977) model of strategic adaptation, outlined in the introduction.

An alternative is to reduce commitment and adopt superficial conformity and personal detachment (Sofer, 1970, p. 62). This is Lacey's mode of strategic compliance. Even here, Sofer seems to feel the drift into internalized adjustment almost inevitable: 'This is a species of identity management, but the distinction between a 'true' identity and a 'managed' identity may prove tenuous, i.e. the contrived identity may become central to the personality' (*ibid*). Lacey (1977) shows how the bulk of psychological research and theory represented the focus behind these changes in terms of psychological traits, while Becker (1977), seeking a corrective to this by bringing the factors surrounding an individual into account, according to Lacey, rescued one from immutable aspects of the self only to make one a slave to the situation. Any self-will or personal resource of the individual which might be employed to *change* the situation seems almost entirely left out of account. We were interested therefore to see if we could detect any signs of this 'strategic redefinition'.

We were concerned to find out if, how and when strategic redefinition occurs in the course of a teacher's career. This constitutes a better test than Lacey's own sample, consisting of student and probationary teachers, since these are experiencing the most difficult period of their careers which might give a distorted picture. They have to 'situationally adjust' during this period, or they do not survive (Hanson and Herrington, 1976; Woods, 1981a). It represents a crucial development in one's moral career (Goffman, 1961), a concept that reminds us that the basis for making judgments about oneself and others, and thus formulating motives and interests, is not a constant, but itself subject to change.

There were signs among our sample of many variations of using these strategical modes. We noted in Chapter 5, for example, how a teacher could simultaneously appear to be both 'complying' and 'redefining'. In the process, there might well be some 'internalized adjustment'. In fact, our material points to a considerable amount of what we might call 'strategic compromise', involving a mixture of internalized adjustment and strategic redefinition. This is a distinctive category, for it represents a merging of the two rather than dual usage of them. We have seen throughout the book a picture of teachers managing typically by provisionally accepting certain elements in the situation, partially modifying their interest, then seeking to secure their partially redefined ends. This process would be repeated many times over a teacher's career in a perpetual dialectic between teacher and external world. Hunter and Heighway (1980, p. 480) recognize this when they talk of 'positive situational adjustment'. Vallely (1978) equates it with 'impression management'. Hughes (1937, p. 137) describes career as 'a sort of running adjustment', Rappaport (1959) a 'cogwheeling between person and society throughout the life cycle', and Burns (1983) talks of 'resistance to situational pressures'. This all suggests a fourth category to be added to Lacey's model, which is, perhaps, the one most commonly employed among teachers.

If this is the 'how' of managing, or 'redefining', we need to ask what it is that is redefined, when, and where. Our teachers have illustrated how they manage the constraints of examinations, educational policy, institutional gatekeepers and resources; how they redefine (or 'make' rather than 'take' — see Plummer, 1975) the role in relation to a concept of 'proper teacher' how they interact with pupils, and how their identities, aims and careers might be reshaped as a consequence.

As to when 'redefinition' of this character occurs, we have shown the importance of critical periods and incidents, and illustrated with the first, initiation, phase of the teacher career, as recalled by older teachers. They were able to show how they were affected by this period and certain key incidents within them; how their conception of teaching changed, how they felt their own identities were altered.

This 'critical period' is one integral to the teacher career. Others are induced by external factors, as with secondary reorganization or the current cutbacks following economic depression and government policy. It has been demonstrated elsewhere (Woods, 1979) how, in a situation of growing constraint and unyielding commitment, teachers' adaptational powers are stretched to the utmost. We might envisage three major responses:

1   Involves no, or little positive adjustment, constituting surrender or resignation in some form or other. This includes leaving the profession, psychological withdrawal, and complete reversal of aims, such as to constitute a counter-culture if others are involved. Riseborough's (1981) teachers, for example, were unable to internally adjust, failed to survive, and could only exist in the school as kinds of living ghosts, haunting the headmaster, whom they saw as their main oppressor.

2   Involves a change in commitment. In figure 1, we have put together analyses from other recent work on this (Lacey, 1977; Woods, 1979; Nias, 1981), with our own indications from this study to provide a composite model.

This shows a vocational 'calling' to teach or dedication to a set of ideals about education; a professional commitment to subject-based teaching, to teaching as an art or craft, and to the institution, such as the school; and an instrumental commitment to a teacher career purely as a useful career to be in. An individual teacher may show one, some, or all, of these types, may vary them from time to time, or at certain ages (Peterson, 1964), and may also vary in intensity of commitment from core to peripheral. We might hypothesize that the teacher career generally sees a shift from left to right as it progresses, with a

Figure 1:   Forms of Teacher Commitment

	Vocational	Professional			Instrumental
	Education	Subject	Teaching	Institution	Career
Core					
Mixed					
Peripheral					

corresponding switch between core and peripheral. As we have seen, the initial phase marks a progression from vocational to professional commitment, and it is not unreasonable to assume an increase in instrumental commitment during the 'settling down' phase of the life cycle, when many teachers acquire or extend their familiar responsibilities. There are several examples of these kinds of shift in Chapter 4 (Mrs Castle's commitment for instance, moved from 'education' to 'pedagogy'). But shifts may be more fluid than this, depending on certain critical incidents. These need not necessarily all be in the same direction. A good crop of examination results, an unexpected piece of good work from a particular child, a generous pay award, an increase in in-service provision, a lowering of the teacher–pupil ratio — such events might induce a shift from right to left in figure 1. Others — for example, a bad experience with some disruptive pupils, an unsatisfactory pay award, a piece of educational policy of which they disapproved, being 'passed over' for promotion — may promote a shift to the right.

During the current critical period, with the profession under contraction, the schools under-resourced by comparison with the previous decade and deep dissatisfaction about salary levels, we might expect a left-right, and a top-bottom shift, or a combination of the two. This might be accompanied by the development of alternative careers outside teaching, in some other occupation or business, in the family, or in a hobby.

3   A third alternative is that teachers might 'strategically compromise', that is to say find ways of adapting to the situation that allows room for their interests, while accepting some kind of modification of those interests. Thus, a teacher who had previously planned a vertical career may begin to see the attractions of operating on a horizontal plane (Becker, 1976). There may be new opportunities made for mobility within schools between posts of responsibility, subjects and courses and between schools within LEAs (Burns, 1983). Or a teacher may develop a related, concurrent career, as art teachers, for example, may do in art, craft and design and other activities outside school (Bennet, 1983).

This is a creative process, that may, in fact, in some instances construct new possibilities out of the debris of the crisis. Such creativity is, of course, institutionally governed and mediated. We have shown, for example, how systems of participatory democracy open up new career paths by virtue of making routes available which were formerly monopolized by hierarchical posts. By contrast, some institutional forms might inhibit such developments. Similarly, Hunter and Heighway (1980, p. 480) remind us of the *advantages* to teachers of falling rolls — more space in the school, easier timetabling, greater accessibility to specialist facilities. The reduction of the teacher force has also made for greater stability within schools. The rate of staff turnover in some schools has been a perennial problem until recently. Also, despite the numbers of teachers lost in recent years, the teacher–pupil ratio has actually been reduced, though it varies enormously between schools and between areas (DES statistics 1983) (and though it may also mean that subjects are lost through shortage of pupils to take them!).

This is not to minimize the overall effect of the crisis on the educational system and process. But in terms of teacher careers, it suggests there are things that can be done at the level of the school. Thus Hunter and Heighway (1980, p. 480) argue for a 'creative turbulence' within schools, and for opportunities for initiative, control, involvement, planning for all staff, regardless of their organizational status. They quote one headteacher: 'One of the things we must do is give people status . . . they must be made to feel important . . . As far as possible we must create situations from people's interests . . . it is a question of developing skills . . . and in any case to make sure leadership roles are not static'. And they give examples of how this might be done. The quotation reminds us quite vividly how strategic redefinition or compromise might be aided or obstructed by important gatekeepers within the school. The matter is complicated further by heads invariably having in their schools teachers of different types, holding to different kinds of commitment, having different interests and aspirations, and championing different forms of organization. Thus, teachers who favour traditional/authoritarian and bureaucratic regimes are unlikely to welcome 'creative turbulence'. There may also be a matter of quality. As one of Hunter and Heighway's headteachers remarked: 'Poor teachers need direction; good teachers need choice' (*ibid*, p. 484).

However, there are other mediating factors, and against this argument that the prime source of higher morale among teachers at the moment lies initially within the school, Bennet (1983) argues that some teachers, and art teachers in particular, gain their rewards primarily from their own work, which may not be directly related to school or teaching. The answer in these cases, she maintains, is to extend their subject knowledge and/or involvement in other non-school interests. If we consider the whole person as compared to the teacher, commitment to the institution and its kind of careers, necessarily constrained by wider forces, might give way to increased commitment to the subject, and to other *self* interests.

Hence the subject is an important mediator. But whereas art, and music and some others might have these external ties, others, perhaps most, and certainly those reliant on an extant body of knowledge, are institutionally bound to a large extent. This would certainly be the case with science teachers. As their teaching careers progress, they get further and further away from the frontiers of scientific knowledge, and more reliant on secondary and tertiary sources. They are likely to become more professionally committed to teaching. For these, as well as opening up new opportunities within the institution, there might be offered the attractions of a heightened professionalism, operated through such things as inservice provision, school-based curriculum development, and more active teacher participation in educational research, as in action research.

Whatever the mode of provision, it has to take into account type of commitment and preferred identities. It is to the latter we now turn.

Self and Career

We have taken an interactionist view of self, that is one that sees the self as a social object emerging from interaction with others, and continually undergoing change as new interactions and new situations occur (Mead, 1934). It is not, therefore, an entity that presents itself to the world ready fashioned, but a process, 'continuously created and recreated in each social situation that one enters' (Berger, 1963, p. 106). This does not mean that there is not some on-going consistency. In fact, the evidence suggests that people strive throughout life for continuity of personal character (Sofer, 1970, p. 39), and that 'the historical self has a rock-like endurance' (Musgrove, 1977). However, if the self is a product of social relationships, and these in contemporary society are complex, then the self also is complex, differentiated and subject to change (Stryker, 1980). This is not as contradictory as it may sound. William James (1915, p. 179) argued that a person has as many social selves as there are individuals who recognize and can identify that person. Such individuals usually fall into reference groups, each of which shares a perspective with the person. The person may then show a different self, or aspect of self, to each of these groups; and as a new reference group is formed, so a new part of self may be developed. Or rather, the two are formed in interaction — as a person meets a new situation — one may discover new resources, desires, abilities, limitations as yet unrevealed or untested — or some half-formulated ones may be confirmed. The reference group aids identification of this new self, and reflects its essential properties back to the person. There may also be a contrastive group, which, through its opposition, also sharpens definition.

At some time or other, a person may formulate a sense of a 'real me' or a 'true identity' (Turner, 1968 and 1976). A person may feel that the 'real me' is reserved for family life, or reserved only for that person alone in total privacy, or expressed only through a leisure-time activity, or an alternative career, or held in abeyance pending retirement or events that have, as yet, not happened. It will be seen that the realization of the 'real me' is as much dependent on social circumstances as on personal choice. In particularly, adverse circumstances where opportunities for self-realization are few, one might expect as one possible consequence, some redefinition of the self. We see this well portrayed in Chapter 3, for example, when Mr Shaw (48, scale 3, Head of Department, rural science), having gained an MA to improve his promotion prospects, failed to gain any promotion:

I'm saying to myself, do I really want the money that much. Promotion means losing touch with rural studies, but I'm 48. I've got twelve years or seventeen. What's rural studies going to be doing in seventeen years time? There's the personal satisfaction, there's the status we all seek in some way or another. Am I going to find it, or am I going to become one of those grouchers of the staffroom corner who complain about everything, and become bitter and twisted? I'm having a crisis of conscience at the moment.

This is as much an identity crisis as anything, and many teachers are currently having to search within themselves for how they truly order their interests, and whether these interests can tolerate some kind of readjustment in order to derive some benefit from the situation. In this scenario, the 'real me' may be slightly redefined or re-examined for realizable and unrealizable attributes if something is to be gained, or totally submerged (so that one ends up a staffroom 'grouch') if nothing is gained.

Mr Shaw, like many others, can be said, then, to be undergoing a 'critical period', but it is an extrinsic, unanticipated one within the context of the teacher career, unlike that of initiation into teaching which is integral to the career and comes during a formulatory period. During the latter, one is concerned with discovering aspects of the self. During the former, with the self already well-formulated, it is more a matter of invention. It is in this sense that they have to 'make' the best of it.

It seems they will recognize any such adjustments for what they are (that is rather than 'internally adjusting'). For the teachers in our sample, of all types, showed a considerable resilience. Nowhere is this better illustrated than in the way they managed the teacher role. Berger *et al* (1973, p. 84) have argued that this kind of attitude and behaviour reflects the superceding of 'honour' as a motive force in society by 'dignity'. 'The concept of honour implies that identity is essentially, or at least importantly, linked to institutional roles. The modern concept of dignity, by contrast, implies that identity is essentially independent of institutional roles ... the latter are only masks, entangling (the individual) in illusion, 'alienation' and 'bad faith'. In resisting the latter, our teachers showed a concern for personal dignity. Musgrove (1977, p. 224) assumed that this would apply especially to younger teachers, but our research indicates it was the concern more especially of those in mid-career, as a consequence largely of the prevailing social climate at the start of their teaching careers. It is not necessarily *age*, therefore, so much as *generation*, and the socio-economic circumstances and the general zeitgeist attending its emergence from childhood into adulthood that seems to be the critical factor.

Further, personal dignity has become more than a matter of personal resistance. As Musgrove (1977, p. 225) puts it, 'The lack of a sense of personal worth is no longer a private misfortune but a public injustice and legitimate base for a social movement'. This, therefore, may lay behind the growth in 'public strategies', as discussed at the end of Chapter 3.

What, then, are the major influences on the teacher self? Hargreaves (1980) argued that the major components of the occupational culture of teaching were status, competence, and relationships. Our research both modifies and expands on these themes. Status, for example, did not appear to be an important career issue for our art teachers (see also Bennet, 1984), although the status of the *subject* was important to them. On the other hand, for most of our teachers it was a matter of considerable concern that they felt underprivileged in bureaucratic hierarchies and that participatory frameworks not only gave them more scope to achieve their ends, but enabled them to 'feel right', in Riseborough's teacher's terms.

Competence was also an issue, but we need a wider conception of it than the 'academic, moral and vocational' connotation Hargreaves gives it. It involves handling constraints, managing the role and career, devising and executing strategies, as well as the ability to teach. It is little short, in fact, of making a success of one's life, of negotiating a way through hazards and around obstructions, of making or seizing opportunities to realize or further one's interests.

As for relationships, this was clearly important for our teachers. However, this is usually taken to imply mainly or even solely colleague relationships. Now while these certainly mattered, as, for example, in the formation of cliques and cabals (Chapter 5), our research points to the enormous influence on teacher identities and careers of relationships with pupils. As Strauss (1959) notes, we need to have our identities upheld in open court — in this case, the classroom and other public arenas of the school, with the pupils as judge, jury, and sometimes executioners. For many teachers in fact, they appear to be the main reference group. They define teacher identities and affect their careers in a variety of ways. It is through them that many teachers achieve their ambitions. A 'good pupil response' may be sufficient reward, and some teachers may conceive of the quest for it as their main career line. This may be through a vocational commitment and a particular dedication to pupils (as was the case with several of our art teachers); it may be through a felt close relationship with them on generational or familial grounds, as friend, parent, grandparent, and so on; or through a particular, high-status skill in handling pupils. In the latter case, as Riseborough (1983, p. 45) notes, 'they may be losers in the promotional, recruitment process, but winners in the process of "natural selection", the "fittest survivors".' Our research indicates, too, despite the crisis, the enormous satisfactions to be had from teaching, derived from interactions with pupils.

By the same token, pupils may be responsible for frustrating a teacher's aspirations. At the extreme, they might force a teacher out of the profession. Otherwise, as we have considered in Chapter 6, pupils can act as teacher stress-producers, as teacher reality-definers, as staff selectors. Pupil response is an ongoing factor in teacher identity, an essential component of reputation, and hence, status.

Pupils are part of society, and attitudes change as the social climate changes. Some current deviant behaviour may simply be an expression of their impacting against an outmoded role — that of the 'proper teacher' — founded on a system of honour and allegiance to inhuman structures and traditions. Teachers who resist this role, and insist on personal dignity, also recognize the personal dignity of pupils, rather than seeing them as faceless occupants of roles themselves. And herein lies the kernel of a new relationship founded on the mutual recognition of their basic humanity. Waller's (1932) often quoted assertion that, to his pupils, the teacher must be 'relatively meaningless as a person' is becoming outmoded.

Pupils, thus, are important for teachers through the relationships they have with them; through the sense of competence achieved through skill in handling them; and through the status that consequently accrues. The same considerations are evident with regard to the teacher's subject — the third major element (with role and pupils) in teacher identity. Ball (1982), Ball and Lacey (1980) and Goodson (1981 and 1983) have demonstrated the importance of the subject community and culture. If the pupils one teaches are one major reference group, one's subject colleagues are another. They help to define continually the area and nature of one's field of expertise, which is subject to change as knowledge and skills advance or recede, status changes, and differential resources are allocated.

We have seen some of the consequences of this for our teachers in Chapter 7. Art, for example, is a comparatively low status subject, and has a poorer allocation than science — a high status subject — of pupils, periods and privileges. But, art as a subject provides a useful cushion against the disappointments this might otherwise entail. For it extends beyond the boundaries of school and pervades the life-world of the teacher in a more complete way than subjects like science. Indeed, the major collegial reference group of the art teacher is likely to be supra-institutional, consisting of teachers in other schools, and those in colleges in the area (Woods, 1984). And the activity of art clearly means a great deal to such teachers in their spare time (cf Gouldner, 1957).

For art teachers, their subject and the pupils they deal with *are* their careers. Their chances of promotion are poor, and few look for it in terms of progress through a hierarchy. But then that kind of career is not in the nature of the subject — humane, marginal, creative, intrinsic (that is, residing within pupils rather than in an extant body of knowledge). Art teachers, therefore, have their satisfactions, and like Bennet (1983) we found these to include a special kind of close relationship with pupils, freedom and flexibility in their work conditions, opportunities to diversify, ongoing involvement with their subject, and perhaps the development of new techniques, processes and skills.

Science teachers enjoy high status, though their qualifications, for men at least, may often be inferior to other teachers — both factors owing to the marketability of the subject, which takes the more highly qualified into industry. There are consequently more rewards available to them in terms of scale points, pupils, the timetable, and so on. The subject is important to them. Like any subject, it marks out the area of a teacher's expertise, and knowledge — it is the basis of a claim to professionalism. They know what it takes both in terms of content and method to pass 'O' and 'A' levels, and this is highly valued indeed within society generally. This subject, in particular, carries extra kudos. It *matters* within the mainstream of the school to be a science teacher, in a way that art does not. However, it is the social position of the subject within the school, rather than its intrinsic nature that appears to be important. As we have noted, the latter counted more when teachers were younger and nearer the sources of their scientific knowledge. But without inservice leave, they find it difficult to keep up with latest developments. Our science teachers exhibited, in consequence, a shifting commitment from 'intrinsic' subject to pedagogy, while maintaining their social positions as scientists within the school; and more of an interest in administrative posts in the upper hierarchy.

Our artists and scientists well illustrate, therefore, in their contrasting ways, how teachers 'manage' their careers and negotiate a path through the different hazards and opportunities that present themselves to them. The basic self is not changed, but different aspects of it respond to different circumstances. As a consequence, some old lines of development may be subjugated, other new ones, that have perhaps lain quiet or dormant, or have been gradually growing, promoted.

We do not underestimate the seriousness of the current educational crisis, and the extent to which that is a product of political and socio-economic circumstances. There are deep repercussions, too, for teacher careers from decisions and policies made at the institutional level, as we have shown. In amongst these difficulties, however, the teacher has personal resources, and is increasingly being called upon to use them. Cultivation of the kind of flexibility our sample have demonstrated would appear to be the best way in which teachers themselves can meet the present crisis — and indeed the future. They then may be able to say, like Arthur,

> I had a good time. I'm not saying it was all sweetness and light, mind, there were some difficult times — all the changes, the reorganization, the comprehensivization, schools getting big, difficult colleagues and some kids who were nasty pieces of work. But you come through it all, and if you like it and if you're right for it, it's a damn good life all round.

Bibliography

ADELSON, J. (1962) 'The teacher as model' in SANFORD, N. (Ed.) *The American College*, New York, John Wiley.

ALUTTO, J.A. and BELASCO, J.A. (1972) 'Typology for participation in organizational decision making', *Administrative Science Quarterly*, 17, pp. 117–25.

ARGYLE, M. (1972) *The Social Psychology of Work*, Harmondsworth, Penguin.

BAIN, G.S. (1970) *The Growth of White Collar Trade Unions*, London, Clarendon Press.

BALL, S.J. (1980) 'Initial encounters in the classroom and the process of establishment', in WOODS, P. (Ed.) *Pupil Strategies: Explorations in the Sociology of the School*, London, Croom Helm.

BALL, S.J. (1981) 'The teaching nexus: a case of mixed ability', in BARTON, L. and WALKER, S. (Eds.) *Schools, Teachers and Teaching*, Lewes, Falmer Press.

BALL, S.J. (1982) 'Competition and conflict in the teaching of English', *Journal of Curriculum Studies*, 14, 1, pp. 1–28.

BALL, S.J. and LACEY, C. (1980) 'Subject disciplines as the opportunity for group action: A measured critique of subject sub-cultures' in WOODS, P. (Ed.) *Teacher Strategies: Explorations in the Sociology of the School*, London, Croom Helm.

BANKS, O. (1976) *The Sociology of Education* (3rd edn.) London, Batsford.

BECKER, H. (1952) 'Social class variations in the teacher-pupil relationship', *The Journal of Educational Sociology*, 25, 4.

BECKER, H. (1966) 'Introduction' to SHAW, C.R. *The Jack-Roller*, Chicago, University of Chicago Press.

BECKER, H. (1977) 'Personal change in adult life' in COSIN, B. *et al.* (Eds.), *School and Society* (2nd edn.), London, Routledge and Kegan Paul.

BECKER, H.S. (1976) 'The career of the Chicago public school teacher' in HAMMERSLEY, M. and WOODS, P., (Eds.) *The Process of Schooling*, London, Routledge and Kegan Paul.

BECKER, H.S. and STRAUSS, A.L. (1956) 'Careers, personality and adult socialization', *American Journal of Sociology*, 62, November.

BELL, R.E. and GRANT, N. (1974) *A Mythology of British Education*, St. Albans, Panther Books.

BENNET, C. (1983) 'Paints, Pots or Promotion? Art Teachers' Attitudes Towards their Careers', paper given at Conference on Teacher Careers, St Hilda's College, Oxford.

BENNIS, W.G. (1968) 'Beyond bureaucracy' in BENNIS, W.G. and SLATER, P.E. (Eds.) *The Temporary Society*, New York, Harper and Row.

BERGER, P.L. (1963) *An Invitation to Sociology*, Harmondsworth, Penguin.

BERGER, P.L., BERGER, B., and KELLNER, H. (1973) *The Homeless Mind*, Harmondsworth, Penguin.

245

BERGER, P.L. and KELLNER, H. (1964) 'Marriage and the construction of reality', *Diogenes*, 46, i, pp. 1–23.

BERGER, P.L. and LUCKMANN, T. (1967) *The Social Construction of Reality: A Treatise in the Sociology of Knowledge*, Harmondsworth, Penguin.

BERGER, P.L. and LUCKMANN, T. (1971) *The Social Construction of Reality*, Harmondsworth, Penguin University Books.

BERNSTEIN, B. (1975) *Class, Codes and Control*, London, Routledge and Kegan Paul.

BERTAUX, D. (Ed.) (1981) *Biography and Society: The Life History Approach in the Social Sciences*, Beverly Hills, Sage.

BEYNON, J. (1984) 'Sussing-out teachers: pupils as data gatherers' in HAMMERSLEY, M. and WOODS, P. (Eds.) *Life in School: the Sociology of Pupil Culture*, Milton Keynes, Open University Press.

BLACKIE, P. (1977) 'Not quite proper', *Times Educational Supplement*, 25 August, 633, pp. 21–2.

BLAU, P. (1955) *The Dynamics of Bureaucracy*, Chicago, University of Chicago Press.

BLAU, P.M. and SCHOENHERR, R.A. (1973) 'New forms of power' in SALAMAN, G. and THOMPSON, K. (Eds.) *People and Organizations*, London, Longman, for the Open University Press.

BLISHEN, E. (1955) *Roaring Boys*, London, Thames and Hudson Ltd.

BLISHEN, E. (1969) *This Right Soft Lot*, London, Thames and Hudson Ltd.

BRIAULT, E. and SMITH, F. (1980) *Falling Rolls in Secondary Schools*, Windsor, NFER.

BROMLEY, D.B. (1974) *The Psychology of Human Ageing,* Harmondsworth, Penguin.

BUCHER, R. and STRAUSS, A. (1961) 'Professions in process', *American Journal of Sociology*, 56, 1, pp. 325–34.

BURNS, D. (1983) 'Teacher identity and some methodological considerations', paper given at Conference on Teacher Careers, St Hilda's College, Oxford.

BURNS, T. (1955) 'The reference of conduct in small groups: Cliques and cabals in occupational milieux', *Human Relations*, 8, pp. 467–86.

BURNS, T. and STALKER, G.M. (1961) *The Management of Innovation*, London, Tavistock.

BUSWELL, C. (1984) 'A comprehensive sixth form' in BALL, S.J. (Ed.) *Comprehensive Schooling: A Reader*, Lewes, Falmer Press.

CAIN, L.D. (Jr.) (1964) 'Life course and social structure' in FARIS, R.E.L., *Handbook of Modern Sociology*, Chicago, Rand McNally.

CARR, R.F. (1972) 'Recruitment for teaching: Problems and possibilities', *London Educational Review*, 1, 1.

COHEN, L. (1969) *Role Conflict in Headteachers*, unpublished PhD thesis, University of Keele.

COLE, M. (1984) 'Teaching till 2000: Teachers' consciousness in times of crisis', in BARTON, L. and WALKER, S. (Eds.) *Social Crisis and Educational Research*, London, Croom Helm.

CONWAY, J.A. (1980) 'Power and participatory decision-making in selected English schools' in BUSH, T., GLATTER, R., GOODEY, J. and RICHES, C. (Eds.) *Approaches to School Management*, Milton Keynes, Open University Press.

CORRIE, M. (1981) *The Social Construction of Teachers' Careers*, report to the Social Science Research Council (HR5423), December.

COULSON, A.A. (1976) 'The role of the primary head' in PETERS, R.S. (Ed.) *The Role of the Head*, London, Routledge and Kegan Paul.

DALE, R. (1976) 'Work, career and the self', Unit 7 in Course DE351, *People and Work*, Milton Keynes, Open University Press.

DALE, R., ESLAND, G. and MACDONALD, M. (Eds.) (1976) *Schooling and Capitalism: A Sociological Reader*, Milton Keynes, Open University Press.

DAUNT, P.E. (1975) *Comprehensive Values*, London, Heinemann.

DENNISON, W.F. (1979) 'Research report: Falling rolls part II', *Teachers and Shrinking Schools*.

DENNISON, W.F. (1981) *Education in Jeopardy*, Oxford, Basil Blackwell.

DENSCOMBE, M. (1980a) 'The work context of teaching', *British Journal of Sociology of Education*, 1, 3, September.

DENSCOMBE, M. (1980b) 'Keeping 'em quiet: The significance of noise for the practical activity of teaching' in WOODS, P. (Ed.) *Teacher Strategies: Explorations in the Sociology of the School*, London, Croom Helm.

DENSCOMBE, M. (1980c) 'Pupil strategies and the open classroom' in WOODS, P. (Ed.) *Pupil Strategies: Explorations in the Sociology of the School*, London, Croom Helm.

DENZIN, N. (1970) *The Research Act in Sociology: A Theoretical Introduction to Sociological Methods*, London, The Butterworth Group Ltd.

DICKS, H.V. (1965) 'Personality' in *The Seven Ages of Man*. New Society Publication.

DODD, C. (1974) 'Comprehensive school teachers' perceptions of role change', *Research in Education*, 12, pp. 35–45.

DOLLARD, J. (1935) *Criteria for the Life History*, New York, Libraries Press.

DORE, R. (1976) *The Diploma Disease*, London, Allen and Unwin.

DOYLE, W. (1979) 'Student Management of Task Structures in the Classroom', paper presented at the Conference on Teacher and Pupil Strategies, St Hilda's College, Oxford.

DREEBEN, R. (1970) *The Nature of Teaching*, Illinois, Scott, Foresman and Co.

DUNHAM, J. (1977) 'The effects of disruptive behaviour on teachers', *Educational Review*, 29, 3, June, pp. 181–8.

DUNHAM, J. (1980) 'An exploratory comparative study of staff stress in English and German comprehensive schools', *Educational Review* 32, 1, pp. 11–20.

DUNHAM, J. (1982) 'Stress in schools', *Times Educational Supplement*, 23 July.

EBBUTT, D. (1981) 'Girls' science: Boys' science revisited' in KELLY, A. (Ed.) *The Missing Half*, Manchester, Manchester University Press.

EBBUTT, J. (1981) 'Science options in a girls' grammar school', in KELLY, A. (Ed.) *The Missing Half*, Manchester, Manchester University Press.

EDELWICH, J. with BRODSKY, A. (1980) *Burn-Out: Stages of Disillusionment in the Helping Professions*, New York, Human Science Press.

ELBAZ, F. (1983) *Teacher Thinking: A Study of Practical Knowledge*, London, Croom Helm.

ERIKSON, E. (1950) *Childhood and Society*, New York, Norton.

ERIKSON, E. (1959) 'Identity and the life cycle' *Psychological Issues*, 1, pp. 1–171.

FARADAY, A. and PLUMMER, K. (1979) 'Doing life histories', *Sociological Review*, 27, 4.

FESTINGER, L. (1957) *A Theory of Cognitive Dissonance*, New York, Harper and Row.

FISKE, D. (1979) 'Falling rolls in secondary schools: Problems and possibilities', paper given at North of England Education Conference.

FURLONG, J.V. (1977) 'Anancy goes to school: A case study of pupils' knowledge of their teachers', in WOODS, P. and HAMMERSLEY, M. (Eds.) *School Experience*, London, Croom Helm.

GEER, B. (1971) 'Teaching' in COSIN, B.R., DALE, R., ESLAND, G.M. and SWIFT, D.F. (Eds.), *School and Society*, London, Routledge and Kegan Paul.

GIDDENS, A. (1979) *Central Problems in Social Theory*, London, Macmillan.

GIDDENS, A. (1982) 'Power, the dialectic of control and class structuration', in GIDDENS, A. and HELD, D. (Eds.), *Social Class and the Division of Labour*, Cambridge, Cambridge University Press.

GINSBURG, M.B., MEYENN, R.J., and MILLER, H.D.R. (1980) 'Teachers' conceptions of professionalism and trades unionism: An ideological analysis', in WOODS, P. (Ed.) (1980) *Teacher Strategies*, London, Croom Helm.

GLASER, B. (1964) *Organizational Scientists: Their Professional Careers*, Kansas, Bobbs-Merill.

GLASER, B.G. (Ed.) (1968) *Organizational Careers: A Sourcebook for Theory*, London, Weidenfeld and Nicolson.

GLASER, B.G. and STRAUSS, A.L. (1967) *The Discovery of Grounded Theory*, London,

Weidenfeld and Nicolson.

GOFFMAN, E. (1961) *Asylums*, Anchor Books, Doubleday and Co.

GOODSON, I. (1980) 'Life histories and the study of schooling', *Interchange*, 11, 4.

GOODSON, I. (1981) 'Becoming an academic stubject: Patterns of explanation and evolution', *British Journal of Sociology of Education*, 2, 2, pp. 163–80.

GOODSON, I. (1983) *School Subjects and Curriculum Change*, London, Croom Helm.

GOULD, R. (1972) 'The phases of adult life: A study in developmental psychology' *American Journal of Psychiatry*, November.

GOULDNER, A. (1965) *Wildcat Strike*, New York, Harper.

GOULDNER, A.W. (1957) 'Cosmopolitans and locals: Towards an analysis of latent social roles — I', *Administrative Science Quarterly*, 2, pp. 281–316.

GRACE, G. (1972) *Role Conflict and the Teacher*, London, Routledge and Kegan Paul.

GRACE, G. (1978) *Teachers, Ideology and Control: A Study in Urban Education*, London, Routledge and Kegan Paul.

HAMMERSLEY, M. (1977) 'Teacher perspectives', Units 9/10, Course E202 *Schooling and Society*, Milton Keynes, Open University Press.

HAMMERSLEY, M. (1980) *A Peculiar World? Teaching and Learning in an Inner City School*, Manchester, University of Manchester, PhD thesis.

HAMMERSLEY, M. (1984) 'Staffroom news' in HARGREAVES, A., and WOODS, P. (Eds.) *Classrooms and Staffrooms*, Milton Keynes, Open University Press.

HAMMERSLEY, M. and TURNER, G. (1980) 'Conformist pupils?' in WOODS, P. (Ed.) *Pupil Strategies: Explorations in the Sociology of the School*, London, Croom Helm.

HANNAM, C., SMYTH, P. and STEPHENSON, N. (1971) *Young Teachers and Reluctant Learners*, Harmondsworth, Penguin.

HANSON, D. and HERRINGTON, M. (1976) *From College to Classroom: The Probationary Year*, London, Routledge and Kegan Paul.

HARGREAVES, A. (1977) 'Progressivism and pupil autonomy', *Sociological Review*, August.

HARGREAVES, A. (1978) 'Towards a theory of classroom coping strategies', in BARTON, L. and MEIGHAN, R. (Eds.) *Sociological Interpretations of Schooling and Classrooms*, Driffield, Nafferton.Books.

HARGREAVES, A. (1979) 'Strategies, decisions and control: Interaction in a middle school classroom' in EGGLESTON, J. (Ed.) *Teacher Decision-Making in the Classroom*, London, Routledge and Kegan Paul.

HARGREAVES, A. (1981) 'Contrastive rhetoric and extremist talk: teachers, hegemony and the educationalist context' in BARTON, L. and WALKER, S., (Eds.) *Schools, Teachers and Teaching*, Lewes, Falmer Press.

HARGREAVES, D. (1967) *Social Relations in a Secondary School*, London, Routledge and Kegan Paul.

HARGREAVES, D. (1980) 'The occupational culture of teachers' in WOODS, P. (Ed.) *Teacher Strategies: Explorations in the Sociology of the School*, London, Croom Helm.

HARGREAVES, D. (1982) *The Challenge for the Comprehensive School: Culture, Curriculum and Community*, London, Routledge and Kegan Paul.

HARGREAVES, D., HESTOR, S. and MELLOR, F. (1975) *Deviance in Classrooms*, London, Routledge and Kegan Paul.

HARGREAVES, D.H. (1972) *Interpersonal Relations and Education*, London, Routledge and Kegan Paul.

HARGREAVES, D.H. (1978) 'What teaching does to teachers' *New Society*, 9 March.

HART, N. (1976) *When Marriage Ends: A Study in Status Passage*, London, Tavistock Publications.

HAVINGHURST, R.J. (1964) 'Youth in exploration and man emergent' in BOROW. H. (Ed.) *Man in a World at Work*, Boston, Houghton Mifflin.

HENDRY, L.B. (1975) 'Survival in a marginal subject: the professional identity of the PE teacher', *British Journal of Sociology*, 26, 4, pp. 465–76.

HER MAJESTY'S INSPECTORATE (1979) *Aspects of Secondary Education in England*, London, HMSO.

HERZBERG, F., MAUSNER, B. and SNYDERMAN, B.B. (1959) *The Motivation to Work*, New York, Wiley.

HILSUM, S. and START, K.B. (1974) *Promotion and Careers in Teaching*, Windsor, NFER.

HOYLE, E. (1969) *The Role of the Teacher*, London, Routledge and Kegan Paul.

HOYLE, E. (1983) 'The professionalization of teachers: A paradox' in GORDON, P. (Ed.) *Is Teaching a Profession?* Bedford Way Papers 15, University of London Institute of Education.

HUGHES, E.C. (1937) 'Institutional office and the person' in HUGHES, E.C. (1958) *Men and their Work*, New York, Free Press.

HUNTER, C. (1980) 'The politics of participation' in WOODS, P. (Ed.) *Teacher Strategies: Explorations in the Sociology of the School*, London, Croom Helm.

HUNTER, C. and HEIGHWAY, P. (1980) 'Morale, motivation and management in middle schools' in BUSH, T., GLATTER, R., GOODEY, J. and RICHES, C. (Eds.) *Approaches to School Management*, Milton Keynes, Open University Press.

HUSEN, T. (1979) *The School in Question*, Oxford, Oxford University Press.

INTERNATIONAL LABOUR ORGANIZATION (1981) *Employment and Conditions of Work of Teachers*, Geneva.

JAMES, W. (1915) *Psychology*, New York, Henry Holt and Co.

JANIS, I.L. and KING, B.T. (1954) 'The influence of role playing on opinion change'. *Journal of Abnormal and Social Psychology*, 49.

JAQUES, E. (1965) 'Death and the mid-life crisis' *International Journal of Psychoanalysis*, 46, pp. 502–14.

JENKINS, C. (1974) 'Male careers in PE', *Aspects of Education*, 16, pp. 71–80.

JUNG, C.G. (1971) *The Portable Jung* in CAMPBELL, J. (Ed.), New York, Viking Press.

KEDDIE, N. (1971) 'Classroom knowledge' in YOUNG, M.F.D. (Ed.) *Knowledge and Control* London, Collier-MacMillan.

KELLY, A. (Ed.) (1981) *Missing Half: Girls and Science Education*, Manchester, Manchester University Press.

KELSALL, R.K. and KELSALL, H.M. (1969) *The School Teacher in English and the United States*, Oxford, Pergamon.

KLEINE, P. and SMITH, L. (1985) 'Innovative teachers: A fifteen year study' in BALL, S.J. and GOODSON, I.F. (Eds.) *Teachers Lives and Careers*, Lewes, Falmer Press.

KRAUSE, E.A. (1971) *The Sociology of Occupations*, Little, Brown and Co.

KYRIACOU, C. and SUTCLIFFE, J. (1979) 'Teacher stress and satisfaction', *Educational Research*, 21, 2, pp. 89–96.

LACEY, C. (1970) *Hightown Grammar: The School as A Social System*, Manchester, Manchester University Press.

LACEY, C. (1977) *The Socialization of Teachers*, London, Methuen.

LACEY, C. (1983) 'Career: Opportunity or Constraint' paper presented at Conference on Teacher Careers, St Hilda's College, Oxford.

LAVELLE, M. (1982) 'Secondary school organization: bureaucracy or community?', *School Organization*, 2, 1, pp. 21–9.

LAWN, M. and OZGA, J. (1981) 'The educational worker? a re-assessment of teachers' in BARTON, L. and WALKER, S. (Eds.) *Schools, Teachers and Teaching*, Lewes, Falmer Press.

LAYTON, D. (1972) 'Science as general education', *Trends in Education*, January.

LEVINSON, D.J. et al., (1978) *The Seasons of a Man's Life*, New York, Knopf.

LEWIS, G. (1980) *Day of Shining Red*, Cambridge, Cambridge University Press.

LEWIS, M. (1979) *The Culture of Inequality*, New York, New American Library.

LOMAX, D. (1970) 'Focus on student teachers', *Higher Education Review*, Autumn.

LORTIE, D.C. (1975) *Schoolteacher: A Sociological Study*, Chicago, University of Chicago Press.

LYMAN, S.M. and SCOTT, M.B. (1970) *A Sociology of the Absurd*, New York, Appleton-Century-Crofts.

LYONS, G. (1981) *Teacher Careers and Career Perceptions*, Windsor, NFER-Nelson.

MACDONALD, A. (1979) 'The opinions of former PE students on the initial teacher training courses', *PE Review*, 2, 1, pp. 63–71.

MACDONALD, A. (1981) 'Career determinants and sources of satisfaction and dissatisfaction among PE teachers in secondary schools', unpublished paper.

McLEISH, J. (1969) *Teacher's Attitudes: A Study of National and Other Differences*, Cambridge, Cambridge Institute of Education.

McNAIR, D. and MACDONALD, A. (1980) 'The first four years in physical education', unpublished paper.

MARDLE, G. and WALKER, M. (1980) 'Strategies and structure: some critical notes on teacher socialization' in WOODS, P. (Ed.) *Teacher Strategies*, London, Croom Helm.

MARLAND, M. (1980) *Comprehensive School: Organization and Responsibility*, National Book League.

MASLOW, A.H. (1943) 'A theory of human motivation', *Psychological Review*, 50, pp. 370–96.

MEAD, G.H. (1934) *Mind, Self and Society*, Chicago, University of Chicago.

MEASOR, L. (1984) 'Gender and the sciences: pupils' gender-based conceptions of school subjects' in HAMMERSLEY M. and HARGREAVES, A. (Eds.) *Curriculum Practice: Some Sociological Case Studies,* Lewes, Falmer Press.

MEASOR, L. (1985) 'Interviewing in ethnographic research', in BURGESS, R. (Ed.) *Strategies of Educational Research: Qualitative Methods*, Lewes, Falmer Press.

MEASOR, L. and WOODS, P. (1984a) *Changing Schools: Pupil Perspectives on Transfer to a Comprehensive*, Milton Keynes, Open University Press.

MEASOR, L., and WOODS, P. (1984b) 'Cultivating the middle ground: teachers and school ethos', *Research in Education.* 31 May.

MERTON, R. (1961) 'The bureaucratic personality' in ETZIONI, A. (Ed.) *Complex Organizations: A Sociological Reader*, New York, Holt.

MERTON, R.K. (1957) *Social Theory and Social Structure*, Glencoe, The Free Press.

MINER, J.B. (1962) 'Conformity among university professors and business executives', *Administrative Science Quarterly*, June.

MORSE, N.C. and WEISS, R.S. (1955) 'The function and meaning of work and the job', *American Sociological Review*, 20,

MULFORD, H.A. and SALISBURY, W.W. (1964) 'Self-conceptions in a general population', *Sociological Quarterly*, 5, pp. 35–46.

MUSGROVE, F. (1971) *Patterns of Power and Authority in English Education,* London, Methuen.

MUSGROVE, F. (1974) *Ecstasy and Holiness*, London, Methuen.

MUSGROVE, F. (1977) *Margins of the Mind*, London, Methuen.

MUSGROVE, F. and MIDDLETON, R. (1981) 'Rites of passage and the meaning of age in three contrasted social groups', *British Journal of Sociology*, 32, 1, March.

MUSGROVE, F. and TAYLOR, P. (1969) *Society and the Teacher's Role*, London, Routledge and Kegan Paul.

NAS/UWT (1979) 'Pointing the Way' a discussion document on salary and promotion prospects, March.

NEWMAN, K. (1979) 'Middle-aged, experienced teachers' perceptions of their career development', paper presented at the annual meeting of the American Educational Research Association, San Francisco, California.

NIAS, J. (1980a) 'Leadership styles and job-satisfaction in primary schools' in BUSH, T., GLATTER, R., GOODEY, J. and RICHES, C. (Eds.) *Approaches to School Management*, Milton Keynes Open University Press.

NIAS, J. (1980b) 'Further notes on the concept of commitment' unpublished paper, University of Cambridge, Institute of Education.

NIAS, J. (1981) 'Commitment and motivation in primary school teachers', *Educational Review*, 33, pp. 181–90.

NIAS, J. (1984) 'The definition and maintenance of self in primary teaching', *British Journal of Sociology of Education*, 5, 3, pp. 167–180.

NUT (1981) 'A fair way forward: Appointment, promotion and career development; NUT memorandum.

PECK, R.F. and HAVINGHURST, R.J. (1960) *The Psychology of Character Development*, New York, John Wiley.

PETERSON, W.A. (1964) 'Age, teachers' role, and the institutional setting' in BIDDLE, B.J. and ELLENA, W.S. (Eds.) *Contemporary Research in Teacher Effectiveness*, New York, Holt, Rinehart and Winston.

PLUMMER, K. (1975) *Sexual Stigma*, London, Routledge and Kegan Paul.

POLLARD, A. (1980) 'Teacher interests and changing situations of survival threat in primary school classrooms' in WOODS, P. (Ed.) *Teacher Strategies: Exploration in the Sociology of the School*, London, Croom Helm.

POLLARD, A. (1982) 'A model of coping strategies', *British Journal of Sociology of Education*, March.

POSTER, C. (1976) *School Decision Making*, London, Heinemann.

PURVIS, J. (1973) 'Schoolteaching as a professional career' *British Journal of Sociology*, March.

RAPPAPORT, D. (1959) 'Introduction' to ERIKSON, E.H. *Identity and the Life Cycle*, Psychological Issues, 1, 1, Monograph 1.

REMPEL, A. and BENTLEY, R. (1970) 'Teacher morale: relationship with selected factors', *Journal of Teacher Education*, 21, Winter, pp. 534–9.

REYNOLDS, D. (1976) 'When teachers and pupils refuse a truce' in MUNGHAM, G. and PEARSON, G. (Eds.) *Working Class Youth Culture*, London, Routledge and Kegan Paul.

REYNOLDS, D. and SULLIVAN, M. (1979) 'Bringing schools back in' in BARTON, L. and MEIGHAN, R. (Eds.) *Schools, Pupils and Deviance*, Driffield, Nafferton Books.

REYNOLDS, D. and SULLIVAN, M. (1981) 'The comprehensive experience' in BARTON, L. and WALKER, S. (Eds.) *Schools, Teachers and Teaching*, Lewes, Falmer Press.

RICHARDSON, E. (1973) *The Teacher, the School and the Task of Management*, London, Heinemann.

RISEBOROUGH, G. (1981) 'Teacher careers and comprehensive schooling: An empirical study', *Sociology*, 15, 3, pp. 352–81.

RISEBOROUGH, G. (1983) 'Pupils, Teachers, Careers and Schooling: An Empirical study', paper presented at Conference on Teacher Careers and Life Histories, St Hilda's College, Oxford.

ROSS, J.M., BUNTON, W.J., EVISON, P. and ROBERTSON, T.S. (1972) *A Critical Appraisal of Comprehensive Education*, Slough, NFER.

ROTH, J.A. (1971) 'Timetables: structuring the passage of time in hospital treatment and other careers', in COSIN, B.R. *et al.* (Eds.) *School and Society,* London, Routledge and Kegan Paul.

ROY, W. (1983) *Teaching Under Attack*, London, Croom Helm.

RUDDUCK, J. and HOPKINS, D. (1984) 'The sixth form and libraries: Problems of access to knowledge', *British Library Research Report*.

RUTTER, M., MAUGHAM, B., MORTIMORE, P. and OUSTON, J. (1979) *Fifteen Thousand Hours*, London, Open Books.

SCHOOLS COUNCIL (1968) *Working Paper 11: Society and the Young School Leaver*, London HMSO.

SECONDARY HEADS ASSOCIATION (1980) *Staffing Our Secondary Schools*, Secondary Heads Association.

SELZNICK, P. (1948) 'Foundations of the theory of organizations', *American Sociological Review*, 13, pp. 25–35.

SELZNICK, P. (1949) *TVA and the Grass Roots*, Berkeley, University of California Press.

SHEEHY, G. (1976) *Passages: Predictable Crises of Adult Life*, New York, E.P. Dutton.

SHIPMAN, M. (1975) *The Sociology of the School*, London, Longmans.

SIKES, P.J. (1984a) 'Teacher careers in the comprehensive school' in BALL, S.J. (Ed.) *Comprehensive Schooling: A Reader*, Lewes, Falmer Press.

SIKES, P.J. (1984b) 'Secondary School Teachers' Perceptions of their Role', paper presented at Conference on The Affective Curriculum, St Hilda's College, Oxford.

SILVERMAN, D. (1970) *The Theory of Organizations*, London, Heinemann.

SMITHERS, A. and CARLISLE, S. (1970) 'Reluctant teachers', *New Society*, 5 March.

SOCKETT, H. (1983) in GORDON, P. (Ed.) *Is Teaching a Profession?*, Bedford Way Papers 15, University of London Institute of Education.

SOFER, C. (1970) *Men in Mid-Career*, Cambridge, Cambridge University Press.

SPOONER, R. (1979) 'The end of the ladder?', *Education*, 4 May, pp. 513–4.

STEBBINS, R.A. (1980) 'The role of humour in teaching: Strategy and self-expression' in WOODS, P. (Ed.) *Teacher Strategies; Explorations in the Sociology of the School*, London, Croom Helm.

STOUFFER, S.A., SUCHMANN, E.A., DEVINNEY, L.C., STAR, S.A. and WILLIAMS, R.M. (1949) *The American Soldier: Adjustment During Army Life*, Princeton, University Press.

STRAUSS, A.L. (1959) *Mirrors and Masks*, San Francisco, The Sociology Press.

STRAUSS, A.L. and RAINWATER, L. (1962) *The Professional Scientist*, Chicago, Aldine Press.

STRYKER, S. (1980) *Symbolic Interactionism*, Menlo Park, California, Benjamin/Cummings.

SUPER, D.E. (1981) 'Approaches to occupational choice and career development' in WATTS, A.G., SUPER, D.E., KIDD, J. (Eds.) *Career Development in Britain*, published for CRAC by Hobson's Press, Cambridge.

TAYLOR, J.K. and DALE, I.R. (1971) *A Survey of Teachers in their First Year of Service*, Bristol, University of Bristol School of Education Research Unit.

TIMES EDUCATIONAL SUPPLEMENT (27 August 1984) article on differential pay of scientists in schools and industry, p. 17.

TOWNSEND, P. (1981) 'The family and later life' Unit 23, E200 *Contemporary Issues in Education*, Milton Keynes, Open University Press.

TURNER, R.H. (1968) The self-conception in social interaction' in GORDON, C. and GERGEN, K.J. (Eds.), *The Self in Social Interaction*, New York, Wiley.

TURNER, R.H. (1976) 'The real self: from institution to impulse'. *American Journal of Sociology*, 81, 5.

VAILLANT, G.E. and MCARTHUR, C.C. (1972) 'Natural history of male psychologic health. 1 The adult life cycle from 18–50', *Seminars in Psychiatry* 4, 64.

VALLELY, M. (1978) Review of Literature (Careers in Teaching Project), Working Paper, SCRE.

WALKER, R. (1976) 'Innovation, the School and the Teacher (1)' Unit 27 of Course E203, *Curriculum Design and Development*, Milton Keynes, Open University Press.

WALKERDINE, V. (1980) 'Learning, language and resistance' *History Workshop Conference*, Brighton.

WALLER, W. (1932) *The Sociology of Teaching*, New York, Russell and Russell.

WATTS J. (1974) *Teaching*, London, David and Charles.

WATTS, J. (1980) 'Sharing it out: The role of the head in participatory government' in BUSH, T. GLATTER, R., GOODEY, J. and RICHES, C. (Eds) *Approaches to School Management*, Milton Keynes, Open University Press.

WEBB, R.B. (1983) 'Teachers' status panic: Moving up the down escalator', paper given at UK conference on Teachers' Careers and Life Histories, St Hilda's College, Oxford.

WILENSKY, H.L. (1960) 'Work, careers and social integration', *International Social Science Journal*, 12, pp. 543–74, reprinted in BURNS, T. (Ed) (1969) *Industrial Man*, Harmondsworth, Penguin.

WILLIS, P. (1977) *Learning to Labour*, Farnborough, Saxon House.

WOOD, D. (1981) 'Handicap of the professional man', *Sunday Times*, 25 October.

WOODS, P. (1979) *The Divided School*, London, Routledge and Kegan Paul.

WOODS, P. (Ed) (1980) *Teacher Strategies: Explorations in the Sociology of the School*, London, Croom Helm.

WOODS, P. (1981a) 'Strategies, commitment and identity: Making and breaking the teacher role' in BARTON, L. and WALKER, S. (Eds) *Schools, Teachers and Teaching*, Leives Falmer Press.

WOODS, P. (1981b) 'Careers and work cultures' Unit 24, E200 *Contemporary Issues in Education*, Milton Keynes, Open University Press.

WOODS, P. (1983) *Sociology and the School*, London, Routledge and Kegan Paul.

WOODS, P. (1984) 'Teacher, self and curriculum' in GOODSON, I.F. and BALL, S.J. (Eds), *Defining the Curriculum: Histories and Ethnographies*, Lewes, Falmer Press.

WOODS, P. (1985) 'Conversations with teachers', *British Educational Research Journal*, 11, 1.

Author Index

Subject Index